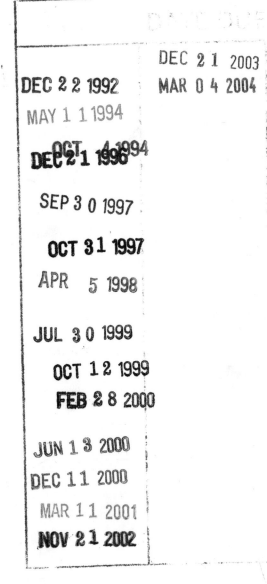

NI

TRUMPED!

The Inside Story of the *Real* Donald Trump— His Cunning Rise and Spectacular Fall

---

JOHN R. O'DONNELL

with JAMES RUTHERFORD

SIMON & SCHUSTER

New York London Toronto Sydney Tokyo Singapore

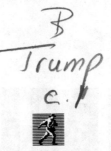

Simon & Schuster
Simon & Schuster Building
Rockefeller Center
1230 Avenue of the Americas
New York, New York 10020

Manufactured in the United States of America

1   3   5   7   9   10   8   6   4   2

Library of Congress Cataloging-in-Publication Data

O'Donnell, John R.
Trumped! : the inside story of the *real* Donald Trump—his
cunning rise and spectacular fall / by John R. O'Donnell with
James Rutherford.
p.   cm.
Includes index.
1. Trump, Donald, 1946—   .   2. Businessmen—United States.
3. Real estate developers—United States.   4. Casinos—
New Jersey—Atlantic City—Management.
I. Rutherford, James.   II. Title.
HC102.5.T78036 1991
333.33'092—dc20
[B]   91-9987
CIP

ISBN 0-671-73735-X

All photographs not otherwise credited are by Florence Garrett
Photo Service.

Acknowledgments

I owe an enormous debt to my wife, Lisa, and to family, friends and colleagues too numerous to mention here, whose advice and support as I wrote this book, and throughout my career, I shall never be able to repay. I am especially grateful to those current and former Trump casino employees and associates who, on condition of anonymity, generously contributed their time to assist me with their recollections and insights. Of those whom I can identify, special thanks go to Roger Gros, journalist, editor and keen observer of the gambling industry, and finally to Joellen Seville and Mary Rutherford, without whose assistance in the preparation and research of the manuscript, the truth might never have been told.

To my sister Pat Seidenfeld and to Donna Hyde, Lauren Etess, and Beth McFadden

—J. O'D.

To Mary

—J.R.

"Those who rise from private citizens to be princes merely by fortune have little trouble in rising but very much in maintaining their position . . . for unless he be a man of great genius it is not likely that one who has always lived in a private position should know how to command, and they are unable to maintain themselves because they possess no forces friendly and faithful to them."

—*Niccolò Machiavelli,*
from The Prince

"People have been waiting for years to watch me fall."
—*Donald J. Trump,*
from Trump: The Art
of the Deal

Prologue

Gamblers are my profession. I've spent my life around many of the richest in the world. I know what excites and lures them. I've learned to think like them. I've plumbed their strengths and weaknesses. I've faced them down across green felt tables stacked high with $1,000 chips and beat them.

For three years I helped run Trump Plaza Hotel & Casino—a $300 million operation, in its day the most glamorous and successful of the great gambling halls that tower over the beach and the Boardwalk in Atlantic City. For the last of those three years I was the boss. In the gambler's world, that made me "the house." In Donald Trump's world it was my job to make him richer.

Of all the gamblers I've known who tempted fortune beneath the crystal chandeliers of Trump Plaza's casino, Donald was the biggest. And for a time he was the luckiest. But fortune is a mercenary, its loyalties are unpredictable, especially in a casino. It was fitting that when I finally walked out on him it was by that same path I took when I first joined him: past the craps and blackjack tables, past the soft tick of the roulette wheels, past aisles and aisles of slot machines just stirring to life that final morning—Friday, April 27, 1990—with the clatter of bells and thousands of freshly falling coins.

From the gambler's perspective, the odds were against me leaving Donald. Certainly to his thinking they were. He never saw it coming, even though our alliance had been rent and we had drifted apart. ("Nah," he said, confiding to one of our attorneys with his typical aplomb, "Jack will never leave me. I pay him too much money.") But then gamblers are an incorrigible lot. And Donald had made the worst mistake a gambler could make: he had become overconfident.

With reason, I guess. He was paying me $260,000 a year. A tough bet to call. In fact, on the morning I quit, he was on his way to Atlantic City to meet with me. I was in my office. He was flying down on his private helicopter, a sleek, black, military-style Aérospatiale Super Puma emblazoned, like everything he owns, with the bold letters of his name. We were going to hammer out an employment contract that would ultimately pay me nearly twice what I was earning.

But in a split second, that ceased to matter anymore, in such a rage that at first I did not believe it myself. Immediately afterward, I angrily paced the carpet in front of my desk. Then the realization set in: I had called his bet and I would not back away from it. The house never sweats the action. No matter how high the stakes or how hot the player's hand, in the end fortune swings back to the house. It is inevitable. It is what I've learned about gamblers, what I live by, the knowledge that the implacable logic of time is always waiting to reclaim their world of dreams and delusions. Most of them refuse to accept that. But like I said, gamblers are incorrigible.

When I had composed myself enough to stop pacing, I returned to my desk and sat down. I took a breath and let it out slowly, and I took another, measuring the oxygen the way I would while pounding out the last leg of a 26-mile marathon.

I read over my letter of resignation one last time, as if to convince myself that I'd really done it:

Dear Donald:

   Effective immediately, I resign my position as president and chief operating officer of Trump Plaza Hotel & Casino.

I signed it simply, "Jack."

I handed the sheet of paper to my administrative assistant and instructed her to deliver it to Donald as soon as he got off the helicopter. After she'd gone, I slid my appointment book into my briefcase and snapped it shut. I sat alone for a moment and tried to construct my next move. But the anger drowned out any thought of a plan. It roared inside my head like the din of the engines on the Super Puma, the last thing I had heard before I slammed down the phone.

1

"I like the casino business. I like the scale, which is huge, I like the glamour, and most of all, I like the cash flow."

—DONALD J. TRUMP

On *February 4, 1987*, I went to work for Donald Trump as senior vice-president of marketing at Trump Plaza Hotel & Casino at the center of the Boardwalk in Atlantic City. I was 32 years old and two rungs down on the management ladder from the top of a multimillion-dollar gaming and resort company. On that day I was reunited with two former colleagues of mine, Steve Hyde and Mark Etess, respectively president and executive vice-president of the Plaza. It was Steve, in fact, who had offered me the job working for Donald Trump. And it was on that day, too, that I first met Donald.

It was about one o'clock in the afternoon when I looked up from my desk and saw standing before me a tall figure in a black overcoat whom I recognized immediately from the newspapers and television.

"Hello, I'm Donald Trump," he said.

Immediately, I rose from my chair. "Yes, I know that," I replied. "I'm Jack O'Donnell."

He stood a full head taller than me, much taller than I had

imagined him. Physically, he wasn't especially solid—I was enough of an athlete to notice that—but he was imposing nonetheless. His presence filled the office, the way he moved— quickly, vigorously and with purpose. He didn't offer his hand. I put out mine, he grasped it and we shook. "Welcome aboard," he said, speaking rapidly with the broad accent of the New York boroughs. "This is the best place in the world to work and I'm the best guy in the world to work for."

I didn't know what to say to that. But who wouldn't have been excited to work for a man who had accomplished more at the age of 40 than most men achieve in a lifetime? As he then added, "I'm America's most successful businessman. And I've made a lot of money in the casino business. I've done things nobody thought could be done. And I've got big plans."

I knew he was about to pocket millions on the greenmailing of Bally Manufacturing Corporation, which owned my former employer, Bally's Park Place Casino Hotel in Atlantic City. He "took them"—that's how he described his profiteering swipe at that company, which was run by "the worst managers in the world," he said. Donald had bought a sizable chunk of Bally stock, then induced the company to buy it back at a premium to avoid a takeover—"greenmail," as the practice is known. "These idiots, they caved in," he said. "I really enjoyed doing it because it put a real scare in them." Even more satisfying, or so it seemed to him, he had just elbowed Steve Wynn out of Atlantic City, the man who had dominated gaming on the Boardwalk for almost seven years, and had lured away three of his top executives— Steve Hyde, Mark Etess and now me. Trump was preoccupied with Steve Wynn, as was clear five minutes into our conversation. With his overcoat still on, he settled into a studio couch against the wall opposite my desk. "Tell me about Steve Wynn," he said.

I was taken aback. After all, I expected some inquiry into my background, my accomplishments. I thought maybe he'd quiz me on my marketing philosophy and my plans for the property. But he couldn't have been less interested. So I described how Steve Wynn, my former employer, had offered me a top job with him in Las Vegas, and how I had declined because I had sunk roots in Atlantic City. My wife, Lisa, and daughter, Laura, were happy here. I preferred to move, as Steve Hyde had done, to the Trump Organization and make my future there. (I did not mention that Steve Hyde was the only man who could have persuaded me to leave Wynn, and that if not for him I would never have gone to the Trump Organization.)

Trump nodded approvingly and said, "Yeah, you'll never have another job like this. There will never be another guy like me. So don't ever leave."

"I don't plan to, Mr. Trump," I said.

"Donald," he corrected me, and he leaned back on the couch. "C'mon, tell me about Wynn. I hear he's a real maniac . . . screaming at his people, hollering, throwing things in his office. Is it true?"

"Well, Steve's a very emotional guy," I said. "He runs his business with a lot of emotion."

"So I hear. Tell me, what did he do?"

"Well, uh, I remember once he crumpled up a piece of paper and threw it at me."

"Yeah? He did that?"

"At a board of directors meeting."

"A board of directors meeting! Unbelievable!" Donald said, shaking his head. He was clearly delighted and wanted to hear more.

I told him how it was routine to get an angry call at home from Steve in the middle of the night because the win at the gaming tables had been unimpressive the day before.

"Really?" Donald said.

"Oh, yeah. Or he'd call you at three o'clock in the morning, you know, to demand an explanation because one of the stars complained about the room service."

"Really?"

Donald was amused by these tales. It was the gossip that intrigued him. So I let them unravel. He listened intently, as if he was hearing a confirmation of what he believed all along, that he, not Steve Wynn, was the better man. He smiled, the corners of his mouth curling upward in an expression that put me in mind of a crocodile.

"So it's true," he said. "I heard stories like that about the guy. He's immature. What else did he do? I hear he thinks he's a real ladies' man, hitting on anything in pantyhose. Tell me about that. Is that why he divorced his wife?"

(Steve and Elaine Wynn were granted a divorce by mutual consent in Las Vegas in July 1986. I remember Steve calling me into his office one day to tell me the news. He mentioned that he had phoned Donald Trump also to inform him. Why, he didn't say. And I didn't ask. But Donald was so struck by that call that he made it a point to talk about it in his autobiographical book, *Trump: The Art of the Deal*.)

"Yeah, this is a weird guy," Donald went on. "He called me when he was getting divorced. Like I give a shit whether he gets divorced from Elaine. I don't even know her. I don't know this guy from beans and he's calling me to tell me he's getting divorced."

I tried to redirect the conversation, looking for an exit from it altogether. "Like I said, Steve can be very demanding," I continued. "He's an emotional guy, passionate about the business. He's really driven by the numbers. He wants to produce numbers every week, every month, every year."

"Well, you're not going to get that with me," Donald said. "I understand what it is to manage people and to work with people. My future is better than his anyhow. I'm a winner. I've always been a winner. I'm going to do great things. Yeah, I know all about Wynn and his property on the Strip. But just so you know, I'm going to be in Nevada in a big way. And I'm going to expand in Atlantic City."

What could I do but act as if I approved? Which, of course, I did. His boldness and acquisitiveness meant opportunity for me as a manager. What I found unnecessary and a little distasteful was the way he rattled it off, as though it was a speech he had memorized and recited to all the new hires. But I shrugged that off.

He sat up and said, "Look, I know what you're used to, but I run my business on a simple rule: I hire the best people from my competitors, I pay them more than they were making, and I give them bonuses based on how they perform for me. That's how I've built a first-class operation. So do great things. Do good work. I'm going to pay you lots of money. I want to be number one. Make us number one."

Then he rose to leave. Again, he didn't offer his hand. "See you later. Remember, I'm a winner. Never leave me." And he was gone.

For a moment, I sat still. So that was Donald Trump, I thought. I was amazed at my disappointment.

When I began working for Trump I already had ten years' experience in the gambling business in Las Vegas and Atlantic City. Marketing, the foundation of any successful gaming enterprise, was my expertise. I had had two of the best teachers there were: my father, William O'Donnell, who built a Chicago pinball machine company into Bally Manufacturing Corporation, the largest maker of slot machines and amusement games in the world, and Steven Wynn, chairman of the board of Golden Nugget, Inc., a brilliant promoter and an operator of vision.

I came up the hard way. Bill O'Donnell insisted on that. At

22, I was building coin-operated bingo machines on an assembly line at a Bally plant in my hometown of Chicago. Factory work turned out to be an education in mass-marketing I could never have gotten at Harvard Business School and one I've been grateful for ever since. As a working man I learned firsthand what motivates working people to spend their leisure dollars. I saw where they spend them and why. Building circuits and wires into boxes of lights and colors that they would reach into their pockets and pay to play engendered in me a fascination for the link between technology and imagination. Later, when I was sent into the field for Bally as a distributor and troubleshooter for the company's slot machines in Las Vegas, I saw the magic of that link at work under the blazing neon of a city whose single theme as a gambling resort made it one of the most fabulously successful vacation spots ever imagined. Combined, the experience was invaluable. That was my father's bequest to me.

Naturally, I longed to put it to work as a casino operator. The chance came when Bally went east to Atlantic City in 1979 to open Bally's Park Place, the third massive casino-hotel complex in the seaside resort. I signed on as director of slot operations. It was my job to ensure that our 1,588 slot machines ran smoothly and, most important, to develop and guide the kinds of promotional programs that would lure people to play our machines more frequently than anyone else's. I learned by doing: such was my introduction to the unique world of gaming in Atlantic City, light years from the worlds I had known in Chicago and Las Vegas.

New Jersey had spun the wheel on legalized gambling in a voter referendum that had passed in 1976. The hope was that the casinos would spark the revitalization of the aging and rundown resort and return it to its former glory as a world-class tourist destination. In the process, they would pump millions of sorely needed dollars into a host of social programs statewide, primarily to benefit the elderly. The enabling legislation, known as the

Casino Control Act, provided for an 8 percent tax levied annually against the gross revenues of every property. In addition, each property was assessed a financial obligation to reinvest in housing in the city. Finally, to guard against the influence of organized crime, the act set down a scrutinous licensing process in which owners, managers and employees at every level had to undergo extensive background investigations to be approved to work in the industry. Internal activities, from hiring and promotions to the extension of credit to the placement of a slot machine, were strictly regulated by the Division of Gaming Enforcement, an arm of the state Department of Law and Public Safety, and an independent five-member body known as the Casino Control Commission.

Economically and socially, New Jersey's casinos accepted public obligations unheard of in the private sector. It was to be a vastly different environment from Nevada and a new frontier for the industry. The potential for profits was enormous, though, at least in the beginning. The first experiment, Resorts International Hotel Casino, which had grafted a gambling hall onto the city's famed old Haddon Hall Hotel at the eastern end of the Boardwalk in 1978, was wildly successful. Caesars World, owner of Las Vegas's famed Caesars Palace, opened Caesars Boardwalk Regency the next year. Several large hotel chains followed with casino projects financed by the voracious appetite of the investment community for high-yield, high-risk "junk" bonds: Holiday Corporation, parent company of Holiday Inns, opened Harrah's Marina; and Hilton Hotel Corporaton built a huge competing property across the street from Harrah's in the marina section of town. The celebrity operators tried their hands. In 1980, *Penthouse* publisher Bob Guccione broke ground for a casino next door to Caesars on the Boardwalk. Hugh Hefner opened the Playboy Hotel Casino a year later. And Steve Wynn, who ran the Golden Nugget on the Las Vegas Strip, entered the market in

December 1980 with a sister property of the same name located at the far western end of the Boardwalk.

In 1984, I was fortunate to be offered an opportunity to work with Wynn as vice-president of slot operations at the Golden Nugget. It was easily the smartest move I ever made. There I met the two men who would become my closest friends and whose lives and destinies would shape my career: Executive Vice-President and Chief Operating Officer Steve Hyde, a kind and quiet man, an astute manager with a talent for inspiring loyalty; and Mark Grossinger Etess, a scion of the famed Grossinger's resort in the Catskills, the Nugget's vice-president of casino marketing, a born showman with tremendous energy and ambition.

What I learned most about gaming and gamblers I learned from Steve Wynn, who had been shown the ropes by his own father, who had run bingo parlors in their home state of Maryland. Steve graduated from the University of Pennsylvania's Wharton School. He was articulate, an avid reader, handsome and possessed enormous charm. He fashioned a career for himself by moving to Las Vegas and buying a small stake in Golden Nugget, Inc. Within a few years he had recruited a core of shareholders loyal to him and he was elected chairman of the board, a position he has held ever since. He was a genius at promoting a gambling hall, and in Atlantic City that genius bloomed to full flower. In contrast to the faceless hotel chains, he was the first of the "superstar" casino owners, appearing in television commercials with his friend Frank Sinatra. The Golden Nugget brought Las Vegas-style flair and glamour to the resort, which was just what it needed.

We were three then, Steve Hyde, Mark Etess and I. Armed with Steve Wynn's extensive connections in the Las Vegas gaming and entertainment communities, we promoted the Nugget as a high-stakes gaming hall, luring the deep-pocket gamblers, the so-called high rollers, with a reputation for action, luxury accommodations, lavish complimentaries and the excitement of big-name stars. The Nugget was the smallest casino in town in square feet and the number of blackjack, craps, baccarat and roulette tables and slot machines, but year after year, we were at or near the top in gaming revenues. From Steve Hyde I learned the importance of involving the employees at all levels in the success of the operation. If the employees felt good about themselves, they'd make the customers feel good. Above all, I learned the profession of hospitality. The heart of the Nugget's success was its ability to make even the nickel slot machine player feel like a high roller. "The only big deal is our customer," Steve Wynn used to say, "not a president or vice-president or chairman."

As the Nugget marched forward, plans were laid for expansion. Wynn had purchased from the MGM Grand Hotels 14 acres of land in the marina section of town next door to the casino under construction by Hilton, and he talked of building a $300-million, 1,000-room hotel tower atop a casino much larger than the Nugget's, one more than 60,000 square feet.

Donald Trump, the deal-maker and builder of Manhattan skyscrapers, as flamboyant and successful as Wynn in his own right, came to Atlantic City in the middle of those early boom years. Like the rest, he was seeking new worlds to conquer. He was lured by the same excitement that worked its magic on us all. Primarily, he saw that the income from New York hotels, even the most luxurious and successful ones, pales in comparison with the fast and easy cash of a gambling hall.

Beginning in 1980 Trump had been quietly buying up or leasing oceanfront property in and around the site of the old My Way Lounge, a favorite watering hole of convicted Philadelphia crime boss Nicodemo Scarfo in the days before casinos. The land sat right at the base of the Atlantic City Expressway, the main highway into the resort. Trump had astutely acquired what he described in the parlance of Manhattan real estate as the "Tiffany location."

His ability to corner the site was eased by a large pool of ready cash and the enormous reputation that preceded him into town. Born in 1946 in the affluent Jamaica Estates section of Queens, he had attended military school and later graduated from the Wharton School before joining his father, developer Fred C. Trump, to learn the business of building and renting middle-income apartments in the boroughs of Brooklyn, Queens and Staten Island, something his father had been doing successfully for four decades. Over the years, Fred Trump had forged strong connections with the city's Democratic party machine. In the late 1970s, his son brought those connections and an estimable family fortune of $200 million to Manhattan, where he parlayed them into a real estate empire that would ultimately be worth over $2 billion. And in doing it, he had changed the face of the Manhattan skyline, first with the Grand Hyatt, a glittering 32-story hotel he built above Grand Central Terminal in partnership with the Hyatt hotel chain, and then with the Trump Tower, his celebrated "Tiffany location" on Fifth Avenue between 56th and 57th streets. In Trump Tower the Trump Organization maintained its headquarters, and Donald reserved the premier apartment, a lavish 50-room triplex, for himself and his family.

Donald became Manhattan's largest private landowner when he purchased from the bankrupt Penn Central railroad an option to develop 76 acres along the Hudson River on the Upper West Side. He announced plans to build "Trump City," a lavish retail and luxury housing complex to be capped by "the world's tallest building."

With every advance, his plans, each more grandiose than the last, leaped farther afield. And the volume of public acclaim grew louder, with Trump himself turning the dial. "I wasn't satisfied just to earn a good living," he once said. "I was looking to make a statement. I was out to build something monumental . . . something worth a big effort." He was constructing more

24

than buildings. He was building a legend. At times, he talked of erecting an actual castle, "Trump Castle," complete with spires and turrets and a moat and drawbridge, on Madison Avenue in the middle of Manhattan. He turned a roving eye to Las Vegas, where he announced plans to build the largest casino in the world and call it "Xanadu." For his real-life getaway he purchased for $10 million the palatial estate of Marjorie Merriwether Post, Mar-a-lago, a 118-room mansion on 20 acres in Palm Beach, Florida. He had taken for his wife the glamorous Ivana Zelnickova Winklmayr, a former fashion model and Olympic skier. All told, under the umbrella of the Trump Organization, he was lord over a host of separate real estate corporations and partnerships with 1,000 people on his payroll. Most of them were in New York, where he was every inch the prince of the city—young, arrogant, flamboyant. In a nation that worships success he had become an American icon.

When he appeared before the Casino Control Commission in March 1982 to testify at licensing hearings for himself and his younger brother, Robert, an executive vice-president of the Trump Organization, he was already larger than life. He stood for wealth beyond measure and the limitless possibilities it offered to rehabilitate Atlantic City and lift it beyond anything even Las Vegas had dreamed of. In less than two hours he cleared review and was granted a casino license. Shortly after, he announced plans to build a 37-story casino hotel on his property at the foot of the expressway, in partnership with Holiday Corporation. It was to be the resort's largest to date, with 614 rooms and a 60,000-square-foot casino. Very high-profile. Very "Trump."

Perhaps it was further evidence of his reputation as a master deal-maker that the terms of the partnership were almost beyond belief, especially considering that he had only recently broken ground at the site. In exchange for a 50 percent share of the income and the inclusion of Harrah's, a Holiday subsidiary at the time, as the operator free of charge, Holiday reimbursed Trump for $22 million in costs up to that time, paid him another $50 million ($20 million of which went as a management fee to Donald), financed a $170 million construction loan and indemnified him against any operating losses for the first five years.

But the honeymoon was short-lived. No sooner had New Jersey Governor Thomas Kean cut the ribbon for "Harrah's at Trump Plaza" on May 14, 1984, in a splashy Boardwalk ceremony, than Donald Trump and Holiday were at war.

In order to meet the $220 million construction budget, Trump quickly threw up a building with escalators that broke down, as I was told, with stairways that led nowhere, a kitchen that was too far from the restaurants and a hotel lobby that was cramped with huge pillars that blocked the line of sight and made it seem even smaller. Ivana Trump designed the interior in ponderous chrome fixtures and wall treatments done in a cacophony of bright reds, oranges, yellows and purples. Her husband called it "the most magnificent building in the world." Holiday was aghast.

Trump claimed he brought the building in on time and on budget. Holiday claimed that he ran millions of dollars over budget.

I had only recently joined the Golden Nugget at the time. All I knew of Donald Trump then centered on his entry into Atlantic City and the bitter collapse of the Holiday partnership, which, as competitors, we were watching with some interest. I heard talk of their enmity, of stormy arguments in the conference rooms with Donald Trump in the thick of it.

From a distance, though, there was something appealing about the brash New York billionaire. I admired his image, his high-velocity competitiveness, probably because I am competitive by nature, in both my public and private lives. Endurance athletics is a devotion of mine, my edge, and I've been competing in marathon and triathlon championships nationally and worldwide for 14 years. It's a peculiar pastime, I guess, for someone in my business, with a career so demanding and time-consuming. But the long hours of the casino and the hard physical training for a race were compatible somehow; the stress of one mitigated the stress of the other. I lived to push myself beyond normal limits. So in my own way I identified with the heroic scale of Trump's accomplishments.

At the close of that first year, 1984, total revenue at Harrah's at Trump Plaza was second to the worst in the city, though it represented only seven months of operation. It began to improve the next year, though not enough to satisfy Trump. He coveted the high-stakes gambling trade that Caesars and we at the Golden Nugget specialized in, which to his thinking was the only play worthy of his name. He was determined to force Holiday out as his partner.

The new year 1985 soon brought dramatic and unexpected developments. In March, Barron Hilton, the chairman of Hilton Hotel Corporation, was denied a gaming license by a 2–2 vote of the Casino Control Commission on the basis of his corporation's association with a Chicago labor lawyer with alleged ties to organized crime. Everybody in the industry was shocked. No one was building anything in Atlantic City when the Hilton hotel was completed that spring. Barron Hilton had already hired more than 1,000 people, and the property was 12 weeks from opening when his license application was denied. For the city and, obviously, for Hilton, a massive investment was suddenly in serious financial trouble.

Steve Wynn jumped in first. Gaming's star player made a hostile bid to take over the entire hotel chain with an initial offer to buy 27 percent of its stock, 6.8 million shares, for $72 per share, $5 above the going market price.

The move sent shudders through the boardrooms of Altantic City's ten casinos. What was Wynn up to? Did he really want Hilton's worldwide holdings? Could he afford them? Or was he squeezing Barron Hilton to sell him the Atlantic City casino at a bargain to fend off the takeover. Steve already owned 14 acres of undeveloped land right next door. With his expertise and the addition of this giant hotel and the potential to expand it further, he could dominate the town with a gaming complex large enough to devour the lion's share of the East Coast market.

Donald Trump, embroiled in his feud with Holiday, his partners on the Boardwalk, abruptly changed course and appeared at the marina as if from nowhere, suddenly weighing in with an offer to buy the property, for Barron Hilton's entire $320 million investment. Donald had never been inside the building. "If I'd told my father . . . he would have said I'd lost my mind," Trump joked afterward. But he was determined to block Steve Wynn, the casino rival he feared more than any other.

Barron Hilton eagerly accepted Trump's offer, and the sale was closed in April. Hilton now had a war chest to beat back Steve's takeover attempt and he withdrew his bid. Trump walked away with an enormous casino hotel covering 14 acres, the first one he owned in its entirety. The property was simply and distinctively designed. It was 26 stories high with 200,000 square feet of public space and a majestic 30-foot atrium. Adjoining it was a 9-story parking garage with space for 3,000 cars. The hotel contained 703 guest rooms. The gaming hall was huge, 60,000 square feet, with 107 tables and 1,688 slot machines. It would ultimately employ close to 4,000 people.

The immediate problem was finding someone to manage it. Trump had neither the knowledge nor the time. His brother, Robert, and his chief New York adviser, Harvey Freeman, were both members of the executive ownership committee of Trump Plaza, but neither was in a position to run a casino, which was acknowledged in the property's filing with the U.S. Securities and Exchange Commission, a requirement in order to sell bonds on the open market: *"None of the members of the Executive Committee devotes a significant amount of his working time to the operations of the Partnership. Accordingly, the Executive Committee has delegated responsibility for day to day operations to certain other persons."*

But the question remained: Who?

Trump credited Freeman, then 46 years old, an attorney and senior vice-president of the Trump Organization, with having "a brilliant analytic mind." Reputedly he was the shark at the negotiating table, the hard-nosed bargainer who got his employer the sweet end of the deals and made them stick. He was an inveterate pessimist, however, "Not too big on laughs," as Trump described him. ("Doom and gloom Harvey," I would later come to think of him.)

Robert, 37 years old, two years younger than his brother, was an executive vice-president of the Trump Organization. His background was in corporate finance. He had graduated from Boston University and followed his brother to Manhattan, taking an apartment in the same building when the two were bachelors. Before joining the family real estate business he worked on Wall Street. He served on the ownership committees of all of his brother's Atlantic City casinos, though he never exerted an especially commanding presence in town and, like his brother and Harvey, brought no direction in terms of casino operations or marketing. But he suited the Trump Organization well from an image standpoint, and he enjoyed the confidence of the New York banks and brokers.

To oversee his new property, Trump turned to his wife, Ivana, who had the requisite ambition, and then some.

Officially, Ivana was executive vice-president in charge of design with the Trump Organization, and, as mentioned, she played a major role in the interior design of Harrah's at Trump Plaza. Her fiery presence and explosive temper were something of a legend on her husband's construction sites in New York—"a natural manager," Trump described her. In defending her as his choice to run his new casino he said, "I'd studied Atlantic City long enough to be convinced that when it comes to running a casino, good management skills are as important as specific gaming experience." Most important, she was family, which to his thinking meant she could be trusted. So on June 17, 1985, the former Hilton property, newly renamed "Trump's Castle," opened its doors with 36-year-old Ivana Trump as senior vice-president and chief operating officer.

Ivana had no reason to doubt that her husband was grooming her to take over his entire Atlantic City operation, which, depending on the outcome of the partnership with Harrah's at Trump Plaza—and Donald was looking every which way to break that—could well amount to an empire.

Holiday Corporation, tired of feuding with Donald over the Harrah's property at the base of the Atlantic City Expressway, approached Trump with an offer to sell its half. The contracts were signed early in 1986. Trump bought out Holiday and became sole owner of the casino, the hotel and the site of a parking garage, which had been a focus of dispute between the partners, for $67 million. It was, he would later say, "one of my most savored transactions."

He soon had something else to savor. In March of that year, he announced that Stephen Hyde, the executive vice-president of the Golden Nugget, was coming to work for him as president of the property, now rechristened "Trump Plaza Hotel & Casino."

Trump had sized up the competition and envied Steve Wynn's success at the Nugget. Steve Hyde was to be his weapon to raid the high end of the gambling market. In truth, though, Trump Plaza wasn't positioned especially well for the assault. Steve and

I remained in constant communication after he left, and I was aware of the Plaza's fundamental shortcomings: no adequate parking, and luxury hotel suites that were well below the best industry standards, certainly nothing compared with what we had at the Nugget.

But with Steve, Trump had chosen wisely. Steve was a native of Kaysville, Utah—a kind, robust Westerner, in love with the outdoors. He was also a devout Mormon—something of an anomaly in our business—40 years old, the same age then as Trump, and the father of seven children. I didn't know Trump beyond the public image as the brash, big-city entrepreneur, confrontational in his approach to business and obsessed with winning. Steve I did know to be soft-spoken, thoughtful, deliberate in his decision-making and compassionate to those under him. And he was an astute operations man, a veteran of the Caesars and Sands organizations in Las Vegas, in addition to the Golden Nugget, and a manager who commanded respect throughout Atlantic City. Through him, Trump was able to lure to the Plaza some of the best departmental brains from every casino in the city.

Steve's top pick was Mark Etess, his protégé at the Nugget, who joined Trump Plaza two months after Steve in May. At 33, Mark was boyishly handsome, sharp, ambitious and supremely confident in his destiny to make history as a casino showman. At Grossinger's he had grown up among the celebrities and entertainers who had made the Catskills resort famous in the 1940s and 1950s. Mark's most valuable connections from those years were in the sport of professional boxing, for which Grossinger's had been equally famous as a training camp, and since coming to Atlantic City, he had been looking for an opportunity to tap them.

Steve offered me a vice-presidency at Trump Plaza. But I declined—for two reasons. First, I had a vibrant career with Steve Wynn, doing what I loved and learning from the best. Second,

Trump had no reputation as a gaming operator; he was a real estate developer, albeit a fantastically successful one, and while his high profile and deep pockets could benefit Atlantic City, his intentions were suspect: he was a deal-maker, the type who might be buying casinos just to sell them and move on. Plus, what I had seen of his noisy business style, based on the breakup with Holiday, left me uncomfortable with the thought of him as my boss.

Steve Hyde understood my concerns but he let the offer stand. The door to Trump Plaza was open for me, he said, whenever I was ready.

In the meantime, my career at the Golden Nugget was soaring. Steve Hyde's departure forced a restructuring, which led to my promotion to senior vice-president of marketing. In addition to slot operations and retail promotions, I now oversaw the marketing of the table games and various aspects of the hotel, jobs previously held by Mark Etess. I was working closer than ever with Steve Wynn now and gaining valuable insights into his vast player-development network through contact with his representatives nationwide. Steve spoke proudly of my promotion, calling me over on the casino floor one day and saying to his wife, Elaine, who was on the board of directors of Golden Nugget, Inc.: "Jack is the man now. A big part of our future is with him."

Steve Wynn loved to strategize on ways to motivate the gambler. We'd brainstorm for hours over ways to know the players better, understand them, market to them in new ways and find better methods to service them. He was emotional, driven, passionate and demanding—he thought nothing of calling you at home at three in the morning or yanking you out to Las Vegas with him for a week at a time—but there was always a lesson behind it; invariably I walked away from the time we spent together having learned something new about our business. His temper could be explosive, his emotional outbursts were legendary, but he was never vicious. He was man enough to apologize, perhaps he'd renew the discussion to make his point in a different way, and afterward it was forgotten; he'd never bring it up again.

What appealed to me most was his love of innovation. He broke the mold of traditional casino entertainment, booking performers as diverse as Mikhail Baryshnikov and the Dance Theater of Harlem in his casino showroom. In the early 1980s he had brought Frank Sinatra to Atlantic City under exclusive contract. The first weekend appearance by the entertainment legend drew record crowds to the casino and resulted in record wagering at the tables. Steve rewarded everyone at the property with double paychecks that week. That was the Wynn personal touch, his largesse and his genius.

He was fascinated by my technological background and was constantly looking for imaginative ways to apply it. We both believed that whoever won the battle for technology in the gaming business would win the war for market share. Steve gave me a seat on the steering committee he formed to advance data processing and computerized management information. Also, I was given oversight of research and development at his properties in Las Vegas and Atlantic City.

But as 1986 drew to a close, events began to change rapidly. In the fall, Steve had announced Golden Nugget, Inc.'s, purchase of 86 prime acres on the Las Vegas Strip on which he planned to build a $600 million gaming and resort complex the likes of which had never been seen. I worked closely with him on the preliminary drawings for this casino, which was to be called the "Mirage," and which would feature an indoor tropical forest, a waterfall, live tigers and sharks inside and a fire-spitting volcano outside.

Trump's two casinos had failed to make a dent in our revenues in Atlantic City in 1986. He was offering to buy Steve's 14 acres in the marina section, which adjoined his new Trump's Castle.

The Mirage forced Steve to shelve plans to develop the site, but he tweaked Trump by asking $60 million for it anyway, an outrageous price, which immediately ended the discussion. Trump also was itching to invest in Las Vegas, and he offered to develop the Mirage property jointly. Steve turned him down. Frustrated, Trump would later lash out at his rival in *The Art of the Deal*, calling Steve "the son of a compulsive gambler," who, he said, "grew up in his father's bingo parlor."

"He's got a great act," Trump would continue in a summation of his competitor that ran with invective. "He's a smooth talker, he's perfectly manicured, and he's invariably dressed to kill in $2,000 suits and $200 silk shirts. The problem with Wynn is that he tries too hard to look perfect, and a lot of people are put off by him."

I was in daily contact with my friends at Trump Plaza, Steve Hyde and Mark Etess, and, to be honest, I missed working with them. Steve invited me to dinner and renewed his offer to me to join him at the Plaza. I again declined. But then Trump launched a series of business moves that had the effect of drawing me to him despite my intentions.

No sooner had he severed his partnership with Holiday at Trump Plaza in the spring of 1986 than he began buying stock in Holiday Corporation. He correctly guessed that the company was vastly undervalued. By the end of August, he owned upward of a million shares and was breezily talking of a takeover.

In a panic, Holiday's board of directors huddled to devise a plan to beat him back. They hastily restructured the corporation, taking on $2.6 billion in new debt to pay off the stockholders with a one-time bonus dividend per share. Then to reduce the enormous debt load, they began selling off hotels. Out of that a new subsidiary was born that contained only two existing Harrah's casinos in Nevada, a few hotels and Harrah's Marina in Atlantic City.

The takeover scare had sent Holiday's stock soaring, which is what Trump figured. In November, he sold his stake in the company and walked away with a profit guessed to be as much as $30 million. He got the additional pleasure of inflicting some sleepless nights on his former partners.

Trump had devoured some easy cash. He found he liked the taste. Within weeks of divesting himself of his Holiday stock, he dived on Bally Manufacturing Corporation, which my father had retired from six years earlier and which owned my former employer, Bally's Park Place in Atlantic City, and two MGM Grand casino properties in Las Vegas and Reno, Nevada. Trump began buying and obtaining options to buy Bally stock. His plan, he announced, was to own 49 percent of the company.

Early in December, Bally appeared to surrender. To stave off the takeover, the company offered to buy the Golden Nugget in Atlantic City. The reasoning was that a second Bally-owned Atlantic City casino would have the effect of freezing Trump out, because if Trump purchased Bally Manufacturing, he would be classified as a holding company with four Atlantic City casinos— Trump Plaza, Trump's Castle, Bally's Park Place and the Nugget property. This would put him over the maximum of three allowed a single owner under New Jersey law. To entice a sale, Bally offered Steve Wynn a phenomenal sum of money, seemingly more than a reasonable businessman could refuse: assumption of the Nugget's $299 million mortgage and an additional $141 million that Steve could put in his pocket, a $440 million deal all told, the highest price ever offered for an Atlantic City casino up to that time.

Steve was anxious to start construction on the Mirage in Las Vegas, and I knew it was in his interest to give Bally's offer some serious consideration. I didn't think he would sell, but he did.

Expensive and foolhardy as Bally's offer was, it worked: Trump dropped his takeover bid. But in the process the Bally's Park Place and the MGM Grands in Nevada were pillaged of cash to fund the purchase of the Golden Nugget, which was renamed "Bally's Grand." When the dust settled, Bally was buried under $1.8 billion of new debt. The deal was ominous for Atlantic City as well. To the insatiable investment market of the time, Trump had driven the perceived value of casino junk bonds through the roof, which made the paper even more popular as a financing tool and made additional borrowing more attractive for properties looking to expand in the relatively small and highly competitive Atlantic City market. Bally went from owning one of the resort's most financially stable casinos to being burdened with four, two in Nevada and now two in Atlantic City, that were hobbled with high interest payments.

Now it was up to me whether to go west to the Mirage with Steve Wynn or stay at the Golden Nugget in Atlantic City, working for a debt-ridden Bally, my old employer. I struck that off right away, though. The manner in which they caved in to Trump was simply poor management, in my opinion, enough to convince me that I didn't want to work for them again. As for Steve Wynn and the Mirage—yes, it was an exciting opportunity, but I had no desire to uproot my family and transfer to Nevada. Besides, in my view, Atlantic City represented a vast, untapped future for gaming. Suddenly, then, my choice was clear. In the new year of 1987, I cast my future with Atlantic City—and that meant Donald Trump.

2

"I've made Ivana a very popular woman. I've made a lot of satellites."
—DONALD J. TRUMP

I n *January 1987*, the board of directors of Golden Nugget, Inc., approved the sale of its Atlantic City casino to Bally. Steve Wynn packed up and went west to devote his time and a newly swollen pocketbook to the development of the Mirage on the Las Vegas Strip.

In Manhattan, in the offices of the Trump Organization on the 26th floor of Trump Tower, the calculators were smoking. A few weeks into the new year, Trump had won permission from the SEC to increase his stock purchases in Bally Manufacturing Corporation. Armed with that, he played his ace: he promised not to block Bally's purchase of the Golden Nugget in exchange for their agreement to buy back his 9.6 percent share in the company at a premium. Bally again caved in. Trump's profit on the exchange was estimated at $20 million.

Within days of my move to Trump Plaza in February, the outlines of the deal were disclosed. Bally's stockholders cried greenmail. In New Jersey, the Division of Gaming Enforcement expressed concern, and for the first time the New Jersey Casino

Control Commission suggested that Trump rein in his investments in competing companies.

From an image standpoint, Steve Wynn's departure deprived Atlantic City of its premier showman. Could Donald Trump fill the void? At that point, he owned two moderately successful gaming halls. Casino revenue, or "win"—the money retained from gaming operations after all winning bets are paid—was $224 million at Trump's Castle in 1986, fifth among Atlantic City's eleven casinos, $35 million less than Caesars, the top-earning property that year, and $23 million behind second-ranked Golden Nugget. Trump Plaza had won even less, $218 million, only sixth best in town.

But the new year opened fabulously for him. He and his glamorous wife, Ivana, were hot news items. His rough-and-tumble business style and his prodigious accomplishments were soon to be enshrined in *Trump: The Art of the Deal*, the autobiography that would climb to the top of the bestseller lists. He traveled in a private Boeing 727. He bought the lavish 282-foot yacht of the Sultan of Brunei from his friend, billionaire Saudi Adnan Khashoggi, for $25 million, and rechristened it the *Trump Princess*.

The wealth he commanded and the promise it represented could not be denied, and it was seductive. His appetite for property was monstrous and he had the seeming financial ability to feed it. His string of stupendous achievements was as yet unbroken, or so it seemed.

His presence had come to exert a hypnotic effect on Atlantic City. The seaside resort was nine years into the gambling experiment and had yet to become the world-class vacation destination that was envisioned in 1978 when the first casino, Resorts International, opened its doors to huge crowds. The market had settled down to 1 million or so visitors, mostly from a hundred-mile radius, who made 30 to 40 repeat trips a year and mostly stayed for the day. They arrived by car or by the hundreds of charter and route buses that rumbled into town every day mostly from the New York, Philadelphia, Baltimore and Washington, D.C., metropolitan areas and subsidized in large part by the casinos themselves. Plans to expand the city's airport about 10 miles west on the mainland, and to build a new convention center had yet to leave the drawing board.

Where was the promise of urban renewal? Where was a city of working families and the affordable housing to enable them to live there? Beyond the glittering pale of the casinos lay block after block of boarded-up, burned-out houses and stores. The central business district was rundown and perceived as dirty and dangerous.

Enter Donald Trump.

His purchase of the Hilton property had bailed out the state and the city from a potential disaster. He had saved thousands of jobs and set a new gaming palace afloat at a time when other construction projects were foundering. Their gratitude and the lengths to which they'd go to keep Trump in Atlantic City and happy were apparent when it came time for him to make good on his promise to honor a commitment Hilton had made to the state to spend $13 million to widen an existing road spur from an old Philadelphia-to-Atlantic City highway, past the Castle and to a bridge to the nearby island of Brigantine. Trump simply refused. It became an issue early in 1987 when he testified before the Casino Control Commission for renewal of his Castle license. He said his initial promise was based on misinformation: he had been unfamiliar with the plans for the road, and when he finally examined them subsequent to his purchase of the property, he realized they were poorly conceived.

Hilton's lawyers testified that the plans were discussed in detail with Trump during the negotiations for the purchase; drawings were even rolled out for him to examine, which he did.

Trump denied ever meeting with Hilton's lawyers on the subject and brought out his own attorneys, who maintained that no discussions had taken place.

The issue then was whether Trump was misrepresenting the facts, which, if proven, was grounds to revoke his license, or at least to deny the renewal pending an investigation. New Jersey's Office of the Public Advocate got involved and recommended precisely that. The Casino Control Commission, however, decided it believed Trump and voted 4–1 to renew his license. He agreed to contribute $8 million for the road improvements.

By this time I had already joined Steve Hyde and Mark Etess at Trump Plaza. I remember when I first called Steve Wynn in Las Vegas to tell him I was resigning and going to work for Trump.

"Please, please, Jack, don't do that," he said. "Don't go there. Go anywhere but don't go there."

I didn't know what to make of that. In any event, I had already made up my mind. Besides, I knew that while Steve preferred to dismiss Trump as an inexperienced interloper, he really had been angry at having lost Steve Hyde, his executive vice-president, and Mark Etess, vice-president of casino marketing, to him.

"Let's call Jack Davis," he said, referring to the then-president of Resorts International. "I'll call Jack Davis. You'll be hired in two seconds down at Resorts."

I thanked him but I declined.

But he was serious. "Jack, you're making a mistake," he said. Then he reminded me of some of the assessments of Trump within the industry: that he knew nothing about gaming, that his ego was overweening and unpredictable, that he would be impossible to work for. He's out of control," Steve said. Steve, who is not at all shy about self-promotion, used to mockingly refer to Donald as "The Trump-et."

At Trump Plaza, Steve Hyde and Mark Etess painted a different picture. They were two of my best friends and I trusted them.

Either way, I couldn't be certain what to expect. But that didn't frighten me. It intrigued me. Trump hired me on Steve Hyde's recommendation without ever having met me. I felt good about that.

So on February 4, I was happy to be reunited with Steve and Mark. We were a management team again. Our mandate was clear: to turn Trump Plaza Hotel & Casino around and make it number one. Trump Plaza hadn't given a stellar performance in 1986. But to their credit, Steve and Mark had managed well, bringing $15 million to the bottom line as pretax profit. And they did it in the face of enormous obstacles. The executive staff had been ripped apart in the breakup between Trump and Holiday. The rank and file were fragmented, inadequately trained, uncertain of their jobs and demoralized. The facility lacked indoor parking, it was poorly designed, horribly decorated, and the hotel suites fell short of the size and luxury necessary to compete for the high-stakes gambling trade that Trump desired.

But Steve and Mark were thrilled by the challenge, an opportunity to build something from almost nothing. Trump had not interfered with them, they said; he was completely supportive and he was prepared to spend whatever it took to make the property the class of the gaming world.

"I've told him I'm here to take care of the business and run it for him," Steve said to me. "I hardly ever see him. If he wants to know something, he calls me. If I need something, I call him. It's better for us that way."

One of the biggest surprises to me was the ambiguous relationship that existed between our property and Ivana's at Trump's Castle across town. My education about this began almost immediately.

With the publication later in 1987 of Donald's autobiography, *The Art of the Deal*, both properties were expected to stock hardback copies in their retail newsstands, which made sense as a promotion. But we had to buy huge numbers of them, which did not make sense, except as a device to make the book appear more popular than it was. In my role as head of marketing for Trump Plaza, I placed our order for 1,000 copies. I learned soon after that I had made a mistake.

"You've got to increase your order," Steve Hyde told me one day.

I asked why. He said, "The Castle put in a bigger order. Donald will go nuts if you don't take more books."

"What is this, Steve, a competition?"

He nodded his head, answering my question with a grim smile. "This is the way it is. They took more, we've got to take more. Donald wants to see who sells the most books."

"How many more should we order?"

"The quota for both properties is 8,000," he said. "We have to take four."

"Four thousand! Steve, that's going to cost us thousands of dollars. How are we going to get rid of 4,000 books? I mean, I'll do it. I'll order 20,000 if you want me to, but I can't promise you I'll get rid of them."

Then Steve's smile actually brightened, his way of telling me he knew it was ridiculous, too. He chuckled, "You're the marketing guy. Use your creativity. Oh, and by the way, Jack . . . there can't be any returns." (Books that are not sold can normally be returned to the publisher for full credit.)

For his sake I made a project out of it. I called together my marketing staff to develop ways to try to turn an oversupply of Donald's paean to himself into a sales triumph for Trump Plaza. We queried various local bookstores for promotional and display ideas; we had large color posters made of Donald's portrait from the book jacket to decorate the hotel lobby and the other public spaces. Even so, the books did not sell fast enough, and months later, we were still searching for ways to unload them. We gave them away at customer parties. We sent dozens at a time to New York for Donald to sign, and then we mailed those to our preferred players as gifts. Then someone hit on the idea of placing copies in all the guest rooms on New Year's Eve 1987 with our normal chocolate turn-down service. "We can get rid of 500 books? Great. Do it," I said.

Moving those copies of Trump's autobiography was my introduction to the practical consequences of Donald's ego. Ivana understood this perhaps better than any of us: after all, she had ordered more books from the start. Steve accepted it as a cost of doing business. But he was mindful, and he made Mark and myself aware, of the lengths to which Ivana would take the competition with us. Unrestrained, she could drive the cost of doing business to absurd heights. I began to see how deep were the waters that divided Steve and Ivana.

Steve told me that he had taken the position as president of Trump Plaza with Donald's word that he would one day manage all the Trump holdings in Atlantic City, whatever form they took. Yet by setting his wife up as operator of the Castle, Donald created an obstacle for Steve and himself. Indeed, we wondered what promises he had made to Ivana in the same regard. In explaining her presence at the Castle, he had said, "What I needed was someone totally competent, totally honest and totally loyal to oversee the project. There is nothing to compare with family if they happen to be competent, because you can trust family in a way you can never trust anyone else."

But it was Steve's opinion, based on conversations with Donald, that Ivana was in Atlantic City because her involvement in Trump's business and her presence at his construction sites in New York had become an embarrassment to him. He had expressed privately to Steve his hope that she'd get bored in Atlantic City and agree to return quietly to her duties as a wife and mother of their three children.

Steve had stronger grounds than Mark and I for such speculation. He and Donald spoke every day, usually several times a day, whether in person or over the telephone. Donald routinely called him at home at night from his Trump Tower penthouse, where, Steve told me, Donald slept in a bedroom alone, apart from his wife. From what I saw, Steve was the only man Donald actively sought out for conversation. And he may have been the only person Donald truly trusted. Often, their late-night phone calls lasted into the wee hours. Steve characterized these conversations as largely personal, and he kept most of their contents to himself. I believe that Steve was as close a friend as Trump ever had.

Nonetheless, Ivana was operating under the assumption that she, not Steve Hyde, would rule over her husband's casino empire. Like her husband, she knew nothing about operating a gambling hall. But she was ambitious enough to want to learn. Initially, she attended the weekly meetings of Trump Plaza's top executives, which were chaired by Steve. She did not participate, but she busily took notes. At that time, she maintained, at the Plaza, a large office which had been hers since the earliest days of the partnership with Holiday. She never visited it after Steve was hired in the spring of 1986. But when Steve suggested the office be given to Mark Etess after Steve brought him over as executive vice-president, she refused to relinquish it. Finally, Donald had to order her to give it up, which she did.

From a marketing perspective, after I joined the Plaza, our most important task was to establish the identity for the property in the minds of the public. Naturally, we wanted to play to our strongest suit, the glamour of the Trump name. Since Steve Wynn had already established a formula for success in Atlantic City based on the market value of the so-called celebrity operator, our strategy essentially emulated his: we were going to pursue the high end of the market, the "rated" table players, the so-called high rollers, specifically those we could expect to wager at least $5,000 at blackjack, craps, baccarat or roulette during an average trip. We believed that Steve Wynn's departure left a void in that market. To capture it, though, we had to be able to offer what would be perceived as an unparalleled level of excitement, which meant the most luxurious accommodations (Steve Wynn, for example, had spent $1 million on each luxury suite at the Golden Nugget), the finest gourmet restaurants and the biggest names in sports and entertainment.

What had Steve Hyde and Mark Etess so excited from the beginning was that they recognized that for all its deficiencies, Trump Plaza had natural advantages even the Golden Nugget did not enjoy. It had size—its casino was 60,000 square feet (13,000 square feet larger than the Nugget), with 115 table games (22 more than the Nugget) and 1,670 slot machines (400 more than the Nugget)—and it had, arguably, the best location in town. It sat directly at the base of the Atlantic City Expressway, the only modern superhighway leading into the resort. Also, it adjoined the city's 60-year-old Convention Hall, site of the Miss America Pageant, which, for all practical purposes, provided it with the largest indoor arena in Atlantic City, one that seated 22,000 people. Convention Hall became the focus of our high-end marketing because it made it economically feasible to stage championship boxing matches, a mainstay of Las Vegas's success and something no Atlantic City casino had been able to do on a large scale. Boxing, as Las Vegas had shown over the years, was an incomparable enticement to the high rollers. We knew that if we could put together a first-rate series of boxing events, we could establish an image of glamour that would lift Trump Plaza's income far beyond its competitors'.

By the time I signed on in early 1987, work was well under way on a ten-story parking garage with space for 2,650 cars and an enclosed pedestrian skywalk—the first of its kind in Atlantic

City—to funnel gamblers from the garage, over Pacific Avenue, and into the second-floor casino. The cost was approximately $30 million, $25 million of which Trump obtained from $250 million in 12.875 percent bonds he floated in the spring of 1986 and secured with a first mortgage against the property. The bulk of the bond issue, $153 million, went to pay off the financing for the original construction of Trump Plaza. Another $50 million was used to buy out Holiday Corporation's half interest, with the balance of $17 million payable over seven years. The remainder, $22 million, was plowed into the property as working capital. With this money, plans were laid to remodel the interior, rip out Ivana's design, refit the hotel lobby and convert 48 guest rooms on the 14th through 35th floors into luxury suites, 19 of which would be extravagant "super suites" done in marble and gold, with living rooms and dining rooms, fully stocked bars, hot tubs and butlered service.

In contrast to what Steve and Mark had told me, Donald was at the property regularly in those first months as the renovations began. I got a firsthand look at his habits and methods.

He neither smoked nor drank alcohol. Both his grandfather and his older brother Freddie had been alcoholics. Freddie died in his forties.

Donald moved vigorously through the property, always in a dark two-piece suit with a red or pink silk tie, always with two burly lookouts, Lynwood Smith and Jim Farr, by his sides. He rarely stopped to acknowledge the crowds he inevitably attracted. If he passed a gift shop, he'd go in and scoop up handfuls of chocolate candy and stuff them in his pockets to eat later; then he'd move on to finish his whirlwind tour or make his next meeting. He had a passion for cleanliness, and depending on his mood, a stray cigarette butt on the carpet or an employee's scuffed shoes could unleash in him a fearful tirade, always accompanied by a stream of expletives. Usually, it was Steve Hyde who bore the brunt of it. (Donald's language was the hardest thing to get used to at first. Donald seemed not to notice it. It was nothing to find him perched on the end of a desk in the secretarial pool at the front of the executive suite, talking on the phone, barking into the receiver the earthiest speech laced with four-letter words as if no one else was around.)

After concluding whatever business required him to be in Atlantic City, he usually returned to New York. Occasionally, though, he'd stay overnight. Then it seemed that he was possessed by an almost unnatural energy. He was uncanny in that he seemed to sleep only in fits. He would wake in the middle of the night and come downstairs to filch bags of popcorn from the newsstand, or he'd send one of his bodyguards downstairs to fetch him a king-sized chocolate milk shake from one of the restaurant kitchens. It was a mystery at times whether he slept at all, especially when he'd come down to the hotel lobby in the morning with the same navy-blue pinstripe suit he had worn the night before, so badly wrinkled that it was obvious he'd never taken it off.

Within weeks of my coming to Trump Plaza, the top floors were closed off for the construction of the new luxury suites. Later, the renovation of the hotel lobby was begun. For the sake of getting the parking garage up and open, the only outdoor lot we had had to be shut down for a time, leaving us with no parking at all.

Donald complained incessantly about the conditions resulting from the remodeling. The place was "a pigsty," he told Ivana; it was not being managed properly and was not making enough money. This was offensive to us, especially to Steve. What was inexplicable about it was that Donald had agreed on the importance of the improvements and had been kept abreast of the progress all the way. It seemed to me that he was terribly forgetful. And there was an endless restlessness about him. Also as

I learned, his attention span was frightfully short. Whatever you said to him you had to say fast. Combine these traits and loose them from any outside control and they could be devastating for business. Steve realized early on, and impressed upon Mark and me, that our most important job might be to shield the Trump Plaza staff from Donald's volatile and unpredictable moods.

Initially, the renovations were a detriment to our competitive position. What hurt more was Donald's failure to grasp even the most basic facts about the performance of the two properties. In *The Art of the Deal,* he claimed that in 1985, the Castle's first year, its gross revenue—the earnings from all operations, including gaming, the hotel, restaurants and cocktail lounges—was fourth best among the eleven casinos in town and "far better," he said, than his Boardwalk property, Harrah's at Trump Plaza, had done in the same period. But it is impossible to assess performance based on six months after opening. Trump Plaza grossed $266 million that year, according to figures published by the Casino Association of New Jersey, an industry trade group, while the Castle's gross in the first six months after it opened was $143 million.

But the retail value of the promotions Trump Plaza spent to drive in that business—the rooms, food, beverages and entertainment given away to customers—was $35 million. The Castle, in six months of operation, spent $15 million. So the Plaza earned more, but a comparatively larger portion of it was its own money. Which is only to say that in a casino, an accurate financial profile is a tricky thing to come by in the short run.

There are two basic gradations of prosperity: 1) "gross revenue," the total of all operations, the "top line," is one; and 2) "gross casino revenue," known as the "win," which is the money earned on the gaming floor after all winning bets are paid.

But perhaps the most useful figure is "operating income," which is best defined as revenue from all operations minus promotional allowances, the cost of goods and services, cash and bus subsidies, advertising, depreciation and uncollected gambling markers. Operating income is valuable in addressing the ability to service debt. Generally, high operating income shows a vibrant cash flow. And operating income also helps to measure how efficiently a property is run. "Net income," or profit—the "bottom line"—is a function of operating income after interest and taxes are paid.

The Plaza was not performing as well as our two principal rivals, the Golden Nugget and Caesars. Steve Hyde saw this immediately, especially the need to improve management of the Plaza's games. The Castle generated $6 million more in gaming revenue and $3.5 million more in gross revenue in 1986 than Trump Plaza. This impressed Donald, who proclaimed, "The Castle is doing great." He added, "But I still give Ivana a hard time about the fact that it's not yet number one."

Ivana, for her part, shunned all communication with Steve Hyde and instead selected her own group of executives and advisers at Trump's Castle, which she molded into an inner circle that revolved around her and in turn depended on her for power and influence.

But when it came to power and influence in Atlantic City, Donald had found the key in Pat McGahn, a portly, ingratiating Irish-American, a "saloonkeeper's son," as he liked to describe himself, a Congressional Medal of Honor recipient in the Korean War, an attorney whose familiarity with the political system and its players in Atlantic City allowed him to command legal fees of $300 an hour. Probably the resort's best known and most powerful lawyer, his fees reportedly were the highest in town.

His brother, Joseph McGahn, a former state senator, was one of the sponsors of the original Casino Control Act. Among its other provisions, the act exempts lawyers from the licensing requirements that apply to nearly everyone else who does business with a casino, from suppliers to vendors to investors, the rationale being that they are regulated by the state bar association. Yet, paradoxically, Hilton Hotels Corporation was denied a gaming license because of its association with a Chicago attorney with alleged ties to organized crime who, incidentally, was a member in good standing of the Illinois bar. And with strict language incorporated into the act banning direct political activity by casino owners and executives, attorneys with Pat McGahn's connections became of inestimable value to the gaming companies.

No sooner had Resorts International broken ground as the city's first gambling hall than Pat McGahn was hired on to provide legal and lobbying muscle. As one of many casino owners seeking political clout, Donald sought out McGahn when he came to Atlantic City. McGahn's first coup for him was his negotiation of a deal with the city that obtained for Donald certain air rights at a cost of $100, which allowed him to extend Trump Plaza over a portion of Mississippi Avenue.

Ivana came to rely heavily on a man named Jerry Segal, a former cement contractor from Pennsylvania who came to Atlantic City in the 1970s and bought a local building trades publication in the early days of the casino construction boom. From that he launched *Atlantic City Action*, a monthly newsletter published under the pseudonym "Al Glasgow" which contains analyses of casino win figures spiced with some rough-hewn advice and predictions.

Glasgow had no casino operations experience. "I learned everything by the seat of my pants," as he once told *Atlantic City Magazine*. "They don't teach you to shoot craps at the Harvard Business School." Operating out of a small office near the Boardwalk in the eastern end of town, he gained a certain notoriety, claiming a subscription of nearly 2,000 and frequent quotes in the *New York Times*, *Barron's*, the *Wall Street Journal*, *Fortune* magazine, the *Philadelphia Inquirer* and the *Las Vegas Sun*.

Donald saw the publicity value of having *Atlantic City Action* in his corner. How he and Glasgow met is uncertain, though I knew Glasgow had ties to Nicholas Ribis, a Newark attorney Donald had hired to represent him at his initial licensing hearing in 1982 and whom he has retained ever since in his dealings with the state's casino regulatory agencies. Nick's law offices are quartered in the same Boardwalk building as the Casino Control Commission's.

Glasgow likened himself to the so-called old-school casino operators, Nevada-style, among whom he held up Steve Wynn as the model: "Like they say, [Wynn] talks to Wall Street in the morning and Mulberry Street at night, and they both understand him," he once said. Donald took an immediate liking to the gruff, thick-set pundit, whose gravelly voice and penchant for silk suits, gold watches and filterless Pall Mall cigarettes lent him the appearance of the archetypal gambling tout. "Al is a true Damon Runyon character who lives and breathes gaming," Donald said. "He knows as much as anyone in town about who's doing what to whom."

Donald signed him on as a consultant at a fee estimated at $10,000 a month, but which, in the opinion of one gaming analyst with intimate knowledge of Donald's Atlantic City operation, may in fact have been as high as $30,000. However the relationship was structured, Glasgow apparently avoided having to apply to the Casino Control Commission for a "casino service industry," or vendor, license, despite a provision in the Casino Control Act which requires that any company or individual doing "regular and continuing business" with a casino be licensed ("real and continuing business" defined as $50,000 in a 12-month period). The commission has no record of such a license under "Jerry Segal," the "Al Glasgow" pseudonym, or *Atlantic City Action*.

Glasgow held no sway at Trump Plaza. Steve Hyde was too well versed in the Atlantic City market for the calculations published in *Atlantic City Action* to add anything to the analyses we computed in-house every week. We considered them no more revealing than the monthly numbers released by the Casino Association of New Jersey, from which they are culled.

But he had influence at the Castle from the moment Donald purchased the property. In *The Art of the Deal* Donald says it was Glasgow who first called him with the news when Barron Hilton was denied a gaming license. Later, when it was Ivana who was in need of expertise, Glasgow found his niche. "She understands the game," he once said of Ivana. "Like they say, there's nothing like having your old lady at the cash register."

It was Glasgow who took credit for starting Ivana on the practice of spending half a workday inspecting and signing every casino disbursement check except payroll. It was her first order of business every Tuesday when she came to Atlantic City in the luxury Super Puma, christened the "Ivana" in those days and decorated with mahogany, plush carpeting, a sofa and wet bar.

On Tuesdays, when the Super Puma approached Bader Field, a small airport on the western outskirts of town, the staff at the Castle made ready. A limousine would be waiting to transport Ivana to the property. After she arrived, two secretaries were summoned to her office. The first carried in a large basket of checks and stood on her right, placing the checks on the desk top in front of her. A second secretary stood on her left ready to lift each one away to make room for the next. Ivana would either sign each one as it passed or, if she saw one she thought was unjustifiably large, toss it on the carpet and say, "I'm not paying it!" This ritual took four to five hours.

Once, a former director of public relations questioned her when a request for a $1.49 envelope moistener for the department's voluminous mailings came back with Ivana's red-ink slash and the word, "Denied."

"My secretary needs it," he said.

"Why is that?" Ivana replied. "Can't she use her tongue?"

Like Steve, she chaired her own executive committee meetings. But something was lost in the translation from the Plaza's format, on which she based her meetings. "The queen's court and her various knights sitting around the Round Table," as one of her former directors confided to me. No one but Ivana had much to discuss at these meetings, which lasted on average about fifteen minutes. She'd say what was on her mind and did not entertain any outside suggestions or objections. These meetings became infamous for her shouting matches with her directors.

But Donald insisted that Ivana was "a great manager who treats her employees very well. But she's also very demanding and very competitive," he added. "Her employees respect her because they know she's pushing herself as hard as she's pushing them."

Whether she understood the casino business or not, Ivana was a legend among New York's beautiful people for her fabulous jewelry and haute couture and she brought an air of glamour to Atlantic City.

Yet she possessed a surprisingly frugal streak. She did not want the soap in her bathroom discarded if the smallest bit remained of the bar. One time, she became extremely upset when she discovered a tube of her Maybelline eyeliner, a brand available in any drugstore, was missing from among her things. Later, she found it in her apartment at Trump Tower in New York and apologized for having insisted earlier that someone at the Castle had stolen it.

Generally, after spending Wednesday evening in the Castle apartment, she left on the Super Puma on Thursday morning to return to her home at Trump Tower in New York. Donald usually waited until she was gone to visit the Castle, so when he did it was mostly on weekends. This incensed Ivana, since it appeared that her husband was shunning her property and favoring Trump Plaza.

But Donald's presence at Trump Plaza was a source of tremendous tension as well. Midway through the year we were installing an exclusive lounge for our preferred customers at the top of the hotel tower, called simply "The Club." In some areas, the tile ceiling had to be lowered almost a foot to accommodate the pipes for the hot tubs in the luxury suites that were being built on the floor directly above.

Donald preferred high ceilings and he swore loudly when he was told this. Every time he entered The Club to survey the construction, he'd get testy and swear again. But the reasons were explained to him every time. Then he accepted it. At least he never gave the order to change it. So the construction proceeded.

Finally, the ceiling was installed. One Saturday, Donald went up to have a look, accompanied by Steve, some of our hotel executives and a group of contractors. Donald looked up at the ceiling as if it was the first time he had seen it; then he looked at Steve. "What the fuck is this?" he said. "Who said to make this ceiling so low?"

"You knew about this, Donald," Steve replied. "We talked about it, if you remember, and the plans—"

Suddenly Donald leaped up and punched his fist through the tile. Then he turned on Steve in a rage. "You cocksucker! Motherfucker! Where the fuck were you? Where was your fucking head?"

I don't know how long this went on. But I happened to see Steve in the hall immediately afterward, downstairs in the executive suite. His shirt and suitcoat were soaked with perspiration. He looked ill. He passed me and went into his office. I followed and put my head in the door. "Steve, is everything okay?" I asked.

He propped his elbows on the desk and rested his head in his hands. "Donald just went crazy up in The Club. We have to redo the ceiling treatment."

I was shocked. "We've been through this for weeks. I thought this was over."

Then Steve told me what had just happened. He had been humiliated in front of twenty people, colleagues and professionals. He was not a man to take that lightly. In fact, he left the property that afternoon and took the rest of the day off.

The Club turned out to be a lovely room, with rich oak paneling, black marble-top bars and a magnificent view of the ocean. And low ceilings. After that day though Donald never set foot inside it again if he could help it.

"Some people have a sense of the market and some people don't. I like to think I have that instinct."

—DONALD J. TRUMP

Steve Hyde was back at his desk the Monday morning after Donald's outburst in The Club, as if it had never happened. But the episode had a potent effect on Steve. He became so equanimous in his dealings with Donald as to be fearless. A shock had been dealt to his system that day which rendered him immune from then on to the billionaire's tantrums. As a result of this, he was more adept than anyone I knew at controlling Donald and anticipating his moods.

It was a full-time job, though, because Donald's erratic temperament distracted everyone from business objectives. He was suspicious of his executives, so he liked to play a game of surprise with us. When we thought he was in New York, he would appear unexpectedly in the property, often in the wee hours of the morning, sometimes alone, sometimes with a caravan of guests. If he did not find us in the property—regardless of the hour—he'd call Steve the next day demanding to know where we were. He expected us to be there working whenever he arrived.

At the same time, we always had to be on guard against his

habit of taking aside employees—dealers, housekeepers, janitors, doormen, anyone—and asking them for information about management, then using that information to rate our performance. More often than not, Donald would take the advice of the last person he spoke to, and he'd form his opinions accordingly. I learned that anyone who had the courage to speak to him could influence him. The executive staff relied on Steve to follow behind and smooth over any damage that might result. It was Steve's steady hand and abiding fairness that supported morale at Trump Plaza and maintained it for the property's assault on the front ranks of the gambling world.

Midway through 1987, the Plaza's massive capital improvements were nearly complete. Most of the new luxury suites were finished, and the lobby renovations were well along. The parking garage was opened to traffic on Memorial Day weekend, the start of Atlantic City's busy summer tourist season. On June 15, we struck our first blow: "The War at the Shore," we billed it—heavyweight champion Michael Spinks against Gerry Cooney at Convention Hall.

Bidding for the "site fee," the right to stage the fight, sparked a battle with Caesars Palace and the Hilton in Las Vegas that drove up the price and ultimately cost Trump Plaza $3.5 million. But it was worth it. The promotional and financial dividends were tremendous. Six hundred sportswriters and journalists descended on Atlantic City to see the champ easily handle the aging but popular Cooney. As for delivering the big gambling customers, the fight exceeded our wildest hopes. Ten of the twelve casinos (the Showboat Hotel & Casino had opened in April) purchased tickets from us for their high rollers to see the fight at Convention Hall. The fight drew $3 million at the gate, qualifying it as the highest-grossing live event by far in the city's history up to that time. Betting at our craps, blackjack and roulette tables was at $100 minimums on Saturday night, the night of the fight.

In the baccarat pit the games were smoking at $500 minimums. For the entire day, the amount of gambling chips and markers placed in circulation, known in gaming parlance as the "drop," exceeded $7 million at Trump Plaza, three times a normal summer day's activity and the most action ever experienced at one Atlantic City casino in one day up to that time. Estimates of the cash pumped into the resort's economy ranged from $5 million to as high as $10 million.

We had successfully launched the first phase of our marketing strategy, which was to fashion an identity for Trump Plaza that the public would associate with the glamour and excitement of big-time boxing. The rest of the summer season unfolded fabulously for us. Donald understood the value of image. After all, it was image that created him in New York, and it was what drove his desire to be in Atlantic City in the first place, sizzling as it was in the early and mid-1980s with the anticipation of huge profits and the names of gaming's most exciting entrepreneurs. But he understood image only to a point, which was how he perceived the Trump image to affect him personally. Because he interpreted it so subjectively, he couldn't take it past the most superficial level.

As a consequence, he failed to understand that marketing a gambling hall, in its simplest terms, is really no more and no less than selling a retail product. Imagine Trump Plaza as one of several gambling "products," and imagine Atlantic City as a shelf in a store. Our job as the "manufacturer" was to give the consumer as many reasons as possible to take our product off the shelf rather than the others lined up alongside it. How is that done successfully? By the same methods that have always sold retail products: a market is identified and understood, the product is manufactured to be competitive in that market, and it is individualized, separated from the others and given an identity with which the consumer wants to be associated.

By the mid-1980s, it was clear that Atlantic City's gambling market had become dependent on high volume: large numbers of middle-income bettors, husbands and wives, 35 and older, who mostly came by car or bus, usually for the day, and mainly to play nickel, quarter and dollar slot machines. The bulk of this market represented a gambling potential between $25 and $150 on an average visit. Most casinos chased this market with bus charters, which daily brought in thousands of low-limit players by subsidizing the cost of their tickets with coin and meal vouchers. These methods, unfortunately, were not cost-effective. Worse still, they failed the first test of successful retailing—they did not identify the market. They failed to distinguish gambling potential. Obviously, given the choice between a $25 player and a $150 player, every casino wanted the latter. Yet bus programs provided no way of knowing which customer a casino would be getting, and why. So marketing, not transportation, was the key for me. I had learned this when I worked for Steve Wynn.

Steve built his success in Atlantic City by tailoring his strategies to the strength and limitations of his property. Necessity dictated the Golden Nugget's high-stakes gambling image, a point many of the experts in town have overlooked. It was the smallest casino in town, with 93 craps, blackjack and baccarat tables and only 1,200 slot machines. To be profitable it had to win the most money possible at every location, which meant that the amounts wagered—the "drop"—had to be, table-for-table and slot-for-slot, consistently larger than its competitors'. At the tables, this meant offering a product that appealed to the gamblers with the deepest pockets, the high rollers, whom he cultivated through a network of player representatives and junket operatives that were the best in the business. Then, once he got them inside the property, he feted them with incomparable luxury in the suites and restaurants, with personal service second to none. He lavished complimentaries on them and dazzled them with the top names in entertainment.

Of course, there is nothing new in extravagance. In New York,

Donald Trump reaped enormous success and publicity with it during the boom in the luxury real estate market of the 1980s. Steve's talent went beyond that. Subtly, he sidestepped the prevailing wisdom that no casino could successfully pursue disparate ends of the market at the same time. He recognized that the glamour of the high-roller image worked like an aphrodisiac on middle-income bettors and could be of practical use as a promotional technique in attracting them to his casino. He avoided bus charters because the Nugget was too small to accommodate masses of people, and it needed the optimum in "win" at every betting location. Instead he tried to identify and track the most consistent bettors within the mass market. And he innovated—for example, introducing four-times odds at craps to lure players with a better deal at the games, and installing ticket dispensers at his dollar slot machines, with the tickets redeemable in coins. He devised other giveaways depending on the level of play, for example, the "24 Karat Club," which was simply an old concept—the "S&H Green Stamp" idea—applied to new circumstances.

But his genius was in stretching the concept of casino "marketing," defining it in the broadest possible terms to develop deep consumer loyalty at both the high and middle levels. Every operator knows how to single out the affluent player. But no casino can prosper on affluent players alone. Financial success depended on how well we attracted middle-income bettors. Steve recognized that all employees in a casino must offer excellent personal service to the gambler of moderate means as well as to the big spenders, touching even middle-class bettors with the trappings of affluence. Most casinos just didn't bother to do this. So Steve saw his edge, realizing that if he could make that "average" player feel special, more than likely he could make that player his for life. "The key is to make the $50 guy feel like a $50,000 guy," he used to say. Steve achieved a partnership between image and reality. The Nugget inspired loyalty in its customers at the high, middle and low levels that has never been surpassed in Atlantic City.

At Trump Plaza, we tried to achieve the same. We had natural advantages over the Nugget—we had size, location and, by virtue of our proximity to the large arena of Convention Hall, the ability to stage big boxing matches to market to the high end. Steve Hyde, Mark Etess and I wanted that high end. It matched the Trump profile of wealth and elegance: that was *our* product. Plus, Donald had the bankroll to weather the stakes and to finance the personal network and the junkets to attract the big players, so it made sense economically. Finally, we believed that Steve Wynn's exit early in 1987 left a void in servicing that market in Atlantic City. Either we pursued it ourselves or we could watch it wind up at Caesars down the street.

From the beginning, we were also looking beyond the continental United States. We set our sights on capturing a share of the high-stakes international gaming clientele, a market that could catapult Trump Plaza into that rarefied air where Monte Carlo and Caesars Palace in Las Vegas breathe. It could mean the difference between great years and spectacular ones. We all had extensive connections from our years in the business. Steve Hyde hired a man named T. J. Tejada, whom he had known from his days at Caesars Palace and who was prized on the East Coast for his ability to bring in the wealthiest South American players. He also brought over from the Golden Nugget a man named Ernie Cheung, who enjoyed strong connections in the Orient to spread the Trump Plaza name among the millionaire gamblers of Japan and Hong Kong. It played perfectly to the Trump image, especially in Japan, where Donald's accomplishments were revered and his name was gilt-edged currency.

Donald wanted this high-end trade, too, and was prepared to spend whatever it took to get it. It gratified his ego. But his thinking on the subject really did not go much beyond that. He had no interest in learning the table games and the theories behind them. He did not understand gamblers. He could not comprehend that a person who comes thousands of miles to stand at a table and wager $10,000 over and over again on a throw of the dice is motivated by something other than money. This surprised me at first, then baffled me. After all, Donald's approach to business was so reminiscent of a gambler's. There was an undeniable image of romance that surrounded it and which was the wellspring of his fame. He was a builder of skyscrapers, his name sparkled with the bright lights of Manhattan, multimillion-dollar deals were his "art." How could he not understand the psyche of the affluent gambler?

Then I learned that what motivated him *was* the money. Never mind that he must have had all that he could possibly want. I began to see that Donald's mind moved between very simple polarities: there were only "positives" and "negatives," to use his own terminology, "winners" and "losers." Everything and everyone fell into one category or the other depending on where the pile of cash was when the dust settled. To his thinking, the high roller was valuable in the gambling world, more valuable than the slot player, because, individually speaking, the high roller brought more money into the casino, therefore he would lose more, thus resulting in the movement of a comparatively larger pile of money from the customer's side of the table to Donald's.

Beyond that simple scenario, he had no interest in what happened. It was avarice on the most primitive level. And consequently, extremely shortsighted. For one, it completely ignored the mass-market character of Atlantic City's gaming industry. To give an example, Donald hated cash sweepstakes and large slot jackpots, both valuable promotional tools, because it seemed to him that they allowed a gambler of relatively small means to win a lot of money. He could not see the importance of these tools in attracting loyal slot machine players. Nor could he seem to grasp the role of the high-end player in creating an ambience for the property that would attract those same mass-market players. He could not see that 20 customers with a gambling potential of $1,000 each were more desirable than one $20,000 player, and that it was foolish to pursue the latter at the expense of the former, since the loss of the $20,000 player meant the loss of the entire $20,000, yet the loss of even five of the $1,000 players would still leave a casino with $15,000.

Donald was ignorant of one of the most fundamental tenets of a successful enterprise—customer loyalty and repeat business. It is not enough to get a player into your casino; you want him to come back again and again, regardless of his stature and whether he loses or wins. But you especially want these players back if they win. Time is on the casino's side in a game of chance. As long as the game is honest, time favors the "house." Eventually, if he plays long enough and often enough, the gambler will lose more than he wins. He may win for a while. But that is why, when the stakes climb to three, four and five figures, the length of time he is willing to commit to the table is a prime factor in the house's decisions regarding betting limits, the extension of credit and the treatment he can expect as far as accommodations, complimentaries, travel expenses and the like.

I saw a player toss the dice at craps, and when one cube happened to roll up the dealer's arm and fall back down, the player cried, "It stopped on his arm! It stopped on his arm! It was a four!" The pit boss called Steve Hyde. A $10,000 bet was on the line. "Give it to him," Steve said without hesitating. He knew we'd win it back in due time.

Donald did not understand this, but then his conception of time was so circumscribed that it was astounding. He did business almost entirely in the moment. He would become extremely anxious whenever sizable piles of money shifted to the player's side. He did not approve of us dealing to customers who beat us for large sums. The result was that he continually squandered the significant drawing power of his name among the affluent players. I noticed early in my career at Trump Plaza that at parties and buffets we sponsored for our high-stakes customers, the promise of an appearance by Donald always got us a stronger response from the invitations. But he rarely attended them. The man who mistargeted his market with cameo appearances in an MTV video and a *Saturday Night Live* broadcast considered it a waste of his time to mingle for an hour with a couple of hundred of his most lucrative customers.

I learned this during my first year at Trump Plaza when I attended one party with him. I watched Donald grow more sullen the closer we got to the casino. "This is bullshit," he complained to me as we walked in. It had been an arduous battle to persuade him to come in the first place. Now he was having second thoughts.

He wasn't smiling when we entered. He stayed near the door and sent his bodyguard, Lynwood Smith, over to the buffet to fetch him a Diet Coke with a straw. One player came over and we chatted briefly. When the player turned away for a moment, Donald said to me, "Christ, doesn't this guy come here all the time?"

"Yeah, he's one of our best," I said, assuming he'd be pleased. But he scowled.

By then several customers had gathered around Donald. Suddenly, and loud enough for all to hear, he replied bitterly: "Tell me about it. I know. And all he does is beat me. I don't know why we're bringing him in. This guy has done nothing but beat me every time he sets foot in the place."

Everyone was surprised. Donald looked about impatiently. He quickly finished his Diet Coke and glanced at his watch. "That's it. I'm going," he said, and without another word he walked out.

It was an uncomfortable moment. But I was becoming accustomed to Donald griping whenever a player got hot and won big at one of our games. Similarly, he never concealed his glee when it was the other way around. One time Donald asked one of our best players how he'd fared after a weekend at the casino. "Eh, not so good," the customer said. "I dropped $250,000."

Donald said, "Great . . . oh, that's great."

We lost many large bettors as a result of this overtly expressed attitude. After one customer party, a highly rated player from the Middle East complained to me because Donald groused to his face about the gambler "beating him." He was getting the impression that Donald resented it. "Maybe I should play somewhere else if 'the Donald' really cannot handle it," he said.

Other players found his attitude amusing and took greater pleasure in trying to beat him. Gamblers at all levels are superstitious, they believe in "luck," and oftentimes they're driven more by their emotions than their wallets. Instincts, devotion to a "lucky" object or location, personal loyalties and, most of all, the experience you created for them during their stay—these figure more into their decision to return than success or failure with the turn of the cards. A gambler's self-importance is based on the fact that he wagers, and he expects to be appreciated in accordance with the level of risk he is taking. I had one sit next to me in The Club one night and very earnestly and confidentially promise to have me killed because I would not guarantee him ringside seats to a championship boxing match. The worst thing you can do is to give the impression that you're interested only in picking the gambler's pocket and sending him on his way.

We were favored with many wealthy players through their devotion to Steve Hyde, and as president of Trump Plaza, Steve took great pride in his personal relationships with them. Donald's behavior was a great source of embarrassment. Steve was constantly trying to soothe sore feelings.

At the same time, Donald was obsessed with appearances that

were irrelevant by comparison. He was a stickler when it came to dress. He wore only suits and expected his executives to do the same, and he preferred that you keep your jacket on, even at your desk. He always did this, and his staff in New York followed in step.

I remember Mark Etess's education in the Trump uniform code. In one of his early meetings with Donald at Trump Tower shortly after he was hired, Mark showed up in a sportcoat, not knowing any better. Donald glared at him. Harvey Freeman promptly took Mark aside and explained, "There are no sport-coats in the Trump Organization."

Later, Mark was the offending party again, this time at the Trump Plaza. He came in on a Saturday morning for breakfast with a wealthy gambler who was staying for the weekend, dressed appropriately for what was to be a casual get-together in a warm-up suit with the casino's logo. Donald happened to pass through the property that morning and saw him. He said nothing to Mark but he called Steve Hyde at home, and he was livid. "What the fuck is one of my vice-presidents doing in the property dressed like he's going fucking jogging?" he demanded to know.

To image-obsessed Donald, a loosened tie was the sign of a sloppy mind. He could not afford himself the luxury of relaxation and would not allow it in anyone on his payroll. But the way Donald applied this principle to employees was nothing compared with his interpretation of it for his properties.

During the renovations at Trump Plaza early in 1987, we decided, and Donald agreed, that the luxury suites would get priority over the hotel lobby. This was in anticipation of the weekend of the Spinks-Cooney fight, when we expected an influx of big players and wanted to be prepared to entertain them in style. The lobby was left in a state of half-construction, but this didn't bother us and would mean nothing to the high rollers. They are preregistered in their rooms and whisked directly from their limousines to their suites. They would never spend any time in the lobby. All this was explained to Donald. But he forgot it when he arrived from New York that weekend for the fight. He saw the lobby and exploded, swearing loudly and berating Steve with a stream of expletives. He complained to Ivana, calling Trump Plaza a "shithouse." He was in a foul mood the entire weekend.

For Donald, image and reality were always in conflict. The Windsor knot in his tie was always pulled tight to his throat. At the same time, he let his sand-colored hair dip down to his eyes and curl over his ears and collar, and he plastered it on the sides with a greasy gel that he believed fostered hair growth. He had a tremendous fear of baldness. He swept his hair across the front of his head like a man trying to hide a thinning patch. He once observed to Mark that he considered baldness a sign of weakness. He gave a tube of the gel he used to Mark, warning him, "The worst thing a man can do is go bald. Never let yourself go bald," as if nature could be circumvented through sheer force of will. Mark, who had a full head of hair, laughed about it. One day, he took the tube out of a desk drawer where he'd stashed it and showed it to me. "Why the hell did he give this to me?" he said. "He should have given it to you."

But Donald's conflict between image and reality had more serious ramifications for us, too. As much as Donald desired the high-stakes gambling trade he prevented us from exploiting one of the greatest promotional weapons in his arsenal, his private jet.

To acquire it, Donald had rummaged for months through America's corporate flea market, looking for a distress sale to his liking. He finally found a Boeing 727 owned by a financially pressed Texas oil company. The aircraft had been reconfigured for the company's purposes to seat fifteen and was equipped with a center conference area, and a full bath and bedroom. "It was a little more plane than I needed," Donald said after he bought it, "but I find it hard to resist a good deal when the opportunity presents itself."

Actually, the outdated, fuel-guzzling 727 was worth, at most, about half the $8 million he paid for it. The oil company must have been more than happy to unload it. Donald sank millions more into the jet, adding a rear conference area, five more seats, two more baths, remodeling the stateroom to make a luxury master bedroom, installing 24-karat gold fixtures, and repainting the exterior with alternating red, gold and black stripes and "TRUMP" in red letters on the tail.

We suggested to him that he allow us to use the jet to fly some of our very top gamblers to Atlantic City, but always he refused. It was a foolish business decision. The jet was costing him $4,000 an hour to keep in the air with a flight crew of four and a mechanic on the ground. On an average of 300 hours a year, it was sucking $1.2 million annually from his personal accounts. He could have recouped that plus his initial investment, and then some, had he let us entertain and fly in select high-paying players from around the country and from overseas. But Donald wouldn't hear of it. "No way," he said. "I don't want these high-roller slobs pissing on my toilet seat."

Donald often boasted that his pilots were the best in the country. He took great pride in their skill. He auditioned several flight crews in New York before selecting one that suited him. Donald was adamant about not wanting to feel any movement during landings or while the plane was in the air. He'd get extremely upset with his pilots over a rough landing, whether it was their fault or not. Normally not inquisitive about anything outside his business, he did have an absorbing interest in the difficulties and skill involved in flying his jet. He liked to ride in the cockpit, especially when the jet was coming down over the Rocky Mountains on the approach to Aspen, and he insisted that all his first-time guests ride up there with him. Mark Etess, who disliked flying and was uncomfortable in the air, told me about being pressed into that duty, squeezed in with Donald, the pilot and copilot while Donald engaged the crew in conversation, constantly asking questions.

(Characteristic of many powerful people, Donald always needed agreement and reassurance. Either you volunteered it or he'd ask for it. He'd say, "God, I think it's a great day today, Jack. Don't you agree?" Or "I think business is going to be strong this weekend, don't you think so?" And so it was the case 30,000 feet in the air.)

But gaining access to Donald's jet was less important to me than getting the $150 gamblers into Trump Plaza—and keeping them there. As senior vice-president of marketing, it was my job to figure out how to do this. We were always experimenting, trying new methods to win a gambler's loyalty. It might be a $10 coin voucher, maybe a birthday or anniversary card, maybe two tickets to a small fight. We freed some promotional money by cutting our massive bus subsidies. We were transporting 5,000 people a day into the property before the garage opened in mid-1987. I immediately began cutting it, ultimately whittling it down to about 3,000.

We hit upon the idea of the "Trump Card," a wallet-size piece of plastic stamped with an account number. These were distributed to our slot customers based on their level of play. The cards contained a magnetic strip that could be inserted into the machine, instantly telling our marketing staff that the player was in the property and enabling us to track his or her play and rate it. With the Trump Card we further sharpened the aim of our complimentaries, even routing them directly to the player on the floor. We developed customer profiles with personal information like birthdays and anniversaries. If a player's birthday was the next day, for example, the Trump Card alerted us immediately, and we made sure to send a host down to the floor to present him or her with a small gift right at the machine. Invariably, our customers were amazed and gratified by this. It was really just a refinement on Steve Wynn's technique, the high-roller philosophy translated to the mass market.

Donald's celebrity would have been of enormous value to my efforts, but he displayed a disdain for the public that was embarrassing. It was yet another contradiction for someone as obsessed with popularity as he was.

Walking through the public areas with him it was impossible not to notice the crowds he attracted. On a busy night, people would stop in the aisles and the corridors to watch him pass. It was something to see, how they'd stand, wide-eyed, and part to let him and his two hulking bodyguards through, as if they knew instinctively to keep a safe distance. Donald had a brusque manner, which, like the characteristic smirk he always wore, was etched in his face.

This was true even when he was in a good mood—as he usually was on Saturday nights, when the place was packed with gamblers and the slot machines were ringing and the tables were alive and boisterous with action. "I feel like we're gonna have a great night tonight, Jack, don't you?" he'd say, demanding reassurance. Of course, I'd agree.

I remember accompanying him one night like this when he and his bodyguards were making their way upstairs from the casino level to Maximilian's, his favorite restaurant. I moved among the knots of people who stared at us, nudging each other and pointing, while Donald strode ahead in his wide, brisk step, unmindful of them, talking all the time to me even though I was three steps behind. We stopped before the entrance to Maximilian's, and he said expansively, "Did you see all those people downstairs? Man, I really feel good tonight. We're going to do great numbers tonight. Yep, Jack, I can feel it."

Just then a middle-aged woman stepped forward boldly and

said, "Mr. Trump, please, I'd love to have your autograph." She took a small writing pad and a marker from her handbag and held them out to him.

Instantly, his mood changed. His eyes narrowed irritably. He resented the interruption. So he ignored her and turned to enter the restaurant. Confused, and thinking perhaps that he hadn't heard her, the woman asked again. So he obliged, though reluctantly. He looked down at the carpet while he wrote, scribbling something illegible, never saying a word to her and handing back the paper and pen without ever once looking at her. He had no patience for civilities if he saw no business purpose to them.

It was painfully obvious how ill at ease he was in public situations. In part, I think it was really beyond his control. He was preoccupied by a fear of communicable disease, especially AIDS. Sometimes he'd joke about it, but he went so far as to warn a high-ranking Trump's Castle publicist to avoid the Jacuzzi in the luxury health spa there because he considered it a potential breeding ground for the deadly virus. Consequently he had an aversion to strangers touching him. It would irritate him to the point of distraction if someone stepped up to whisper in his ear, or if an elderly woman who abandoned her slot machine in hopes of meeting him got close enough to peck him on the cheek. He did not like to shake hands. As often as business required him to do it, he was never at ease with the custom. He always spoke of how he detested it.

On the rare occasions when the crowds got a little too close, he'd almost panic. Ivana was more gracious in that respect. It was a source of frequent arguments between them. He scolded her unmercifully one afternoon at Trump's Castle as they walked together through the hotel lobby and she stopped to acknowledge a couple of customers, elderly women, who recognized her and asked to meet her. One had been so bold as to touch her dress. "I told you a hundred times, don't talk to these people," he shouted after they'd gone. He was still fuming over it as they continued on their way and stepped onto the escalator to go down to the car. "I don't understand you," he grumbled. "Why do you let these people touch you? Forget them. Don't pay attention to them. Just forget them!"

Whether he applied it to his personal life or to the marketing strategy of his casinos, "forgetting" the average person was a cornerstone of Donald's philosophy.∨

4

*"I said you can't bet against Ivana, and she
proved me right even sooner than I expected."*
—DONALD J. TRUMP

he Spinks-Cooney bout on June 15, 1987, presented Las
Vegas with a serious challenge to its dominance of the fight
game. But for Trump it was only a first step in a larger
strategy aimed at capturing the fight for the undisputed heavyweight crown.

Boxing's official governing bodies had not recognized Spinks's
victory over the unranked Cooney. Meanwhile, two heavyweight
titles had been snapped up in rapid succession by a fearsome 21-
year-old with wrecking balls for fists—Mike Tyson. In November
1986, he had knocked out Trevor Berbick in the second round in
Las Vegas to win the World Boxing Council heavyweight title.
Five months later, he was recognized as champ by the World
Boxing Association after a twelve-round unanimous decision over
James "Bonecrusher" Smith, also in Las Vegas. Even as Mark
Etess nailed down the arrangements for the Spinks-Cooney
match, the fight we really wanted was a bout between Spinks
and the fearsome Tyson. By virtue of some very savvy negotiating,
Mark was able to sew up that bout for Trump Plaza.

In August, Mike Tyson captured his third crown, the International Boxing Federation's, in a twelve-round decision over Tony Tucker in Las Vegas. Now the stage was set for Trump Plaza to stage the new champ's first two title defenses, against Tyrell Biggs in October and against former heavyweight champ Larry Holmes, scheduled for January 1988.

Trump Plaza's revenues steadily climbed the summer of 1987 in anticipation of these major bouts as our pool of big players grew larger, flooded by customers looking to enhance their "ratings" in hopes of obtaining choice seats to the upcoming fights. (Gamblers are "rated" for their economic value to a casino by the supervisory personnel at the various locations, or "pits," where they play. Note is made of how many chips they buy, their average bet and the length of time they play. In determining a gambler's value to a casino—his "trip worth" or "gambling potential"—other factors also come into play: the theory of the particular game as well as the gambler's skill are important considerations in calculating the house advantage over a player. Obviously an unskilled player who wagers $1,000 a bet is "rated" higher than a masterful player who wagers the same amount, since the former is more likely to lose the bet.)

Across town at Trump's Castle, Ivana was hard-pressed to keep up. "Ivana is almost as competitive as I am and she insisted she's at a disadvantage with the Castle. She says she needs more suites," Donald explained early in 1987. "She isn't concerned that building the suites will cost $40 million. All she knows is that not having them is hurting her business and making it tougher for her to be number one. I'll say this much: I wouldn't bet against her."

As it turned out, Donald probably should have. Ivana persuaded him to build her 97 luxury suites at the Castle alongside its existing hotel tower. The "Crystal Tower," as the luxury suites came to be known—14 stories high with a ballroom at its base and a private club on the 12th floor—would take almost three years to build and would prove to be astonishingly expensive, much more costly than the $40 million Donald anticipated.

It was the perfect example of how Donald was misreading the market and failing to understand the real basis for his success in Atlantic City. And it was my first glimpse into the murky reality underlying this empire of his, in which properties were not operated to be profitable but to spew cash, to advertise the Trump name so that he could continue to acquire more property based on his ability to borrow from banks and bondholders. The casinos, cash fountains by nature, were the bedrock upon which everything else rested, everything he owned. But he needed to project strong gross revenues to support the pretense that every Trump asset was extremely liquid. Trump Plaza was indeed liquid, winning $25 million more in its casino in 1987 than it did in 1986, despite spending only $3 million more in complimentaries. Operating income increased by $10 million, and profits were up $2 million to $17.8 million. By contrast, the Castle spent $8 million more than the year before in complimentaries, more than twice Trump Plaza's increase. It generated $15 million more in casino win than the year before. But its operating income in 1987 was down by $2 million, and profits decreased from $3.7 million to $1.7 million. Clearly, the Steve Hyde team at the Plaza outperformed Ivana's group at the Castle in 1987.

Donald's response to this situation was to set both the Plaza and the Castle in pursuit of Atlantic City's limited pool of high-end players. He foolishly decided that the best way to generate revenues was to foment a war between his two casinos for them.

I saw early signs of it the first summer I was at the Plaza. We invited a couple of hundred of our best customers to a party in the Imperial Ballroom for a celebration of Donald's 41st birthday. Donald was in an expansive mood that evening. He took the microphone amid hearty applause and said, "It's nice to see all you folks. Thank you all. I'm inviting everyone to come over to the Castle. You have to see what Ivana has done over there. It's a wonderful place, beautiful, the best suites . . . and we're adding more. . . ."

I was shocked.

"You know," he continued, "I tell Ivana that I'm paying her one dollar a year and all the dresses she can buy." This got him some laughter. After that, it became a running gag with him. "But she really is doing the greatest job in the world over there."

So he went on, praising the Castle to the Plaza's customers at an event we were sponsoring at considerable cost. He did this all the time, much to the dismay of the staff. It really wounded morale. And it surprised the customers, too. One gambler I was sitting with at the birthday party scratched his head and said, "Hey, will somebody tell me where I am?" As a joke he picked up a book of matches, studied the cover and said, "I thought I was at the Castle. No, I guess I'm at the Plaza."

Donald played the same game at the Castle. His tactic there, as our success surpassed the Castle's in 1987, was to shove the Plaza's performance in Ivana's face, like a mirror, holding it up for her to see the reflection of a less than successful manager. She would become apprehensive before his visits and visibly nervous when they were together. They would meet in her office and he would harangue her over the weekly revenue rankings, which were circulated to executives at both properties. "What the hell are you doing down here, Ivana?" he'd say when the standings weren't satisfactory. "What's going on here? Where's the business?" For Ivana, it was maddening.

It was a sore subject as well with Steve Hyde. Not long after I joined him, Steve told me, "She hates Trump Plaza. Despises it. Whatever she can do to undermine this organization, she will. She would rather a competitor receive business than see us get it. It's almost a compulsion with her."

The way I saw it, she was fanatically ambitious and probably had been led to believe in the beginning that she was going to manage Donald's entire Atlantic City operation. Having been demoted, so to speak, to management of only one component of it, she desired above all to impress her husband with her skill. But then, beginning in 1987, the Plaza's fortunes rose as the Castle's seemed to be declining: this was a tremendous embarrassment to her. She responded by driving her staff all the harder. As she put it to one of them, "You are taking my husband's money, so your performance must be stellar." Seven-day weeks, 14-hour days, 24-hour beepers were the rule. She had all her executives and directors tied up in service contracts to guarantee loyalty and devotion to duty. A monitor was installed in her office so she could watch the parking garage through the security cameras and note what time her executives arrived for work. (One of them took to leaving his overcoat home in the winter so she'd think he had already been on the premises when, in fact, he was just arriving.)

The cleanliness of the property's public spaces was as much a passion with her as it was with Donald. The sight of a crumpled coin wrapper or an empty drink cup, even in the heavily traveled slot machine aisles, would send her into a screaming, foulmouthed rage. On one occasion she summoned the director of housekeeping to the spot on the casino floor where she had discovered a bit of litter, and let loose with a tirade of choice expletives in front of hundreds of customers. (Donald later fired that director's successor in absentia one Saturday night when he took a back stairwell, one used exclusively by the casino dealers to get from the employee lounge to the gaming floor, and found four cigarette butts on the floor. On Donald's order, Harvey Freeman, the senior vice-president of the Trump Organization, who happened to be with Donald that night, was dispatched to confront the then-president of the Castle, Paul Henderson, with the four offending stubs in the palm of his hand.)

Ivana did sincerely care for the place and really wanted to make it special. She gave her attention to every detail. Every amenity in the guest rooms was thought out. She selected everything herself. Donald called her "the most organized person I know." He boasted that "no detail escapes her." But by refusing to delegate authority, evidenced, for example, by her insistence on signing every check, she caused the property to stagnate administratively.

Ivana lacked the one essential quality of a good manager, objectivity. She refused to speak to vice-presidents she did not like personally or who displeased her, making her will known through their subordinates instead, which resulted in the splintering of her executive staff into various factions. After-hours in her office, she entertained an inner circle of aides, managers and directors with glasses of vintage white wine or high-priced bottles of Roederer Cristal champagne. There are many people who attest to Ivana's graciousness on those occasions, and to her generosity, a rare, dry wit, and a ribald sense of humor. But outside those office doors, resentments were allowed to fester. It became impossible to plan and carry through long-term operational and marketing strategies because Ivana was unable to distinguish between those offering sound advice and those simply currying favor. Power could shift from one faction to another, from month to month, which further weakened morale, sapped energies and disrupted the pursuit of objectives.

The Castle was running up large legal bills every month to handle employee contract terminations and alleged wrongful dismissals. By one former staff member's estimate, three law firms were retained just to settle the claims. Ivana, for instance, could not stand to see a pregnant woman working on the casino floor. It was first apparent during the period of the Holiday partnership, when she walked through one of the gambling pits at Harrah's at Trump Plaza one night, accompanied by the casino manager. She stopped before one table, pointed to an employee, turned to the manager and said, "Fire this girl. She's pregnant." When she was told that this was against the law, she became furious. At Trump's Castle, she took to having pregnant cocktail servers transferred off the casino floor. Whether they depended on the tips or not did not concern her.

Ivana, who had borne three children, maintained a strangely ambivalent attitude toward pregnancy. Once, she assembled her staff at the Castle for a baby shower at the hotel.

In one of her more endearing gestures she had become fond of one of her department directors, a childless woman in her 30s; and when she learned the woman had adopted a baby, she hosted the shower herself and bestowed on the child an elaborate and expensive wardrobe.

"You know," she said, when it was time to address the happy gathering, "Donald has always wanted me to have more children. But I tell him, 'The baby factory is closed.' "

As imperious and unpredictable as she could be, still, many on the staff attested to Ivana's capacity for generosity and her thoughtfulness. Unlike Donald, she made it a point to attend every "Employee of the Month" awards ceremony. Executives' birthdays were occasions for champagne in the boardroom. Once a year, she'd treat her managers to dinner at one of the Castle's finest restaurants. But in spite of the rewards and the demands she made on the staff and herself, the Castle did not perform up to expectation. The arguments between Ivana and Donald over the property's performance degenerated into tremendous rows. Typical, as I was told, was one that ended with Ivana screaming in her thick Czech accent, "Fuck you! Get the hell out of my office!"

Donald tried to object. She yelled back, "I don't want to talk to you! Get out! You don't know what the fuck you're talking about!"

"But Steve says—"

"Steve Hyde is nothing but a big fat piece of shit!"

Donald threw up his hands and walked out.

Ivana pursued our customers vigorously. Whatever she could do to lure away Trump Plaza's business, she would. Mark and I were convinced that the Castle had developed some mysterious ability to track our new customers. Steve dismissed the notion with a laugh. But Mark and I believed they had somehow tapped into our computer lines or had planted an operative in our data processing branch. Sometimes within hours after we entered a new name into our files or preregistered someone into the hotel for the first time, we'd get a call from the casino marketing department at the Castle, asking for background or credit information on the same player.

Ivana carried the feud to absurd lengths. If we gave a gift to a preferred player, Ivana gave him a more lavish one. If we presented a $100,000 player with a gold Rolex watch, the Castle gave him two. It was that ridiculous, needlessly driving up the cost of doing business for both properties.

In one instance, Ivana set her sights on one of our top players, a close friend of Steve's and a regular at the old Golden Nugget, who had followed Steve to the Plaza. This player liked to shoot craps at five-figure minimums. The Castle courted him for months through its representatives in New York until, as he later told me, he agreed to visit one night for a drink, if only to pacify them. Informed of this, Ivana made ready for his arrival, instructing her casino manager to reserve a dice table for him. It was a Saturday night in the summer of 1987, one of the busiest weekends of the peak season.

At midnight, he still hadn't arrived. But Donald had. The casino was humming, packed with players at every slot machine and every craps and blackjack game—except for one dice table, which was roped off, empty, with three attendants standing by idly. Donald stopped when he saw the empty table. He summoned the pit boss. "What's this? What's the matter here? Why is this table dead?"

The pit boss called the casino manager, who explained, "We're holding that for——, Mr. Trump."

"Holding it?" Donald said.

Both men looked at him blankly.

"Where's my wife? Get Ivana down here," he said. When she arrived, Donald turned on her fiercely. "How could you close one of my tables on the busiest fucking night of the year!" he shouted. "I can't believe you could be so stupid. Do you know how much money I'm losing here? Stupid! You're costing me a fortune! This is the stupidest fucking thing I've ever seen!" He ordered the table opened. Our player never did show at the Castle that night.

Steve complained frequently to Donald about the costs of the feud. But as harshly as Donald could turn on his wife, he'd defend her to us.

"C'mon, Steve, the competition is good, don't you think?" I remember Donald telling him one time.

Steve disagreed.

Donald said, "Hey, it's not as bad as you think it is. You're just trying to protect your turf. Are you worried she's going to do a better job than you? What are you worried about Ivana for? She's just a woman. She can't take the business."

Donald loved the confrontation, even crowed over it. "There is no way Ivana will be happy until she's far outdistanced the field."

But in the fall of 1987, Trump's Castle was dealt a serious and unexpected blow when Bucky Howard, vice-president of casino operations and one of Donald and Ivana's close confidants, was indicted on charges of conspiracy, commercial bribery and misconduct by a corporate official. The Castle's marketing vice-president, one Jerome Palma, had told state investigators that he and Bucky had split some $300,000 in kickbacks over a four-year period from airline and charter bus operations. Neither Donald nor Ivana would comment on what was clearly a personal as well as a professional dilemma for them.

At the end of October, the Casino Control Commission suspended Bucky's "key employee" license pending the outcome of a trial. Without his license, Bucky had to be let go at the Castle.

In September 1988 Bucky Howard was acquitted on the kickback charges. Exonerated, his license restored, he promptly took the top casino post at the Showboat Hotel & Casino at the far eastern end of town. At the Castle, Bucky's customer representatives, all personally loyal to him, resigned en masse—ten key executives and support staff from the marketing and player-development departments—and joined him at the Showboat. It was a crippling blow to Ivana and the Castle.

This was the state of relations between Donald's two properties when the Plaza staged Mike Tyson's first title defense against Tyrell Biggs on October 16, 1987, in Convention Hall— the "Clash for the Crown." The fight was a huge success. Bettors dropped $7 million in our casino that weekend to see Tyson dispatch the challenger with a knockout. The celebrity turnout was as impressive as Tyson's performance—Robert De Niro, Dustin Hoffman, Robert Duvall, Julius Erving, Sugar Ray Leonard, Darryl Hall and John Oates, James Caan. Donald loved to bathe in the spotlight along with the stars. He had no particularly strong connections with them, the way Steve Wynn did, for example. He suffered them for the luster they lent to his name.

By and large, Donald detested the Manhattan glitterati. He had no time for cocktail conversation; he preferred stock tables to Picassos. The celebrities, in turn, found his arrogance humorous. Some tolerated him for his deep pockets, as an investment of sorts, based on a belief prevalent in show business circles that he could be finagled into overpaying for the entertainers who performed in his casino showrooms. But there is a natural affinity the rich and famous feel for each other. The stars were like Donald, after all. They identified with anyone they perceived as wealthy and powerful. They sought out each other, as if to draw power from each other. For that reason, celebrities have always fed off the excitement of the prizefights. Ivana may have considered the fights barbaric and a waste of time, but Donald loved them. If he had a genuine interest in anything outside business, it was boxing. He considered himself a student of the sport. I believe he viewed it as an analogy for success in business, a metaphor for his own career.

I remember sitting with Donald at ringside for a fight once and feeling the anticipation before the bell clangs, when the fighters are loosening up in their corners, like gladiators in the arena. Ten thousand people are watching. You can feel the electricity in the air. I compete in triathlons for that same feeling, that athletic experience. In 1986, I had competed in the triathlon world championships in Nice, France. But even as a kid at the University of Wisconsin, all of 5 foot 8 and 170 pounds, I joined the Big Ten varsity football team as a walk-on, just to know the experience of mixing it up with 6-foot-4, 250-pound linemen. I always thought that someday I'd attempt to climb a mountain for the same reason, to know that fear, that anticipation, and vanquish it.

As I sat next to Donald that night, waiting for the bell, I said to him, "I love these few minutes before the fight. The nervousness. It's almost like competition. But, you know, I can't really correlate it because I don't know what it's like in the ring. I don't think you can truly relate to the sport unless you've been in the ring."

Donald turned to me and said, "You're nuts. Not for anything in the world would I want to know what that's like. I wouldn't want to be in a fucking fighter's shoes for two seconds. I wouldn't want anybody punching me in the face."

But the only times I ever saw Donald happy were when he was ringside for a fight. We had to make sure to seat him on camera, so that his face would be flashed onto thousands of closed-circuit screens throughout the country. We made sure to seat our best customers with him. Steve would usually sit somewhere nearby. But Donald would always arrive early to watch the undercard bouts. Most of our customers wouldn't show up until the main event. This made Donald furious.

"Go get some people and put them down here in these seats," he'd demand.

"Donald, we can't do that," I'd say. "We've got customers we want to put there."

"Fuck it," he'd say. "I don't want some schmuck sitting in Las Vegas watching this fight thinking I don't have a full house here."

"Donald, it's not even the main event yet, for godsakes. Let's wait to get to that point, and if people don't show up, I promise we'll fill the seats in."

He'd shoot me a sideways look and say, "Jack, just get some people down here now."

So we'd move spectators downstairs from the upper sections. Of course, then the customers for whom the seats were promised—players we expected to gamble $50,000 or $100,000 that weekend—would start filtering in, only to find their places occupied. It would be disaster.

Donald caused endless problems with his personal guests, too. He would say, "Jack, I need three seats and that's all I need. I need three seats in the front, and then you can put customers around me. Okay?"

"Fine, Donald. That's good."

Then he'd show up with an entourage of ten, and we'd be left to try to make it up to a gambler who had just lost thousands of dollars at the craps tables, trying to keep him from finding out that his front-row seat had been given to someone whom Donald had met last week at Regine's in New York, someone he considered important in his world in some vague way.

One of the denizens of that world went completely unnoticed in Convention Hall that October night when Mike Tyson tucked in Tyrell Biggs for the evening.

But at 24, Marla Ann Maples burned with the desire to be recognized as a star. Her escort that night was a former New York City policeman named Tom Fitzsimmons, not exactly the profile to open producers' doors for a model and would-be actress. But Fitzsimmons had been a driver and occasional bodyguard in New York for someone who could help Marla's career—Donald Trump, whose real guest for the evening she was. Marla had dated Fitzsimmons for a time while he was driving and protecting Donald.

For some time now, I had been hearing talk of Donald's association with this beautiful blond model, who was described to me at the time as the girlfriend of New York Giants punter Sean Landeta. I still hadn't met her. I was told that she represented a challenge for the billionaire, a chance to prove he was more attractive than a professional athlete to this woman, who was considerably younger than he. Donald was a "player," as Steve Hyde put it, when it came to women. Donald talked about them all the time. It seemed to me that he was always on the prowl. "Jack," he'd say, "you know what I like—blond hair and long legs."

The first mention of Marla came in a conversation I had had with Steve Hyde late that fall, in which he recounted for me an incident at a book signing in New York for *The Art of the Deal*, which Steve had attended. Donald stood up to say a few words to the reporters there, and as he did, he flashed a wink at someone across the room, standing up in the balcony. "I don't believe he's out there doing that," Steve said to me, telling me how, when he looked up at the balcony, there was Marla Maples winking back.

That was my introduction to the existence of someone "special" in Donald's life. It made sense. Knowing his outspoken fear of AIDS and sexually transmitted diseases, I assumed—I guess, cynically—that he had found someone who was "safe." Donald was too enamored of his own fame, too restless with his celebrity, to submit to the constraints of marriage. Not when he could be the ultimate "pickup" if he wanted to be. But whatever the extent of Donald's relationship with Marla at that time, we were more concerned by his growing presidential aspirations that fall.

After a trip to Moscow in July, Donald had taken to speaking out regularly on foreign policy. He adopted popular, can't-lose stands, advocating nuclear disarmament while criticizing the Reagan Administration for being too soft with America's allies.

In September, he launched his celebrated attack on Japan in a full-page ad that ran in the *New York Times*, the *Washington Post* and the *Boston Globe*. I remembered picking up the *Times* on the morning of September 2 and seeing it—his "open letter," as he called it, from "Donald John Trump" to "the American people," which began: *"There's nothing wrong with America's Foreign Defense Policy that a little backbone can't cure."*

Donald's ad weighed into the Japanese and the Saudi Arabians with ferocity. It was a shot from the spleen, tailored to play to blue-collar resentments over the trade deficit and to rally Middle America against the machinations, real or supposed, of our foreign allies.

"For decades," it went on, *"Japan and other nations have been taking advantage of the United States. . . . Make Japan, Saudi Arabia, and others pay for the protection we extend as allies. Let's help our farmers, our sick, our homeless by taking from some of the greatest profit machines ever created. . . . Tax these wealthy nations, not America. End our huge deficits, reduce our*

taxes, and let America's economy grow unencumbered by the cost of defending those who can easily afford to pay us for the defense of their freedom. Let's not let our great country be laughed at anymore."

It was hard for me to believe that Donald's motive was a patriot's concern for the federal deficit and the balance of trade. Five of his ten principal banks—the Bank of Tokyo, Fuji Bank, Tokai Bank, Yasuda Trust and Mitsubishi Trust—were based in Japan. His real estate acquisitions in New York, Atlantic City and Florida were responsible for nearly a quarter-billion dollars in foreign debt. Also, Japanese wealth was a key to the marketing of his luxury condominiums and his casinos in Atlantic City.

The ads cost Donald some $94,000, a small price to pay for the media speculation that raged like wildfire that autumn of 1987 over his political ambitions. The damage to our efforts to promote Trump Plaza in the Far East was incalculable.

There were people talking about Donald as a presidential candidate in the 1988 election. I was horrified at the thought of it. "C'mon," I said to Steve. "Is it possible that this guy has hoodwinked the American people into thinking he's a legitimate contender for the presidency?" I was holding out for the hope that it was all a publicity stunt. But Steve said, "He's serious. This is a serious test of the political waters. Jack, if things shake out, I wouldn't be the least bit surprised if he decided to do it."

A week after Donald returned from Moscow, a Republican organizer in New Hampshire launched a campaign to draft Donald to run for president. Donald disavowed any knowledge of it, but he said he was "honored." In October, Donald's black Super Puma helicopter touched down in Portsmouth, New Hampshire, where he had been invited to address the Rotary Club as a guest of the "Donald Trump for President Committee." He drew a larger turnout than any of the other Republican candidates had before him. Donald told a packed auditorium that he was tired of the United States "being kicked around" by Japan and Saudi Arabia. "We should have these countries that are ripping us off pay off the $200 billion deficit," he proclaimed to loud applause. "There is a way you can ask them," he said, "and they will give it, if you have the right person asking." And he went on to suggest that the United States should attack Iran and seize its oil fields. The crowd cheered louder.

The *New York Times* covered the New Hampshire speech and later called Donald's office in New York for comment. Norma Foederer took the call and responded that her boss was genuinely concerned about the budget deficit and his nation's declining position in the world. "He's so American, like mom and apple pie," she said. "He loves our country."

In Portsmouth, New Hampshire, the wife of a former Rotary president gushed over the appearance of the billionaire entrepreneur in her town: "He's very exciting. Money is power and power is the ultimate aphrodisiac."

So it was. And not only for the wives of New England Rotarians. There was no end to the published rumors linking Donald amorously with a variety of starlets and female celebrities. The rumors were especially persistent about television's *Dynasty* beauty Catherine Oxenberg, a regular visitor, like the Trumps, to Aspen and Palm Beach, and who was Donald's guest on the *Trump Princess* when the luxury yacht arrived in Atlantic City in the summer of 1988. Donald allowed himself to be photographed with her. But if that can be taken as an indication of his esteem, he was also photographed with Marla, as I was told by the photographer who took the pictures.

At first, it seemed that Ivana hadn't the slightest clue about what was going on. Steve, Mark and I suspected that she was kept busy shuttling three days a week between New York and Atlantic City so that her husband could have that interval to secretly live as a bachelor. As she would later tell her friend and

New York Daily News columnist Liz Smith, she was too preoccupied with Donald's business interests to note any extramarital ones. On Christmas Eve 1987, two months after Marla's appearance at the Tyson-Biggs fight and shortly after she and Donald saw each other at Donald's book signing in New York, Donald handed Ivana a stack of documents for her signature: it was the fourth update of their nuptial agreement—this one guaranteeing her custody of their three children, their 45-room mansion in Greenwich, Connecticut, and $25 million. Ivana signed it.

Two weeks later, the simmering feud between Ivana and Steve Hyde and Trump Plaza boiled over. This time the issue was seating arrangements for the Mike Tyson—Larry Holmes contest at Convention Hall on January 22, 1988.

Steve came to my office one day early in the new year and asked, "Did you get a call from Ivana?"

"I got a call from her office. They said Donald wants all the seats in the front row."

"That's strange," he said. "I just got off the phone with Donald. He told me he only wants two seats in the front row. He wants one for him and one for Ivana. That's it. The rest are ours to do with as we please."

It was customary at every title fight to reserve the ringside row for Donald. Sometimes he'd fill it, but more often, he'd tell us to save only a few seats, which gave us the opportunity to fill up the row with customers (until he arrived, as he frequently did, with an entourage of guests, or he'd insist on arranging his own seating, which invariably resulted in us having to offend prized customers by bumping them from ringside seats). Aside from customers, everyone else was charged the going rate for seats, whether it was another casino or a celebrity such as Jack Nicholson. As a courtesy, though, after our seating was established, we always gave our sister property at Trump's Castle first choice.

We went down to Steve's office together and he called Ivana.

We learned she intended to reserve Donald's row for Castle customers.

"Ivana, you can't do that," Steve said.

"And why not?" she said. "I'm coming to sit with Donald."

"Well, that's fine. But the Plaza is paying for the fight and you can't sit Castle customers in the Plaza section."

She said, "Well, I'm coming with Donald, and I want to be able to sit with some customers."

"You've got your own seats," Steve said.

"I will sit where I want to sit. I will sit with whomever I want. . . . I have some friends coming up from Florida," she said.

"That is not going to take place," Steve said. He was angry now. "I have to put Plaza customers in that front row. If you want to sit with a Castle customer then you're going to have to sit in the Castle section."

"I will sit where I want," she said. I could tell Steve was losing his patience.

"No you won't," he said. "This is totally inappropriate for you to demand that row from us, and you know it."

"I will sit where I want," she insisted in her deepest, most imperious tone.

Steve refused to be intimidated. "You're crazy," he fired back. "There's no way."

"Well, then, I'm not coming," she said.

"Then don't come!"

"I'll have to talk to Donald," she said.

Then Steve said something I never heard him say before and never heard again. "Bullshit, Ivana! Let's get Donald on a conference call right now. Because you see what you're telling me? It's bullshit!"

Steve and Donald talked that afternoon, and Donald laughed about it when he heard. "Boy, you really got Ivana charged up," he said. But he agreed with us. The Castle did not get the seats.

"Forget her. She's nuts," Donald told Steve. "You don't have to take any shit from her."

In the meantime, Donald was keeping Marla on the move, shifting her among various locations around Manhattan and in Atlantic City. He set her up for a time only six blocks from Trump Tower, at the St. Moritz Hotel, which he owned. She stayed for a while at the beachfront home of former Resorts International president Jack Davis, a friend of Donald's who lived at the western edge of Atlantic City. Donald even stashed her for a time at the hotel at Trump's Castle, right under Ivana's nose.

As the new year, 1988, unfolded, Marla assumed more of a presence and more influence in his life. Personally and professionally, his stake in Atlantic City and the risks were growing.

*"People think I'm a gambler. I've never gambled
in my life."*
—DONALD J. TRUMP

T hanks to Trump Plaza, 1987 was Donald's most successful
year to date as a casino owner. With the parking garage open
and the prestige of two major heavyweight fights, the
amount we won at the tables and slot machines was up $25
million over the year before, and it was the second-highest increase in town. Only Caesars' take was larger. The Plaza jumped
from seventh to fourth place among the twelve casinos in revenue
from all operations, including the hotel and sales of food and
beverages. Even after deducting the retail cost of complimentaries, we enjoyed the highest percentage increase in revenue of any
gambling hall in town.

The Castle hadn't fared as well. It won $15 million more in its
casino than the year before and $24 million more on combined oper-
ations. But Ivana had spent lavishly to attract the business. Expen-
ditures for complimentaries increased by 21 percent to $38 million,
$3.5 million more than Trump Plaza's and second only to Cae-
sars'. But correspondingly, casino revenue rose by only 6 percent.

Donald's presence in Atlantic City was beneficial, providing thousands of jobs, for example, but he also exerted a chilling effect on the competition. The Castle and the Plaza together accounted for nearly 20 percent of the city's total gaming revenue. Consequently, Donald entered 1988 as the most important player in the $3 billion casino industry. (He would eventually own approximately one-third of the city's total gaming capacity, which would make Atlantic City dependent on the fortunes of Donald Trump.) Fed by an image of limitless wealth and the fearlessness to use it, Donald vigorously pursued every opportunity to buy himself control over the industry.

Since 1985, only one new gaming hall had opened its doors in Atlantic City, the Showboat Hotel & Casino, which commenced operations in April 1987. Since Donald first entered the market three years earlier, five operators had left town or were looking to leave. With the exception of Hugh Hefner's ongoing licensing difficulties with the state of New Jersey, which dated back to a 20-year-old bribe scheme involving the Playboy Club in New York, and which ended in Playboy being denied a gaming license, Donald would be involved in four of those five episodes.

I think it can be argued that the city would have been better off with a greater diversity of owners and styles of casino management.

First, in 1983, the Casino Control Commission forced Hefner's partner, Elsinore Corporation, to buy out his half-interest in the Playboy Hotel Casino. Elsinore, which also operated gaming halls in Nevada, had to assume a pile of new debt to become the sole owner of the casino, which it renamed Elsinore's Atlantis Casino Hotel.

Then, in 1985, Donald hastened the departure of another potential competitor, Barron Hilton, who had been denied a license by the Casino Control Commission after his casino was already built and ready to open. Donald acted out of fear that his rival Steve Wynn might buy the property.

A year later, in 1986, Donald's hostile bid to take over Holiday Corporation forced that company to restructure its holdings and relinquish ownership of Harrah's Marina in Atlantic City.

Then, the following year, 1987, Donald saw an opportunity to extend his hold over the neighborhood surrounding his "Tiffany location," Trump Plaza, and the adjoining Convention Hall at the base of the Atlantic City Expressway, the heart of the resort's gambling activity, an area known as "center Boardwalk." *Penthouse* publisher Bob Guccione had been trying since the late 1970s to build a casino on the Boardwalk at Missouri Avenue, between Trump Plaza and Caesars. Guccione had invested $70 million but was forced to halt construction in January 1980 when his financing dried up. The mass of piles and steel girders that remained had been gathering rust for six years before Atlantic City and the state of New Jersey ordered him to finish construction, sell it or tear it down. The Sands Hotel Casino in Atlantic City offered to take it off his hands but failed initially to strike a deal. Donald weighed in with an offer of between $16 million and $18 million, which Penthouse president David Myerson spurned as "ridiculously low."

Meanwhile, the construction site was costing Penthouse $600,000 a month in leases, taxes and carrying charges, and the company was desperate to unload it. In the spring of 1987, the Sands returned with a new offer, which Penthouse welcomed as a basis for negotiations. Donald, determined to block any competitor from building a casino next to Trump Plaza, allegedly called Sands president William Weidner that summer with the warning: "Don't screw up my deal." He hastily tried to revive his talks with Penthouse, and in August, he claimed that Penthouse would never come to terms with the Sands. But that same month, Penthouse agreed to sell to the Sands for $61 million. The Sands immediately announced plans for a $265 million gaming complex, the "Sands Hollywood," with a 50,000-square-foot casino, scheduled for completion in late 1989 or early 1990.

The deal, however, was contingent on Penthouse being able to deliver a clear title to the site (there were some lingering property disputes) and on the Sands' ability to obtain financing and the necessary zoning approvals from the city, particularly for parking, which the property lacked. Donald, however, challenged the Sands' zoning requests and, represented by Pat McGahn, he succeeded in delaying the zoning approvals.

While this was taking place, Al Glasgow emerged as a sort of *agent provocateur* in an increasingly nasty battle. He claimed that Penthouse president David Myerson had threatened Donald with blackmail if he continued to oppose the project. According to notes Glasgow said he kept on some thirteen separate conversations with Myerson and other Penthouse representatives over the spring and summer of 1988, Penthouse had a line on Donald's mistress, Marla Maples, which Myerson threatened to publish in the magazine as an exposé. "Check out the fourth floor at the St. Moritz," Myerson allegedly told Glasgow over dinner on July 19, 1988, at an Atlantic City restaurant. Glasgow claimed to have brought two state police undercover officers who "monitored" the conversation from an adjoining booth but did not tape-record it. Glasgow, or so the Sands would later contend in court papers, then offered to arrange a meeting between Donald and Myerson at which, presumably, a deal could be reached for Donald to buy the property out from under the Sands.

On December 15, 1988, the Sands' option on the Penthouse site expired. Donald's opposition had been costly. The extension Penthouse granted until February 1 of the following year came with a warning to the Sands that "time is of the essence."

A couple of weeks into the new year, 1989, the Sands submitted its plans for the Hollywood casino to the city for final approval. Within weeks, the rumor was flying that Donald and Penthouse

were locked in intense secret negotiations. The February 1 deadline came, and technically the Sands' extension expired. Donald,
his lawyer Pat McGahn and Penthouse's negotiators were meeting at Trump Plaza.

In the wee hours of March 19, in Pat McGahn's Atlantic City
offices, Penthouse and Donald put their signatures on a deal that
gave the casino property to Donald for $35 million, only a little
more than half the price Penthouse had negotiated with the
Sands, and the Columbus Plaza parking site across the street on
Atlantic Avenue for another $17 million. Donald dismissed the
Sands' claim to the property.

In Dallas, Jack E. Pratt, the chairman of the Pratt Hotel Corporation, the Sands's corporate parent, vowed to "sue Trump like
he's never been sued before."

Donald responded laconically, "They had an option to buy the
property, and the option expired."

But in 1987 Donald's chief concern was still Steve Wynn. Steve
Wynn was supposed to have been elbowed out for good in 1986
when Bally Manufacturing Corporation, in an effort to fend off
Donald's hostile takeover attempt, offered the outrageous sum
of $440 million for the Golden Nugget. When Steve sold, Donald
exulted, saying, "Steve Wynn left Atlantic City where he made
much of his money, in all fairness, to go to Las Vegas because
he just likes Las Vegas. He likes the atmosphere, he likes the
environment, and I think you know what he thinks of the Atlantic City environment."

But no sooner was the sale concluded in January 1987 than
Donald had reason to worry that maybe Wynn hadn't left Atlantic
City after all, at least not for long. The rumor then making the
rounds of the industry's executive boardrooms was that Steve
Wynn had made a secret offer for Resorts International, owners
of Atlantic City's first casino, then in the midst of building a
second one next door, a giant gaming palace called the "Taj
Mahal," which it intended to be the largest in the world.

Resorts had been leaderless since the death of its founder, James Crosby, in 1986, and the company had been on the market ever since. Dallas-based Pratt Hotel Corporation had a standing offer of $135 a share for a controlling interest of the Resorts' Class B stock, which accounted for the dominant voting power of the company and most of which was in the hands of the Crosby family. There were also millions of outstanding shares of Class A stock, which only held a small fraction of the voting control. The Taj Mahal, on 17 acres fronting the ocean at the far eastern end of the Boardwalk, was being designed as Atlantic City's first themed gaming and vacation resort, larger than anything the city had ever seen—4.2 million square feet, three football fields long, with 1,250 hotel rooms and a 120,000-square-foot gaming hall, the city's largest by far. A month after I joined Trump Plaza in early 1987, Donald made his move and matched the Sands' bid of $135 a share.

Unlike Donald's previous raids on the gaming industry, this deal offered no prospect of a quick killing. Resorts had invested five years and $500 million in the Taj Mahal. By early 1987, the exterior of the Taj was mostly complete and the 42-story hotel tower was up, but the building was still far from completion. It had been dragged through several costly design changes, and was buried in cost overruns. Construction was limping to a halt. Resorts, once flush with cash as the city's first casino in 1978, had been bled white by the effort. Its flagship, carved from the stately old Haddon Hall Hotel, had been left to deteriorate over the years. It had lost its competitive edge and needed millions of dollars in renovations. But Resorts' head start in 1978 had left it in a unique financial position. In those early years, with only two or three competing casinos, it enjoyed profit margins other operators dreamed about. As early as 1976, before the state referendum legalizing casino gaming was passed and speculation sent land prices soaring in Atlantic City, Crosby's vision had led his company to invest heavily in real estate in the city. When he died ten years later, Resorts was teetering near bankruptcy, but it was the city's largest private landholder, controlling more than 10 percent of all developable acreage, with a value conservatively estimated at $700 million.

For someone with the financial reserves to put the company back on its feet, Resorts presented a tremendous opportunity. Casino stock was still a popular buy on Wall Street, enough to insure financing for more suitors. Pratt's standing offer of $135 a share had been matched by oil tycoon Marvin Davis, fresh from his abortive attempt to acquire CBS. But Resorts was Donald's kind of a deal, a virtual fire sale encompassing a treasure chest of undervalued developable real estate assets, along with the Taj Mahal, maybe the brightest jewel of the lot. And there was no shortage of adversaries—Pratt, Wynn, Davis, maybe more. This inspired him, providing him with the only method he understood for making qualitative judgments. He could check off the "losers" and "winners" in his mind. Thus victory acquired its taste.

Three days after he entered the Resorts sweepstakes, a tentative deal was announced giving him a 73 percent controlling interest in the company for $79 million. It was a friendly takeover. Sentiment was as much a factor as business in the Crosby family's decision to reject Pratt's offer and sell to him instead. The family believed that Donald was so strong financially that he would not need to sell off the company's assets to pay its debts. The unfinished Taj Mahal was the most important asset to the family. As veteran casino financial analyst Marvin Roffman of Janney Montgomery Scott in Philadelphia observed at the time: "The Crosby people are loyal people. They see the Taj Mahal as a last memorial to Jim Crosby. They feel Trump has the reputation for following through on things and getting it done in a first-class manner. . . . Trump is a hands-on operator. If anyone can get [the Taj] done, it's him."

But the maneuvering was not over. On March 24, Davis countered with a new offer, a complicated proposal believed by some experts to be a front for Pratt. Donald heard the news while at a party thrown by his friends Barbara Walters and her husband, Merv Adelson. Referring to the fact that Davis was overweight, he snapped, "He should focus on losing 200 pounds instead of wasting time trying to break my deal with Resorts."

This time he could be content with insults. His bid had the inside support of Resorts president I. G. "Jack" Davis. Plus, the brokerage house hired to advise Resorts' shareholders happened to be Donald's own brokers, the Wall Street firm of Bear Stearns, which had floated the junk bonds to finance all his major projects.

In April, Davis's offer was formally rejected and the Crosby family sold out to Donald. He had bought his first public company. Jack Davis called it "a great contribution." In the weeks that followed, Donald increased his holdings to 88 percent of the voting control—an outlay of about $100 million in all for a company worth at least seven times that. With the Haddon Hall property, he now owned three operating casinos, the limit permitted an individual under New Jersey law. He also owned the unfinished Taj Mahal, which, depending on his next move, could push one-third of the city's entire hotel and gaming capacity to his side of the table. In addition, he was technically the city's largest private landowner, in undisputed control of a company with real estate holdings that included the site of a proposed new high school and most of the available land for the low- and middle-income housing the city so desperately needed. At that moment, Donald Trump held the future of Atlantic City and its 35,000 residents in his hands.

From all corners, the purchase was greeted with hope. This "glamorous national figure"—as powerful local Republican State Senator William Gormley characterized Donald—is "sitting in a unique position" with a chance "to spur a large portion of the

redevelopment of Atlantic City." Everyone in town hoped, specifically, that Donald would fulfill an obligation Resorts had been
stalling on for years to build 1,200 to 2,000 units of housing on
a 56-acre plot, one-third of which was already taken up by the
Taj Mahal and the Showboat. In exchange for its pledge to build
the housing, Resorts got an option from the city to buy the plot
for an initial investment of less than $4 an acre. The new owner
of the property, Donald Trump, proclaimed, "I want to do what
is good for Atlantic City and good for New Jersey." But Atlantic
City Councilman Harold Mosee, whose First Ward encompassed
the neighborhoods living in the shadow of the Taj, among the
city's poorest, did not put great store in the billionaire's noblesse
oblige. "Most people are awed by him without looking at the
type of individual he is," said Mosee. "He's a power-crazed in-
dividual. He's not familiar with the human element."

In truth, housing was not at the top of Donald's agenda. The
interest was mounting on the hundreds of millions in financing
to build the Taj Mahal. Its vast interior spaces, its huge ballrooms
and arena, and the casino itself were still incomplete. Four win-
ters and the corrosive salty ocean air had taken their toll on the
structure. Estimates of the cost to complete the building now
ranged as high as $250 million. As Donald's first order of business,
he stopped construction and closed off the site. His second was
to award himself a multimillion-dollar "management services"
contract. Resorts' Class A stock, which had been trading at $60
a share when Donald bought the company, plummeted to $12.

Meanwhile over at the Plaza we had our own concerns about
repercussions from the buyout of Resorts. We already had two
properties feuding with each other. How would a third fit in?
Would the operator of the third casino come on the scene to
battle it out with Steve Hyde and Ivana? Was it even possible to
successfully operate three casinos within the limitations of the
Atlantic City market? Steve doubted it. Moreover, he believed a

property the size of the Taj Mahal was a threat to the profitability of both Trump Plaza and Trump's Castle because it would have to pillage large numbers of their preferred customers.

Donald responded with classic Trump bravado. No one had ever managed three properties because no one before him had the guts to try, he said. But again he was betraying his superficial understanding of the market, as well as his totally mistaken impression of how his own properties did business. Yes, he said he recognized the probability that the Taj would bite into existing market shares, but only those of the so-called weaker properties, as he termed them, and only because their facilities were inferior to begin with, or so he believed. The Trump properties would not feel the pinch because they were "trophies" in their own right and enjoyed distinct identities as luxury gambling halls that catered to the high-end players. Donald failed to grasp that none of the casinos was making money in Atlantic City by appealing to only one segment of the market. Trump Plaza, for example, flourished precisely because of a healthy mix of high-, middle- and low-level players. Due to its sheer size alone, the Taj certainly would need all three markets to survive.

What we had accomplished at Trump Plaza, expanding on what Steve Wynn had done at the Golden Nugget, was to build an image as a high-end casino, which we were. But that was only the superstructure. It rested on a foundation of large-scale retail programs targeted at the mass market. That had been my job: working quietly behind the curtain of glamour to develop and implement direct-mail and telemarketing programs to lure the masses of slot machine players of moderate gambling potential, the customer who paid the bills. It was perception and reality working in tandem. Paradoxically, Donald Trump, the master mythmaker, had swallowed his own image. He was unaware of the importance of the mass market of middle-class gamblers in sustaining his casino operations.

But this much was clear: Donald wanted the Taj Mahal. It was the image property, the "trophy." This spelled a certain excitement for me amid the uncertainty. As Steve Hyde put it to me, "Jack, this looks like it's going to happen. This is what I meant when I brought you in here. Things could change very, very fast. You may go from senior vice-president of marketing to running one of these properties in a very short period of time."

Donald told Steve Hyde and others privately that he would never allow someone else to develop the largest casino in town, Atlantic City's first genuine theme resort, a property of the style and scale to entice a showman like Steve Wynn to return to the market.

That summer, Donald went gunning for his rival. "Steve Wynn bailed out of town," he told the *Atlantic City Press.* "He made his money in New Jersey and he's spending it in Nevada."

Then, after learning that Steve was trying to increase his holding in Golden Nugget, Inc., Donald began buying stock in the company in an effort to block him. On July 9, he announced the purchase of 4.9 percent of it, the maximum allowed under law without having to disclose his intentions to the SEC. *Business Week* seized on the episode with a cheeky story on the Trump-Wynn rivalry, taking note of Donald's failed attempt to buy Steve's marina property next door to Trump's Castle. Donald fired off a rather shrill letter to the magazine: "I have zero interest in that land," he said. It is "the last thing in the world I need or want. . . . If Steve is trying to build up the value of his ridiculous and wasteful land acquisition, let him not use Donald Trump as a potential purchaser of this somewhat inaccessible and hidden parcel of land."

Donald followed with another salvo, calling Steve "an underachiever."

"After 25 years in business he owns 10 percent of a company that owns one relatively unsuccessful hotel in Las Vegas," Donald said. "As a stockholder in Golden Nugget, I am counting on Steve to finally live up to his potential . . . and I always wanted to have him working for me."

"I always wanted to work for Ivana," Steve shot back.

And more seriously he vowed never to pay Donald "one penny" of greenmail. Trump, he said, "has as much chance of taking over the Golden Nugget as he has of turning into Mary Poppins."

On July 21, 1987, Donald had himself elected chairman of the board of Resorts International. Two days later, he was serving notice that Atlantic City housing officials had better not rely too heavily on his largesse. He said that while he recognized the housing obligation his company had undertaken, "It's very important, obviously, for Atlantic City and for the company itself to save the Taj Mahal." He was the man to do it, he said. "I believe the leaders want very much to have the Trump stamp on it in some form." Consequently, the housing would not be built until he was certain he could make a financial go of the Taj Mahal. He would need to float hundreds of millions of dollars in junk bonds to complete the construction.

But the housing issue would not go away. Through the offices of local attorney and power-broker Patrick McGahn, Donald met privately with Mayor James Usry, Business Administrator Carl Briscoe and city housing officials. With the Taj Mahal as a hostage, along with some $5 million in back taxes owed by Resorts, which the city needed to balance its budget, Donald walked out of the meeting with an alternative to Resorts' existing housing obligation. He also obtained the city's promise to rezone the area around the Taj so no competing casinos after the Showboat could be built there. In exchange Donald proposed to build housing closer to the Boardwalk—on which he'd pay no taxes. The deal-maker had painted another work of art.

But local community activists were outraged and sued. They were joined by the state Office of the Public Advocate. The city's housing authority backed off and finally rescinded the deal with Donald. Early in 1988, it was amended: Donald promised to buy the land originally designated for the housing and to build it, though the nature and size of the development would be subject to negotiation. In return he got the city to alter the deed to the land under the Taj Mahal, essentially removing the encumbrance of the housing obligation, which Donald said he needed to obtain the financing to complete the Taj.

With the new year 1988, Donald moved to take Resorts private, offering the holders of its Class A stock $15 each for their 5.7 million outstanding shares. The board of directors rejected the price as "grossly inadequate." The shareholders sued, charging that Donald was trying to take the company off the market at a steal. In February, Donald settled the lawsuits by upping his offer to $22, which still would have gotten him the company for a relatively meager $125 million. The deal was within days of approval by a judge when former television personality and game show mogul Merv Griffin suddenly appeared with an offer of $35.

Now Donald had what he always wanted in any potential deal, an adversary. He called the entertainer's offer "illusory" and sued him. Griffin countersued, charging that Donald had misled the stockholders and was "talking down" the value of their shares in an effort to acquire Resorts "on the cheap." He also claimed that Donald had failed to disclose his own recent appraisal of the company's assets, which placed a much higher value than previously thought on its extensive real estate holdings. He said Donald was using his voting control of the company (actually, he owned only 12 percent of the outstanding stock) to block the shareholders from considering his higher offer.

The battle between the celebrity billionaire and the entertainer made for sensational reading that spring: "War at the Shore" . . . "Griffin, Trump Trade Jabs," headlines proclaimed. There were reports of agreements struck and agreements angrily abandoned, charges and countercharges.

In April, the outlines of a deal emerged. Donald and Merv called a truce. They agreed to carve up the Resorts empire between them. Merv would get the Haddon Hall casino, the real estate and property in the Bahamas. Donald would get the Taj Mahal. There was more wrangling in the months ahead, but by early fall, a final deal was struck. Donald claimed victory, and on the face of it, it looked like he was right. He got $93 million for his Class B voting stock and $63 million for his management contract. Merv sold him back the Taj Mahal for $273 million, which represented only a little more than half Resorts' six-year money-losing investment in the property. Donald also got the three helicopters of Resorts International Airways, which he immediately renamed Trump Air, and the old Steel Pier, which he planned to revive as an entertainment and amusement park. Additionally, he walked off with seven of Resorts' top executives, among them Walter J. Haybert, a former vice-president of finance at Trump Plaza.

Resorts International was now piled under close to $1 billion in debt. On top of some $600 million in existing debt, most of it related to the construction of the Taj Mahal, Merv had to float $325 million in junk bonds to acquire the Class A stock and take the company private. Shortly after the deal was concluded in November 1988, Resorts posted a third-quarter loss of $339 million. "This is the only deal I've ever done where I had no idea why the other guy was doing it," Donald crowed publicly.

This had made Donald even more aggressive in his pursuit of the Taj Mahal, the "trophy" property, which he needed in order to claim victory. To hide the disheveled state of the Haddon Hall casino, Donald hired a squadron of painters, carpenters and paperers to perform some cosmetics along a route carefully selected for Merv to tour.

The dismemberment of Resorts International, concluded in November 1988, was one of Donald's most treasured deals, one with just enough "moral larceny," as a Trump associate once put it, to make it worthwhile for him.

Steve Hyde was not convinced that Donald had made a good deal. Steve always believed it would be impossible to operate the Taj, the Castle and the Plaza simultaneously and still make money. But I don't believe Donald ever understood the intricacies of what he'd gotten himself involved in beyond the split of the assets and the gross dollars involved. He was more concerned lest any perception exist that Merv had somehow outmaneuvered him. As I was told, he asked one former Castle insider: "Why is this playing so bad in the papers?"

The reply, that "maybe some people think Merv got the better part of the deal," infuriated him. (As he admitted in *The Art of the Deal*, "Sometimes part of making a deal is denigrating your competition.")

"Oh yeah? All right," he fumed. "That's what they want to believe? I'll show them."

Donald ordered us to use our publicity department to attack Merv, which, of course, we did not do. Donald sent me a videotape of a *Saturday Night Live* skit that spoofed Merv savagely. He wanted me to show it at management meetings and customer parties. Needless to say, I did not.

Al Glasgow, Donald's adviser, embraced the party line. For the next 16 months, his industry newsletter, *Atlantic City Action,* trumpeted the purchase of the Taj Mahal. He called it "the steal of the century." Merv, he said, "should have stayed in show business. I think he's got a better shot at getting Eva Gabor pregnant than making money with Resorts."

Jack Nussbaum, the attorney who structured the Resorts deal for Donald, said of his billionaire client, "He's only recently gotten into the public company arena. His appetite for companies and his ability to feed it are both enormous. You'll see him become much more acquisitive."

But some people in the gaming industry said that Donald had not made as shrewd a deal for the Taj as he thought. So late in 1988 Donald met with the editors of *Casino Journal,* an industry trade monthly, at Trump's Castle. I was told that he had asked for the interview in order to dispel the lingering suspicion that perhaps Merv had bested him on the Resorts deal. But he kept the newspaper's editors waiting over an hour. When he finally arrived, he was scowling and barking orders at those around him. The first question about Merv and Resorts drew an angry response. "What did you ask me about that for?" he said. "That's a stupid fucking question. I'm not going to answer that. Ask me something else."

Donald got the bond sale for the Taj Mahal off the ground in November 1988 and raised $675 million. The notes were payable in 10 years at 14 percent interest and secured with a first mortgage against the unfinished casino. The original offering statement contained the prophetic advisory: "No assurance can be given that once opened the Taj Mahal will be profitable or that it will generate cash flow sufficient to provide for payment of debt service."

Donald took off for Aspen with his family at the end of December for their traditional holiday vacation. This trip was a break from tradition that promised some genuine excitement for him for a change. Marla was secretly flown in and ensconced in a private apartment at the posh ski resort. Wife and mistress brought together, and only Donald knew it! "Take care of the downside and the upside will take care of itself"—such was his prudent counsel in *The Art of the Deal.* He ignored his own advice as the year drew to a close and he discovered the sensations of life and business on the edge. He was moving into an illusory world where he believed the rules no longer applied to him. He

was writing his own rules. He had been dazzling the banks and
bondholders for years. Atlantic City willingly handed over its
future to him. With the enormous capacity of the Taj Mahal
added onto what he already owned he could remake the resort
town in his own image—a "Trump City," at last. His hubris was
practically boundless. At the Aspen home of his friend Barbara
Walters, where he was celebrating New Year's Eve, he was asked
to make a wish for the coming year. He said, "I wish I had another
Merv Griffin to bat around."

In *the early months* of 1988 it was apparent that Trump was making the first of the massive financial blunders he would be unable to correct. The 97 luxury suites Ivana had commissioned for Trump's Castle bore her personal touch and were frighteningly expensive. The 14-story addition, the Crystal Tower, incorporated 23 selected marbles, oak and mahogany finishings, more than 100 window, wall and bedding fabrics and carpets of pure wool that cost $100 a square yard. The gold faucet assemblies in the bathrooms ran $1,800 each. Adding to the project's cost was the construction of a helipad on the garage roof and renovations of an adjoining state-owned marina. The idea was to transform the rundown docks into a Catalina-style showplace with slips for 600 pleasure craft and a restaurant overlooking the water. Upon completion the Castle planned to lease the marina for an initial $300,000 a year.

The suites were supposed to have cost $40 million. But as the new year began, six months into construction, Donald had to take a $50 million bank loan secured against the equity of the property to finance them. And even that wasn't enough. We had discovered during the renovations at Trump Plaza that Donald's expertise in construction was nowhere near the level his reputation led us to expect. Now the Castle's management was to learn the same lesson. And his attention span was so limited that it was impossible to discuss problems with him in any detail. Nor did he anticipate them on his own; he never got involved to that degree. We had Steve Hyde, who was gifted with enormous patience and a talent for identifying problems and finding the solutions for which Donald had no interest. The Castle was not so fortunate. Left to his and Ivana's devices, the suites and the marina met with cost overruns in the tens of millions of dollars. Donald was looking at a final price tag of more than $100 million for the construction and renovations.

Once the construction was under way and it was too late to stop it, he was furious that he had agreed to such exorbitant costs. So he blamed Ivana—"motherfucking" her all the time, as I learned from one former insider, whom Donald told, "I can't believe she's so fucking stupid."

Weekly construction meetings at the Castle became a regular scene for his tirades. He would come in and shout at the staff, satisfied then that he'd performed his managerial duty. Usually it was too late to correct the problem or mistake. As his visits to the Castle became more frequent, Donald grew more frustrated. His manner became more surly and abusive. "That's dirty, look at that!" he cried, pointing to a smudge on the floor during a tour of the hotel lobby with several executives. Everywhere he turned he saw something that annoyed him. "That's no good over there. . . . That's a piece of garbage. . . . You people are no good. You're not making it." On one visit, he passed a signboard outside a convention room. "Who designed that? That's the ugliest fucking thing I ever saw," he said, and kicked it across the hall. Out at the marina, he dressed down the construction manager because the nails had split the ends of some of the dock planks. Then, as he headed toward the casino, he passed a wooden platform, stopped and kicked it into the water because he didn't like the paint color. "This place is a shithouse!" he said, storming back inside.

But Donald continued to spend money on the Castle, lots of it. Under Ivana's management, the Castle was outspending every casino in town in terms of its ratio of complimentaries to total revenues. Yet casino revenue was only sixth best in town. The Castle was busing in nearly three times as many visitors as its closest competitor, Harrah's Marina, but its operating income was less than half that of Harrah's and had dropped $4.6 million from 1987 to 1988, an 11 percent decline.

Trump Plaza was turning into Donald's cash cow, providing the money he needed to spend elsewhere.

On Saturday, January 22, 1988, we hosted our biggest fight yet at Convention Hall—"Heavyweight History": Mike Tyson versus the most respected of his recent champion predecessors, Larry Holmes. The celebrity crowd, lured by the thrill of big-time boxing, turned out in force—Barbra Streisand, Jack Nicholson, Kirk Douglas, Don Johnson, Peter Falk, Bruce Willis, to name a few.

We paid $2 million for the Tyson-Holmes fight, outbidding Caesars Palace in Las Vegas. But the stars and the cash set the winter air crackling with electricity. We knew we had a promotional spectacular. Fourteen thousand people turned out at Convention Hall to see Tyson send the former champ and his comeback bid sprawling to the canvas with a knockout. We made $2.6 million at the gate. The drop at the tables the night of the fight was a record $8.4 million. And we held well, a little better than 25 percent, which means we won some $2.4 million of that.

I knew we were in for a great night because the back pits, where the craps and blackjack tables are located, were jammed with gamblers hours before the fight started. This pushes up the betting limits, much like demand for a product drives up its price. In a casino, as long as the seats at the game are full, your "product" is in demand, and, theoretically, you can get a higher price for it. So you push the minimum betting limits higher, watching how many players stay in their seats; and you continue to push the limits as long as they stay, but not so high that you force them to leave. Gauging and directing this process, known as the "spread," is the job of the casino manager. A good one is worth his weight in chips. At Trump Plaza, Steve Hyde had hired one of the best.

It was always my habit before and after a fight to work with our casino manager to devise a strategy for spreading the games. And I always checked the blackjack tables in the back pits at the rear of the casino, closest to the skywalk and the garage. It is a highly congested area dominated by slot machines. Consequently, the tables generally attract the lowest-limit players, $5 and $10 minimums on an average night; on a good weekend night in July or August, $10, with a couple of tables at $25. On the night of the Tyson-Holmes fight, in the middle of January, these tables were holding steady at $50 and $100 minimums. This pushed up the limits on the rest of the floor. Our choicer tables were commanding stakes of $500. For the weekend, our drop approached $14 million (including the $8.4 million the night of the fight). An event of such magnitude spills over in increased business to the competition, who buy seats for their preferred players and design promotions and parties around the fight. City-wide, the one-day $1 million win mark was exceeded ten times that weekend. This increased level of business was the reason we got involved in heavyweight boxing matches in the first place.

Trump's Castle, thought to be the jewel of Donald's casino portfolio, lost its luster. As hard as she drove her staff, Ivana could not change that. The Castle's profitability was deteriorating. Ivana's influence with Donald, the cement of their marriage, was her value as a businesswoman, and it was quickly ending.

Donald was spending more and more time with Marla Maples. She was flown down from New York by helicopter to attend the Tyson-Holmes fight, once again officially escorted by ex-cop and bodyguard Tom Fitzsimmons. For the first time, word leaked to me that Ivana was accusing Donald of entertaining an affair. They battled openly in the aftermath of the fight, as I was told by a close associate of Donald's. But the billionaire was growing bored with discretion and with his wife, and her anger and suspicion failed to stop him. Marla took to coming down to Trump Plaza regularly, spending the night, sometimes the weekend, checking in under the name "Fitzsimmons." The hotel staff couldn't help but notice her—Donald's archetypal long-legged, curvaceous blonde, a perfect size 6 with fashion-model looks, who preferred tight sweaters and eye-popping leather miniskirts. Everyone assumed that she was just someone Donald occasionally spent the evening with. But as it became apparent that she was something more, his mistress, in fact, her presence brought out employees high and low—dealers, desk clerks, secretaries, department heads, housekeepers—coming out from the offices, the casino, kitchens, craning their necks to get a look at her as she strolled through the lobby.

I first saw for myself how pretty she was when I met her early in 1988. But I was struck more by what she didn't have. She was unlike what I expected to see in the mistress of a man whose name was synonymous with riches. She wore no expensive jewelry; her clothes were chosen to accentuate and display her shape, but they weren't especially expensive or fashionable: in fact, they looked rather used most of the time, as though they had done long service. In that respect, the well-heeled Ivana was much more impressive—the Chloe dresses, shoes by Jourdan, the dazzling diamond earrings and necklaces. Her abrasiveness and her vulgar speech aside (those manners she had learned from her husband), Ivana cut a presence in public that was striking and that enhanced her finery. She was erect, poised, with a regal air about her, all sophistication and sharp Slavic accent, constantly aware of her body and its movements, like the wife of a head of state on a foreign goodwill tour.

If Marla's wardrobe was any indication of how Donald really felt about her—and I always believed, perhaps wrongly, that it was—her future with him was not long. Then again, there may have been a method to it. After all, a model sporting a four-carat diamond ring was sure to raise questions Donald didn't want to have to answer at the time.

Or maybe he was just cheap. Incredible as it may seem, I had reasons to think that.

After dining with Donald in expensive restaurants like Maximilian's or Roberto's at Trump Plaza, I'd have to quietly motion for the check to be brought to me to sign so I could be sure the waiter would get his tip. I had learned that Donald never tipped anyone, not waiters, waitresses, doormen, bellhops, not even his drivers. He never gave it a thought. Like other very wealthy people, it seems he never carried any money. He used to laugh about it. Cornered by a newspaper reporter about it once, he playfully reached into his pockets and turned out the linings. He found, much to his surprise, two crumpled $1 bills. Not that that was any consolation to our waiters and cocktail servers, who depended on tips to live and worked hard for them, especially when the billionaire owner was at their table. Their complaints made their way to me. Without mentioning anything to Donald, I instructed our vice-president of food and beverage to include a 20 percent gratuity in any bill rung up by Donald or his guests. At least this way, we wouldn't have to double back after him to see that a waiter got the few extra dollars he'd earned serving him.

Donald's needs and tastes, however, were simple, almost Spartan—steak or hamburger for dinner, maybe a simple pasta dish, with a diet cola that he drank from a straw for fear of disease. For all his possessions it seemed that there were none that he ever had the time or peace of mind to enjoy. Ivana couldn't have been more different in that way. She adored the wealthy life and its trappings and worked diligently to educate herself in the ways of the rich and famous. But Donald had no time for anything outside business and rarely beyond the issue of the moment. He cared nothing for art, music and books. He had no hobbies or diversions, not even a passing interest in gambling and the games that made him so much money. Even sports failed to interest him, except for boxing, which he loved.

Whenever I met Marla, I couldn't fail to notice the contrast with Donald—her youthfulness, how vibrant and alive she was, eager to taste the pleasures and enjoy the privileges of a life that now revolved around a love affair with America's most famous tycoon.

She wasn't especially bright, but she was far from boorish. She liked to laugh and have fun. She was sweet in that way, just as her dewy Southern drawl was sweet, almost a parody, the way she consciously laid it on a little thicker at some times than at others. She was no femme fatale, though. More the opposite: She was flighty, insubstantial, enveloped in her scene and unaware of anything outside it. But somehow this made her seem ingenuous, and combined with her youth, it lent her a certain charm. She'd giggle like a schoolgirl at the mention of Donald's name— "my little honey" or "my sweetie," she'd call him, which seemed totally inappropriate for the circles he moved in. But her lack of sophistication was bearable because it was the thing about her, aside from her sex appeal, that was genuine. She was writing a book about "famous and successful men," she said when I met her. I rolled my eyes. But she asked us to set up interviews with some of the entertainers who played Trump Plaza. Later, Donald approached me and said, "See what you can do about it. Pacify her." So through our entertainment department an interview was set up with pop singer Jeffrey Osbourne, who kindly agreed to speak to her, and I was told she did interview him after one of his performances.

That's how it was to be. Atlantic City, Trump Plaza in particular, was designated as her playground. Initially, it was Mark Etess who explained the setup to me, as it had been explained to him by Steve Hyde. She had free access to all the amenities, as if she were a high-rolling customer. She had no interest in our business, never asked about it and never gambled recreationally. But she loved the restaurants and the health spa and the beauty salon, and she enjoyed all these compliments of the house, paid for first on Steve's complimentary privilege, briefly on Mark's, then on mine, but never signed for by anyone under the level of vice-president, for secrecy's sake. We were never to bump a preferred player from a luxury suite to accommodate her, though her stays often denied us the use of a suite we could have given to a betting customer. If a suite was open, however, she would get it. If we were full, a room would have to do. In the beginning, she accepted this.

For Donald, both Marla and Ivana were "trophies," ideals of a type, which he believed were necessary to complement different stages of his life. Now that he had reached the point where he seemed to own everything he could possibly want, he clearly enjoyed pursuing what he was not supposed to have, a gorgeous mistress in addition to his glamorous wife. But it was a glaring mismatch. Marla was young and energetic, Donald was moody and reclusive when they were together, showing obvious signs of middle age.

Ivana was rigid to the point of being overbearing. Her sophistication was studied, the affectation of a runway model, the pretense of chic aloofness. Donald had grown bored with it. He was

tired of a wife who was part business associate, part social secretary and part competitor, though he had molded her in that
shape, believing at the time that it was what he wanted. At best,
their marriage had deteriorated to a business partnership, each
consumed with their separate agendas. By the spring of 1988,
with the Crystal Tower debacle and the Castle's mounting losses,
even the business relationship was deteriorating. Donald was
dragging himself through the motions. They barely spoke in public, never touched or exchanged intimate remarks, and usually
walked several feet apart.

At social gatherings, he continually frustrated and humiliated
her in her desire to be gracious for the sake of the marriage and
their image.

Ivana planned a special weekend at Mar-a-lago on one occasion,
flying down sixteen of the Castle's best customers and their
spouses, wealthy people in their own right. She hosted a regal
feast in the main dining room, surrounded by fabulous tapestries,
with golden china plates and six-sided blue-crystal stemware she
had recovered from the basement, each facet intricately hand-
painted in gold and so delicate that when you touched them they
quivered. (They were virtually irreplaceable, as she found out
when she broke two of them and new ones had to be crafted in
Italy at a cost of $1,800 each.)

Earlier that day the guests had been brought out to the patio
for brunch. Donald appeared briefly. He said nothing to Ivana,
perhaps tabulating the cost of this weekend in his head. All he
said to her customers was, "I understand you all beat my brains
out while you're up in Atlantic City," joking with his typical
questionable taste. "Well," he added, "thanks a lot. Don't get too
lucky." Then he excused himself and left to return to New York.

That evening, Ivana sat without her husband at the head of
the splendid table. When her three young children came down
she let them stay. She enjoyed herself with her dignity unruffled,

laughing and sipping her Roederer Cristal, every inch the perfect hostess.

But when she returned to Atlantic City, Donald needled her constantly over the Castle's flagging performance, pressuring her—"busting her," as his tactics were described to me, "breaking her down."

For the cost of the Crystal Tower's luxury suites he could have built 500 guest rooms or something along the lines of the so-called mini-suites that Harrah's Marina across the street was successfully marketing to the middle-income players who favored the marina section of town. In this regard the Crystal Tower vividly points up how Donald misunderstood the mass-market bedrock of his profitability, focusing again, as he always did, on the much smaller percentage of high-end customers.

Donald's problems with the Castle went all the way back to his purchase of the property from Hilton in 1985. He bought the hotel without ever having been inside it. At the time he had no experience in operating a casino and no experienced management to run one for him.

He paid $320 million for the property and personally guaranteed a $280 million loan at 10 percent from Manufacturer's Hanover Trust to finance the purchase, something he always said he would never do. Then in an effort to take himself off the hook, he floated bonds in an aggregate principal amount of $351 million at an equivalent of 13.75 percent interest, in effect adding three percentage points to his debt service. The bonds were secured with first mortgages on an unopened casino, one with no track record to indicate it could generate enough cash to meet the $41 million in annual interest on the notes and buy down another $22 million of the principal in 1990.

No sooner had he swamped the property with debt and sent his wife down to make it a success than he set about remodeling it to accommodate his desire to have two casinos chasing Atlantic

City's limited pool of affluent gamblers. Ivana, determined to outdo Steve Hyde and Trump Plaza, eagerly pursued this misguided effort.

From a marketing standpoint, her rivalry with Trump Plaza had devastating consequences. Compare the Castle's performance with its sole competitor in the marina, Harrah's. In 1986, its first full year of operation, the Castle spent as much on complimentaries as Harrah's Marina but won $12 million less in its casino and earned $21 million less overall. Operating income—the balance of revenue after subtracting operating and marketing costs and depreciation and allowing for uncollected gambling markers—a prime indicator of cash flow, reflected that disparity. Harrah's generated operating income of $65 million. The Castle's was $44 million. Harrah's brought $48 million to the bottom line as net income, the highest in town that year by far. After lopping off $41 million in interest payments, the Castle's net income was $3.7 million for the year, seventh out of the eleven casinos. In subsequent years, it would never rise higher than that.

For 1987, Donald projected total revenue of $310 million and an operating income of $70 million. Ivana poured on the spending, lavishing $38 million in complimentaries on her customers, more than any other property except Caesars. It was a 21 percent increase over the previous year, the second-highest percentage increase in town after Bally's Park Place and nearly twice the rate of increase of the industry as a whole. Also, it was the highest in town as a percentage of total revenue. She came close to Donald's projections, generating almost $307 million in total revenue, fourth best in town. But costs incurred on one end have to be deducted at the other. Operating income fell to slightly under $42 million. After subtracting another $41 million in interest, actual pretax profit fell by $2 million to $1.7 million.

Hilton had studied Harrah's success in the marina and had planned to copy it. It correctly understood that the property would ultimately settle down to a mass-market attraction. It designed a hotel-casino for that market: large buffets and smaller, moderately priced rooms with the potential to add on as many as 2,000 more. There were plans to add on recreational facilities and a 1,600-seat theater.

But the concept was too plebeian for Donald and Ivana Trump. Hilton had set its sights on a sizable convention trade and built what are known as "breakout rooms," meeting spaces that can be divided or enlarged with movable walls, a feature of most modern hotel chains. These and the buffet area were ripped out by Ivana and replaced with cocktail lounges and gourmet restaurants. Thus the original architectural design was compromised, and a physically large facility was deprived of its capacity to service the mass market. The redesign entailed enormous costs early in the Castle's history. Depreciation, though a nonoperating expense, exceeded $20 million in 1986 and 1987, twice the accepted annual industry standard. At the same time the Castle lacked the luxury accommodations to gratify the high end and compete for Trump Plaza's customers. Which is why, by its second year, Ivana was badgering Donald hard for the luxury suites.

Donald made matters worse by pitting his two properties against each other, egging on the rivalry and pressuring his wife to produce flashy revenue numbers. It seemed he was more concerned with rankings, as far as monthly casino win figures, than he was with profitability. In response, Ivana simply juiced up spending without any apparent clear-cut strategy. Her pursuit of Trump Plaza's customers ran up the cost of doing business on the high end. Underneath, she subsidized massive charter-bus programs and giveaways, which trapped her in that unhealthy cycle of spending to win her own money back. Worse still, service suffered. The enormous crowds those programs brought through the doors overwhelmed the restaurants, bars and bathrooms and made the experience of coming to Trump's Castle less than desirable for many people. Nothing can be more damaging in the hospitality business because it is virtually impossible to recover a customer who's had a bad experience.

For the longest time Donald refused to confront the problems at the highest level of management at the Castle or even to admit they existed. Instead he hyped the property publicly. Privately, he was distraught over its poor performance, as he put the question to one top manager there: "Isn't this the best property in town? What's wrong? Why isn't this place working?" But when told that there were serious problems that needed to be addressed, his mood soured. "All that's just excuses," he said. "I don't want to hear that crap."

Midway through 1988, it was clear that Donald had come too far too fast. He was at the point where image superseded reality. In the same way that he believed a man could retain his hair by willing not to go bald, he thought he could redress the operational shortcomings of a multimillion-dollar company and make it successful by stating and restating that it was. For Donald, this is what passed for salesmanship. "Truthful hyperbole," as he called it in *The Art of the Deal*, stretched to its logical consequences.

Publicly Donald continued to praise Ivana as a brilliant manager. Privately he described her to me as a devoted, almost slavish wife who was always waiting at home for him in the evenings and wanted nothing more than to dote on him. He needed to preserve both images. He actually vacillated between firing her and placing her in charge of his entire gaming operation.

But the ground was giving way beneath Ivana that spring. As if she could feel it, she moved quickly and got to Donald in New York. She secured his assent to an employment contract for an executive whom she recruited from a competing casino. As I was told, this executive expected to report to Trump Plaza as a vice-president. It was a swipe at the president of the property, her rival, Steve Hyde. Ivana was attempting nothing less than a coup d'etat at the Plaza. If successful, Steve's authority would have been permanently undermined. It probably would have forced his resignation.

In Atlantic City, Steve was tipped off by one of Donald's lawyers, who had helped draw up the contract. Steve called Mark and me into his office. He told us the news and said that since Donald had approved the hire, it appeared that Ivana might gain control of both properties. He said, "I hate to tell you this, but, guys, if you have any offers out there, you better take a good, hard look at them. If you don't, you better put some feelers out. Because I don't think this is going to last."

Mark and I were stunned.

"What are you going to do?" I asked Steve.

"I'm going to try to get to the bottom of this," he said. "But the fact that it's happening and the fact that Donald is letting it happen, even if I'm able to put this off—this isn't the organization for us. So it's every man for himself. If you find something, take it. That's my advice. Don't hang around here."

Steve called Robert Trump first. Robert was shocked, Steve later told me. He knew nothing about it. Robert and Harvey Freeman met with Donald in New York for what was later described to me as "a passionate discussion." Apparently they were able to talk Donald out of it. He withdrew his support for the contract. The executive was hastily placed in a senior hotel position at Trump's Castle.

After that, Steve indicated to Mark and me that he believed Ivana's days in Atlantic City were numbered. Donald had finally decided that the problem at the Castle was Ivana. Besides, Atlantic City, removed by 90 miles from friends and family in New York, was a preferable location for his liaisons with Marla Maples. The question was, how to get Ivana out of Atlantic City and back to New York. Then he bought the Plaza Hotel in Manhattan, in March, and with that venerable old building, whose gilded turrets he could see every day from the glass wall behind his desk at Trump Tower, he found his answer.

The 82-year-old landmark Plaza Hotel, just south of Central Park on Fifth Avenue, cost him an estimated $400 million, nearly all of it borrowed money. On top of that he took out another bank loan for somewhere between $25 million and $50 million to renovate it. All told, he was carrying some $430 million in mortgages on the property at interest rates of at least 10 percent a year. To meet those costs and turn a profit, he'd have to book all 814 rooms every night of the year at $500 a room.

The same month that he confirmed the purchase, Donald announced the appointment of Ivana as the hotel's president. Whether Ivana herself had been told is questionable. Immediately after his announcement, the Castle released a statement that said: "Mrs. Trump remains fully in charge as chief executive officer of Trump's Castle."

But Donald thought otherwise. He summoned his wife and Steve to his office at Trump Tower one afternoon shortly afterward and explained to them his plan to restructure his management in Atlantic City. Ivana was returning to New York to run the Plaza Hotel, and Steve was being promoted to chief executive officer of all Donald's casino holdings. Ivana must have already been given her orders. She said nothing to Steve that day. They had taken chairs on opposite sides of Donald's office and Ivana stared straight ahead as he talked.

So within weeks of the announcement that Ivana was staying in Atlantic City, it was announced that Ivana was leaving.

With Steve in charge of everything, including the unfinished Taj Mahal, management of the Castle went to Paul Henderson, who had been hired the year before to replace Bucky Howard and who now became president. Mark Etess was promoted to president and chief operating officer of Trump Plaza. I moved up to second in command as executive vice-president.

Ivana said goodbye to her 3,800 employees at the Castle in a brief ceremony on the afternoon of Thursday, May 19, 1988. The night before, a more intimate affair for the executives was held in one of the ballrooms. Cocktails and hors d'oeuvres were served for an estimated 130 guests. Ivana was emotional as she addressed the room from the ballroom stage. She thanked all for their hard work, and she told them how much she'd miss each of them. Her voice broke in a quiet sob, which lasted for only a moment. Then she said goodbye and returned to her seat next to the podium.

Donald then walked up to the microphone. "Look at this," he said, turning to her. "I had to buy a $350 [sic] million hotel just to get her out of here and look at how she's crying. Now, that's why I'm sending her back to New York. I don't need this, some woman crying. I need somebody strong in here to take care of this place."

The audience suddenly fell silent. He quickly added, "No, really . . . this has all been too much. It's been a strain on her and the family."

Ivana dabbed a tear from her cheek. If she was insulted by what her husband said, she didn't show it. But Paul Henderson hastily stepped up to the microphone to attempt to defend her. "I have to say I've really enjoyed working for Ivana Trump. Her level of perfection is something I've never had the opportunity to work for before. I appreciate all she's taught me . . . and she really has. . . . I think she has a unique ability to put together a level of quality that is really unsurpassed in just about any place I've ever experienced and anyone I've ever worked for."

Donald, who was milling around among the guests at the banquet tables, suddenly turned and looked at Henderson with a fierce glare in his eyes.

7

"We were selling fantasy."
—DONALD J. TRUMP

Donald Trump's casino wave crested on June 27, 1988, when the bell sounded and Mike Tyson and Michael Spinks emerged from their corners to do battle for the undisputed heavyweight crown. At Trump Plaza, we billed the historic clash "Once And For All." Twenty-one thousand fans and 1,500 newspaper and television reporters and photographers came to see it at Convention Hall, where a seat at ringside cost $1,500.

The tremendous hype that had preceded the fight for the better part of a year drove the bidding to host the match into the stratosphere. During the haggling earlier in the year, in January and February, Caesars Palace and the Las Vegas Hilton ran the price up to $8 million. But Mark had already sewn up contractual control over both fighters with the "right of first refusal" clauses he had negotiated with Butch Lewis, the manager of Michael Spinks, and Tyson's comanagers at the time, Bill Cayton and Jim Jacobs. We would have to match the top offer, and we wondered how high Donald wanted to go. But when Steve Wynn entered the bidding on behalf of the Golden Nugget, we were certain that the fight would be ours. "I'll pay $10 million," Donald said when he heard. "Don't fuck around. Get me the fight." Anything to top Steve Wynn.

The final price was $11 million. It was the most expensive boxing match in history. The deal was concluded at the end of February. When it was announced to Trump Plaza's employees, Mark was showered by applause on the casino floor. Trump Plaza, he said, was giving the competition "a fast history lesson" in marketing. "This will be viewed as a bellwether day in Atlantic City history."

Steve Hyde quipped to reporters, "I know there are some people in Vegas sobbing in their beer right now."

Even Don King, who was no more than Tyson's promoter at the time and who had been outmaneuvered in his desire to see the fight at the Hilton, had to concede: "Trump has the ability to transform dreams into reality. He's the kind of guy who makes things happen."

But on the night of June 27 it was all over in a little more than a minute. Tyson stunned the visibly frightened Spinks with a left hook seconds into the first round, then he buried him with a right hand. Spinks sprawled backward against the ropes and dropped onto the seat of his silk trunks. The round was 1:31 old. Many in the record crowd were still taking their seats. In Las Vegas they jeered and called the fight a "bomb."

"I'd like to have a bomb like that every year," Mark fired back. With good cause. That weekend, the drop at Trump Plaza's tables exceeded $18 million. Of that amount we won more than $2 million. Our net income for the second quarter of 1988, which included the month of the fight, was $8,562,000. In the same period the year before it had been $404,000.

For the rest of the city the spillover in gaming revenue, in retail spending, in the restaurants and hotels, not to mention the promotional recognition, was enormous. The twelve casinos took in more than $40 million for the weekend, the best weekend the city ever had. In fact, our competitors bought a full-page ad in the *Atlantic City Press* to proclaim, "Thank You, Mr. Trump." The combined take at the gate—which went to Trump Plaza— and for the closed-circuit and pay-per-view television broad- casts—which we did not share in—was $70 million, making it the highest grossing event in the history of boxing. The celebrity turnout was magnificent. Economics aside, it was by far the most exciting night of the casino era in Atlantic City.

At Trump Plaza, we had hit upon the idea of staging a "celeb- rity buffet" before each fight in our Imperial Ballroom, which allowed us to sequester the stars before the main event, get them to mingle with the big customers and at the same time take some pressure off our crowded restaurants. They were expensive affairs. The Tyson/Spinks feast cost $45,000. Donald always attended them and we'd get prize promotional photos of the billionaire chumming it up with the likes of Jack Nicholson or Paul Simon or Barbra Streisand, which we rushed out over the wire services for distribution to newspapers and magazines nationwide and around the world. But as soon as the photos were taken, Donald would dash the event and defeat its purpose by demanding dinner afterward for himself and 40 friends and celebrities in a private dining room.

The stars were an important ingredient in the promotion of every fight. They enhanced the Trump mystique, and they were a valuable advertisement for Trump Plaza. The icing over it all was that we didn't have to solicit them. They would call us for tickets, and they were willing to pay retail. But we insisted on that. It was more important for us to reserve as many choice seats and hotel rooms as we could for our top customers, since the only way to come close to breaking even on an $11 million event is at the craps and blackjack and baccarat tables. But Donald was an obstacle we couldn't overcome. The more clever celebrities or their agents would bypass us and call him in New York, and then they'd get in for free with a couple of $1,000 tickets each that would have been worth tens of thousands of dollars more in gambling revenue if we could have put them in the hands of high-rolling customers. It was another example of how Donald permitted fame and celebrity to take precedence over the bottom line.

Such poor business judgment would amaze me. But as I came to know Donald, I realized that he had been clawing all his life for a place alongside the other stars in the firmament.

No spotlight was too bright for either Donald or Ivana. If celebrities entered the casino, the billionaire who swore he never fell over himself for anyone always made sure that he was introduced to them and photographed with them and they received special treatment. He had no time to stop and scratch an autograph for a fan or housewife who had come for the day to play at his casino, but he was captivated by anyone he perceived as powerful or wealthy or influential, whether it was in commerce, politics, sports or show business. And he was not going to be denied a chance to impress them or exert a little power of his own.

The night of the Tyson/Spinks spectacle, Donald was in finest form, joking and hamming it up for the cameras at ringside with Ivana at his side as well as his Manhattan entourage, whom he'd brought down by helicopter and limousine, courtesy of Trump Plaza.

We staged a lavish victory party for Mike Tyson in the Imperial Ballroom. Donald and Ivana were there, but Donald was restless the whole time, and as was his way, he became edgy and brusque. Finally, Ivana left and was driven alone across town to spend the night in their apartment at Trump's Castle. Donald stayed until the party ended and came down with some celebrity guests to see them off into a caravan of silver limousines lined up at the curb in the porte cochere. But he wasn't returning with them to New York. He had other plans, only he seemed uncertain at first how to bring them off. Marla Maples, who had watched the fight from a safe distance across from Donald at Convention Hall, now stepped out from the crowd and stood alongside him. He showed her to one car, then quickly changed his mind and said, "No, over here, get in here." She climbed into a second car. He started off, then he stopped. "Fuck it," he said, and he got into the back seat with her.

It was soon after, according to friends, that Donald and Ivana had their most serious argument to date over the young model from Georgia. A month later, I happened to be sitting with Steve in his office one day when he took a newspaper clipping from his desk drawer and showed it to me. It was a short item from the *New York Post*, no byline, which linked Marla with "one of New York's biggest tycoons, a married man. . . . The shapely blonde," it read, "supposedly goes around to all the stores in Trump Tower saying, 'Charge it to Donald.' "

"He's nuts," I said.

Steve nodded. "It's funny. He told me not that long ago he was going to break it off with her. Now I hear Ivana went to see a lawyer."

But by midsummer their dalliances at Trump Plaza were routine. Donald might conduct several hours of business before he'd disappear with her upstairs in one of the suites. Then again there were times when we thought he was coming down for a meeting or function, where his presence was expected, and he'd say, "Don't count on me. I'm not going to be there. I'm not coming down." Usually he'd have their dinner sent up to the room— steak or a hamburger or pasta for him, shrimp or oysters and champagne for Marla—for he preferred to be alone with her. But Marla took to complaining more and more of being cooped up in a suite. She'd beg Steve to invite Donald to dinner because, if he offered, Donald would always accept and she'd get to eat in a restaurant. Steve always found a polite way to decline. He refused to act as her escort and insisted that none of his executives be pressed to perform that duty. He believed no good could come of being that close to Donald and his paramour and advised us to avoid it. But we had to be on guard, anyway, for Donald was always looking for someone to act as a diversion for them, even if it was just to walk with Marla across the casino floor. And he was sly in that way. I'd be with the two of them, walking alongside Donald. Then he'd slowly slip back from the group, and the next thing I knew, I was escorting Marla.

Whether it was due to Marla's influence or his exploding celebrity, his vanities began to take on more exaggerated forms. Always somewhat soft in the middle, he began taking himself through cycles of binging and starving. For days he'd eat nothing but red meat, then he'd fast, then he seemed to get by for days on nothing but candy and popcorn.

He became more dependent on his bodyguards, especially his Atlantic City muscle, Lynwood Smith and Jim Farr. They were always by his side. Yet for all the care he took to ensure his personal safety, he never seemed fearful for it. Sometimes he'd refer to what a "crazy world" it is. "You've got to have these guys. You just never know what's going to happen." But he was not especially secretive about his movements. He'd detail his entire schedule for the day if I asked him. He never thought twice about dismissing his bodyguards when he wanted to move about undetected. Usually he traveled to Atlantic City by air, flying down on the Super Puma, in which case our casino marketing department, which handled VIP services, would be alerted to have a limousine waiting for him at the airport. Lynwood and Jim would accompany the car or post themselves in the hotel lobby to await his arrival. But sometimes his random movements bedeviled everyone. A couple of times he drove down himself in a white Mercedes-Benz convertible with New York tags that spelled "IVANA." Once, he suprised the staff at Trump's Castle when he pulled up to the porte cochere in the middle of the night, alone, behind the wheel of an old jalopy whose provenance was never determined.

As for bodyguards, their real value to him lay in the image they projected. That fact was driven home to me one night as Donald and I ate dinner at Maximilian's.

"God, what a life you guys got. . . . Look at you, eating steak," he said, interrupting the conversation to lean back and needle Lynwood and Jim, who were seated at the next table. He turned back to me. "Go ahead, Jack . . . you were saying." He stabbed a chunk of meat with his fork, dabbed it with ketchup and popped it into his mouth. I continued with whatever I was saying. He listened, but from time to time he'd break away to look over at his two big protectors and joke with them. Neither was the type who would hesitate to put out the forearms whenever the crowds got a little thick. As Donald explained to me good-naturedly, "You know, these guys get a little carried away sometimes, but they're basically good guys. . . . But they need that, Jack. It's good for their minds to rough people up a little bit every now and then. Keeps their heads on. You know what I'm saying?"

He spoke often of his bodyguards in that way, with the affection a man holds for a pair of trusted canines. These two, Lynwood and Jim, especially Lynwood, were his favorites. Lynwood was a trusted confidant, a role he thoroughly enjoyed; he liked to stroll through the casinos late at night in his boss's absence to report back to him on the cleanliness of the floors or to say which executives he had seen or not seen.

Donald's star burned its hottest that summer. He liked to draw our attention to references to himself in newspaper or magazine articles. Often, to make a point, he'd quote himself as if it was fresh conversation.

It was an odd contradiction, one I believe he never quite understood himself: how he could be so intensely concerned about what the public thought of him, yet care so little about their sensibilities. The fact that they were guests in his hotels and players at his tables seemed to mean nothing to him, other than that they were a necessity to be suffered for the sake of making him wealthier.

He continually disappointed them with his behavior, as he did at a huge dinner party we hosted in the Imperial Ballroom at Trump Plaza for a couple of hundred guests and their families for the promotion of "Wrestlemania IV," a nationwide pay-per-view television event we staged in Convention Hall that March in conjunction with the World Wrestling Federation. All the wrestling stars were on hand—Hulk Hogan, Jake "the Snake" Roberts and the like—to mingle with the crowd and sign autographs for the children. Donald came in, saw me at a table tucked away in a far corner of the room and joined me to avoid having to greet the public. (My daughter, Laura, then nine, was with me. She had never met Donald Trump. When I introduced her, Donald said, "Oh, does your daddy take good care of you? Yeah? Well, he better because I pay him an awful lot of money.") Inevitably a crowd soon gathered round our table. It was a celebrity event, though, precisely the place where autographs were expected. Donald signed a few, then waved his hand, as if to say, "No more. Forget it." For the rest of the evening he ignored everyone, adults and children, who passed the table and asked him to scrawl his name. He simply wanted nothing to do with them.

His patience for small considerations had run out as he and Ivana basked in a dazzling spotlight. The brightest moment came that summer on his 42nd birthday, celebrated at Trump's Castle and heralded by the arrival of his newest trophy, a 282-foot, $25 million yacht he christened the *Trump Princess*, which steamed into Absecon Channel early in July and weighed anchor in the marina. The celebration attracted eleven film crews. President Ronald Reagan dispatched a telegram of congratulations. Hollywood's hottest stars called, like fans, seeking invitations and a chance to play aboard the elaborate yacht.

More accurately than anything else, the *Trump Princess* illustrated what Donald and Ivana's life together was. It was Ivana's royal barge and she loved it. Its eleven suites, all named for precious and semiprecious stones, were opulent beyond compare. The master suite, the "Diamond Suite," was the largest and most magnificent. But when she was on board alone she preferred the "Sapphire Suite," with its large bathtub carved from white onyx and fed by two waterfalls.

She expected her guests to refrain from smoking on board. Hors d'ouvres were served only on the outside deck, and no dark-colored liquors were served at all so there could be no risk of staining the thick snowy carpets and 3,500 yards of chamois leather. She was determined to enjoy the yacht every chance she got. Often she brought her three children down with her to stay on it. She'd take it for weeks up to Martha's Vineyard.

Donald took pleasure in showing off the boat. But he never went on it if he could avoid it. He sailed on it only one time, on its maiden voyage from the Azores to New York Harbor, and it so terrified him when they weighed anchor—the movement convinced him it was sinking—that he would never sleep on it. All the time it was docked at the marina, he went on board only to watch boat races or occasionally to entertain important customers or business associates—"out chiseling with the lawyers," as Ivana joked.

But the *Princess* cost far too much money to be of more than marginal value as a marketing tool. It was leased to Trump's Castle for $400,000 a month, plus operating costs. In addition, the Castle had to pay more than $1 million to dredge Absecon Channel to make room for it. The last year it was docked at the marina, 1989, it cost the struggling property $5.7 million. Paradoxically, the *Princess* became the most identifiable image of his wealth. Donald was too caught up in the publicity associated with that to care about much else.

Donald's interest that summer was not yachting but boxing. He thought he saw a path that would lead him to control of the heavyweight champion of the world, Mike Tyson, who had fought his way to the top of the boxing world literally under Trump Plaza's sponsorship:

The relationship between us as site sponsors, on the one hand, and Mike, his managers and promoters, on the other, had been extremely beneficial to everyone concerned. It was an expensive and delicate relationship. Steve and, even more so, Mark were shocked when eleven days after Mike had belittled Michael Spinks in the ring, Donald announced during a trip to the West Coast that he had been asked by Mike to act as the champ's official adviser on business and boxing matters. Mark and Steve tried to talk him out of it, warning him that such tactics could jeopardize all the relationships we had established in the sport. But Donald refused to discuss it. Instead he jumped into a conflict of interest that had to hurt either Trump Plaza or Mike Tyson. As it turned out, it hurt both.

But first Donald did even worse damage closer to home. For all our success in penetrating the high-stakes international market, our most lucrative player was found right here at home. He was a broker of racehorses, who bought them as yearlings, trained them and sold them when they were ready to don racing colors. He was internationally known, having developed several champions in the recent years. Of course, his expertise had made him rich. He liked to shoot craps at $10,000 a toss. Steve and I had known him from the Golden Nugget, where he had been a regular customer, and he followed us to Trump Plaza. He was a great admirer of Steve's. Plus he enjoyed the renown, the "mystique," as he put it, of the Trump name. He was one of the ultimate high rollers because he played frequently and lost consistently. In three years, he'd gambled and lost more than $13 million with us, which made him the equivalent of a dozen buyers of Donald's high-priced New York condos.

The customer, thinking it would be a triumph to bring the famous Donald Trump into the sport of kings, approached Steve in the spring of 1988 with an offer to sell a colt he had bought in Kentucky as a foal the year before. The horse was "bred in purple," as he liked to say. Alibi was his name. He had been sired by Raise A Native, the champion stallion that had also fathered Alydar. Alibi had Triple Crown potential and was going to be entered in the Futurity at Belmont Park that fall, the Champagne Stakes and the prestigious Breeders' Cup held that year at Churchill Downs. The winner of any of these was automatically a top contender for "Two-Year-Old of the Year." After that, it was on to the Kentucky Derby the following spring.

Trump in the racing game! Steve instantly seized on the publicity value of it and brought the proposal to Donald. The horse, he was told, was a potential Derby winner, another "trophy." When Donald heard the asking price, $500,000, for an animal easily worth three times that the minute he won his first race, he agreed. The deal was concluded in the Super Puma in the air over the New Jersey coast. Donald glanced at some photos of the magnificent colt he intended to buy: Alibi was a luxurious chestnut brown, with a shimmering coat and princely bearing. Then, rather absentmindedly, he handed them back to the customer.

"It's a great horse, Donald, a champion," the customer said. "He's gonna be another Secretariat, maybe another Man O' War."

Donald looked out the window and turned back to his guest. "Yeah, okay. Done. It's done."

Down in Florida, at the Ocala training track, Alibi was running what are known as "bullet workouts"—five furlongs in a minute flat, the equivalent of maybe 58 seconds on a racetrack and already as fast as many of the older prize thoroughbreds running in stakes races across the country.

Donald insisted that the colt's name be changed. At first, the customer protested: it was a violation of racing tradition, bad luck to change a colt's name. But Donald persisted and got his way. Summer approached, racing colors were chosen, silks purchased, and Alibi became "DJ Trump."

But then weeks passed and Donald didn't come up with the money to pay for the racehorse. The customer was complaining, attorneys were involved and letters began flying back and forth. So Donald negotiated down the asking price, claiming that since his name was worth at least $250,000—in cash!—he should be required to pay only half what he'd agreed to earlier.

Steve was trying to mediate, and in the end, the customer, partly as a result of pressure from his colleagues, who were eager for a Trump investment in the racing industry, caved in. Donald assured Steve on the phone that a check would be cut and signed within days. But he insisted that Steve get the customer to ship DJ Trump north so the horse could start racing.

As it was, DJ Trump's workouts were already being pushed to the limit to satisfy his new owner. The horse had been "breezed," that is, run almost full out, on seven occasions. It is a process that takes place over several weeks. After each breezing, a colt has to be cooled down, walked the next day, then paced for the next four or five days before it can be given its head again. It was the opinion of the trainer in Florida that at least two more workouts were needed, about two weeks at most, before the horse was ready to come north to race. Donald was furious when he heard this. He demanded the animal be breezed immediately and brought up. A compromise was reached with a final workout scheduled for the following Saturday. DJ would be walked the next day, transported north that Monday, walked again on Tuesday, then galloped to be made ready to race.

That week, a virus swept through the Ocala barn where DJ Trump was stabled, spread by the foals shipped in from breeding farms and immunized on their arrival. The disease, known in racing parlance as "sniffles," is akin to a 24-hour bug in humans and normally nothing to worry about as long as the horses are watched and rested until the sickness runs its course. Rest, however, is vital. Physical stress, such as running at full gallop, could weaken a horse's resistance and bring on high fever, even death. DJ Trump was showing no symptoms of the virus, but as a precaution the trainer suggested that his final workout be postponed for a week.

The customer phoned Donald's office with the news. The same day, as he later told me, he got a call from Steve, who was upset as he relayed his orders from Donald: "He wants the horse to work."

Saturday morning broke warm and clear in Ocala. The summer sun had baked the training track to a hard, dusty crust, ideal for speed and good for a colt's muscles. DJ was saddled and led out of the barn. The trainer waited at the rail with a stopwatch as the jockey mounted the horse, rode him out to the far side and opened him up for all he was worth. The horse ran bravely, but when he was reined in after five furlongs, the trainer's stopwatch showed his time at 1:03, a full three seconds off his best breezings. The trainer knew instantly that something was wrong.

Within a couple of hours, DJ Trump's body temperature was soaring. His front legs began to quiver, then they buckled under him, and the huge magnificent animal went down on its side.

The veterinarians who were called in immediately diagnosed an acute case of the virus, aggravated by the strain of the workout. The horse's condition worsened. By nightfall, it had lost blood circulation in its forelegs. Its front hooves, like two gangrenous appendages, were dying and would have to be amputated if the horse was to survive. The hooves would grow back, but the great animal would never race. The customer got the word by phone from Florida. He later told me the trainer was sobbing on the other end of the line.

The customer phoned Atlantic City and broke the news to Steve Hyde. Steve was shaken, and he promised to call Donald in New York immediately. A few days later, a meeting was arranged in Steve's new office at Trump's Castle. The customer came prepared with an update on DJ Trump's condition and the costs for the amputations and subsequent medical treatment. It was his guess that it would be a year before the horse could stand on its front legs again.

Steve later told me all about the conversation. No sooner had the customer described the horse's problems than Steve calmly replied, "I've got worse news. Donald doesn't want the horse."

At first, the customer didn't understand.

"I laid the situation out for him just as you explained it to me," Steve said. "His response is that we're trying to pass off a lame animal on him. The horse has 'health problems,' he says, and he says he's not going to put a dollar out of his pocket for a horse with 'health problems.' "

The customer was stunned. "What the hell are you talking about, Steve? He was the one who ruined the animal. We had a deal. He bought the horse. It's his."

Steve just looked at his premier player, a multimillion-dollar customer. What could he say?

The customer left Steve's office, swearing that he'd never gamble at Trump Plaza again. "The great Donald Trump," he grumbled bitterly. "Ritz and glitz sonuvabitch. We ruined a $20 million animal. We denied the world this horse."

Donald had never given a thought to the animal's welfare, and he ignored the consequences from a business standpoint. Although the horse would never race, it still had considerable value as a stud with champion bloodlines and was worth the $250,000 investment. Add in the loss of a player who was gambling millions of dollars a year in his casino, and whether or not he should have followed through on the purchase was not even a question. But Donald could not have cared less. Once he realized that there was no chance he would be at Churchill Downs on Derby Day, that he would not stand in the winner's circle, he simply lost interest in the horse.

We did not see the player at Trump Plaza for the rest of the summer, but Steve stayed in contact with him, patiently trying to woo him back and looking for a way to smooth over the damage.

The operation and subsequent treatment to save DJ Trump's life cost our customer close to $50,000. A blacksmith had to be flown in from Texas to fit the maimed colt with special rubber shoes so he could stand on his forelegs.

Steve and our player made a deal in which Steve's wife, Donna, bought DJ Trump for $150,000. The deal was sealed with a handshake. It was Steve's entry into horse breeding, a pursuit from which he ultimately derived a great deal of joy. He even talked me into buying a horse, and soon we were discussing plans to buy a third as equal partners.

The entire episode made a profound impression on Steve, though. That fall, he began to talk frequently of the day when he would leave Donald.

8

*"Despite what some people may think, I'm not
looking to be a bad guy when it isn't absolutely
necessary."*

— DONALD J. TRUMP

In 1988 we had everything in place, and Trump Plaza enjoyed its best year up to that time. Total revenue was the highest in town. For the first time we won $300 million in the casino, one of only two properties (Caesars being the other) to do so. Our profits exceeded $33 million.

Trump Plaza was the place to play in Atlantic City. Steve, Mark and I had accomplished Donald's goal and succeeded in what we set out to do sixteen months before. We had made the property number one.

The Castle's total revenue rose by a lesser margin over 1987 and reached $316 million. But after costs, its income from operations was not enough to carry $41 million in interest payments, and the property recorded a $3 million net loss, the first in its history. The debt brought on by the construction of the luxury suites was now costing the Castle dearly.

As the new chief executive officer of Donald's casinos, Steve moved his office to the Castle to attempt to sort through the years of mismanagement and try to set the property right. But

despite Donald's frustration at the Castle's losses, he was unwilling to accept Steve's cost-cutting recommendations. Steve
strongly advised him to send the *Trump Princess* sailing somewhere else to remove that multimillion-dollar drain on the
property. Donald disagreed. Instead he ordered more costly
renovations. All of the property's relatively new carpeting was
ripped out and replaced at a cost of almost $2 million because it
did not match the color in the new showroom that was under
construction as part of the Castle Tower project. Then he decided
the name of the property should be changed—specifically, he
wanted the apostrophe and the "s" deleted from "Trump's" and
the new name to read simply "Trump Castle." It was a major
undertaking. Every sign, logo, decal and fixture, plus the huge
letters on the outside at the top of the hotel tower, had to be
replaced at a cost of more than $1 million. In an effort to save
money, some outside letters, each about six feet high, were found
in the Castle's warehouse to spell "Trump." They had cost over
$50,000 themselves, but they would be cheaper to install than
new ones. So these were shipped out, the old letters were taken
down from the top of the building, and the replacements were
carted up and mounted in their place next to the word "Castle."
But when Donald saw the new sign he flew into a rage: the letters
that spelled "Trump" were slightly smaller than those that
spelled "Castle." He immediately had the entire sign dismantled.

With the Castle bleeding costs and interest payments, Donald
pushed ahead that fall. Elsewhere, events seemed to be unfolding
in his favor. He closed his deal with Merv Griffin for the Taj
Mahal and reached an agreement with Merrill Lynch to sell $675
million in high-risk bonds to jump start construction and finish
the giant project.

In November, Donald and Ivana and Mark Etess and his wife,
Lauren, went to Las Vegas for four days. Steve Wynn invited them
to stay as his guests at the Golden Nugget. For Mark, the trip

was a personal triumph. More than Steve Hyde or myself, this charismatic, energetic executive, so popular with Trump Plaza's customers and employees at all levels, sought Donald's friendship and longed for a greater share of the Trump spotlight. He returned from Las Vegas more excited and enthused than I'd ever seen him. He spoke warmly of Donald and Ivana and said he and Lauren got along fabulously with them.

Donald, in turn, showed what he thought of Mark's talents and the Plaza's stellar performance that year. With Steve's blessing, he appointed Mark president and chief operating officer of Trump Taj Mahal Associates. He was going to run the largest casino in the world. For me it was the turning point of a nine-year career in gaming. On Steve's recommendation, I succeeded Mark as president and chief operating officer of Trump Plaza, the most successful and profitable of Donald's enterprises.

A couple of weeks before Christmas, Donald called me and invited me to lunch at Trump Tower. We could spend "some quality time together," he said.

"We'll have lunch and shoot the breeze for a couple of hours," he said. "It'll give you a chance to see me in my environment. So we're all comfortable with the way things are going."

Steve and Mark chuckled about it when I told them. Mark said, "So you're going up for your tuna sandwich with Donald"— a reference to the time when Mark and Donald had had a similar get-acquainted lunch. When Mark arrived at Trump Tower, the billionaire ordered tuna sandwiches for the two of them and they ate at Donald's desk.

Two days before Christmas, I flew up to New York in a six-seat Navaho airplane. A freezing rain fell the whole time. When I arrived at LaGuardia Airport a silver Trump Plaza limousine was waiting for me. Shortly before noon, I was deposited in front of Trump Tower's gleaming facade on Fifth Avenue.

I didn't know what to expect. I had been in Donald's office

before but never for any length of time. On the elevator to the 26th floor, I remembered Mark telling me Donald's "tuna sandwich" joke. Donald was not known for mixing business with pleasure. As he liked to say, "I don't give good lunch."

Norma Foederer, his administrative aide, came out to greet me and led me through the open door of Donald's office. He was on the phone and didn't look up when we came in. I took one of the two dark velour chairs in front of his desk and waited. I glanced at the framed magazine covers of Donald decorating the walls—everywhere except behind his broad cherrywood desk, where there is a huge window with a spectacular view of the elegant Plaza Hotel and Central Park.

Finally, Donald concluded his conversation and hung up the phone.

"So how're you doing?" he said cheerfully.

"Good, Donald. I feel pretty good," I said.

"Great," he said. "Well, I hope you're prepared to make 1989 a record year because I'd like nothing more than to see you beat the shit out of all of Etess's records."

Here we go, I thought. I shifted around and told him instead how all our projections pointed to another great year. He seemed pleased with that. We chatted a few more minutes, then he said, "C'mon, let's eat." He stood up and called out to Norma in the reception area. "Call them downstairs. Tell them we're coming down for lunch." That set the security procedures in motion. There had been only one uniformed guard in the reception area when I arrived. Now, when we came out together, two bodyguards were waiting to board the elevator with us.

Downstairs, the atrium was crowded with Christmas shoppers. The moment Donald stepped off the elevator, he turned left and walked off ahead of me. Keeping up with him is hard work. Not only does he walk fast, but he invariably draws crowds of onlookers. Knowing this he always selects the path to his destination ahead of time, and with his bodyguards a few feet in front, he makes a beeline along it.

Lunch this day was at a little Italian restaurant whose owner came out to greet us and show us straightaway to a table in the center of the room. The two bodyguards kept watch outside by a railing at the entrance. Everyone in the room looked at us, which is to be expected with Donald. He rarely takes notice. He handed me a menu and did not look at one himself. He said, "It's a funny thing. This restaurant was one everybody thought would fail. The location, the setup . . . all wrong, they said. But the guy wanted to come in and do it, and Trump was behind him all the way. Now look at it. It's a tremendous success. The food is tremendous. It's a real positive for us. Here's this little place just sitting in the middle of the lobby and I think it has the best pasta in New York City. . . . You've got to try the mozzarella sticks. Out of this world. Believe me."

His conversation skipped across a dozen topics. Then he said, "How about Wynn, huh? He's a fucking madman, isn't he? It must have been hell working for the guy." So we ended up talking about Steve Wynn for a few minutes, always a favorite subject of Donald's, as much now as it was the day I first met him almost two years ago.

Then he suggested again that my prime focus for the year should be to surpass "Etess's records" at Trump Plaza.

I hesitated for a moment, thinking to choose my words carefully. "Well, Donald, it's really been a team effort. I don't think Mark has ever tried to claim that he was responsible for everything that's happened at Trump Plaza. Steve was a contributor, Mark was, I was, all the 4,000 people were. It's something different. It's not—"

"Yeah, yeah," he interrupted, "but you know the guy at the top gets all the credit. You know. So you've got to kick the shit out of all of Etess's numbers. You can do it. Nineteen eighty-nine is the year to do it."

"I happen to think, Donald . . . and this is not from the standpoint of beating Mark . . . but 1989 is going to be a great year at Trump Plaza. We're going to win more money at our table games. We expect to see big gains in certain areas. And not only are we going to win more money than we ever have in the past, I think we're going to be number one over Caesars in casino revenue for the first time in the company's history."

Donald leaned forward and smiled. "That's it! I love that competitiveness. I love to hear it. I knew you'd say this. This is just what I wanted to hear. I wanted to hear you tell me that you are going to blow the shit out of all the records that Mark put up there.

"Tell me about yourself," he said. "I want to get to know you. Tell me a little bit about your philosophy. Tell me about . . . you know, where you think we can get better. What are your ideas for marketing the building?"

I discussed my plans but none of this seemed particularly interesting to him. But he was going to let me talk. He had accepted Steve's recommendation and turned the property over to me, but I was still something of an unknown to him and he wanted to be certain of me in his own mind. So I continued, touching also on the international market and our efforts there. I reminded him that we were spending a lot of money to attract those high-stakes gamblers, but I said I thought we were going to see the fruit of that effort soon, specifically among the Japanese.

"Develop it," he said. "Definitely. I like it. Get the business. Do whatever you have to do. Hire the people you need to hire. Whatever you need."

I had to laugh to myself, thinking of the considerable roadblocks Donald had thrown in front of us in this market.

Donald had first announced his entry into the high-stakes international gambling market a couple of years earlier with a bid for the rights to build and operate what was to be the largest casino in the world in Australia, in Darling Harbor in New South

Wales. He later changed his mind, and, as it turned out, the government of New South Wales backed away from its support for the casino project, too.

But Trump Plaza's spokesman in Asia, Ernie Cheung, with the assistance of Jeff Patterson, a Trump real estate agent and casino customer, had been actively pursuing two Australians, both among the world's wealthiest gamblers. One of them was Alan Bond, a billionaire entrepreneur, winner of the America's Cup in 1983. In the fall of 1988, they had finally gotten Bond to come to New York to meet Donald, after which we made arrangements to bring the two of them to Atlantic City together, where we hoped to get Bond to the tables. When Bond arrived at Trump Plaza, he, Donald, Steve Hyde and some friends had dinner at Maximilian's. By the time the coffee was served, he had bought the St. Moritz Hotel from Donald for $180 million.

Donald had acquired the hotel in 1985 from a group of 500 investors. The legendary 60-year-old Art Deco palace on Central Park, 33 stories high with over 700 rooms, cost him $31 million, he said. Later reports put the true price at closer to $70 million.

Donald insisted he made a profit on the St. Moritz every year he owned it. It also proved convenient for a time as a hiding place for Marla Maples, though I heard that even she complained about the condition of the building. Then in the spring of 1988, he bought the Plaza Hotel on the same block, which put him under some pressure to sell the St. Moritz.

That night across the table with Alan Bond at Maximilian's, Donald saw his chance and seized it. As Steve told me, Donald was at his smoothest, most convincing best. What made Donald deadly in these circumstances was that he embellished facts so often that he often believed the embellishment himself. "Jack, you just wouldn't believe the charm of this guy when he's selling something," Steve said.

The price that Alan Bond agreed to pay, an astounding $180 million, was at least a $100 million profit for Donald. Bond offered Van Gogh's "Irises" as equity, but Donald turned it down. ("What would I do with 'Irises'?" he was reported to have said. "You know what 'Irises' is? It's a piece of canvas with some paint on it.")

Bond returned to New York to close the deal with Donald, without ever betting a single dollar in Trump Plaza's casino, by the way.

As it turned out, the deal left considerable bad feelings in its wake. Donald told me he was certain that Bond didn't fully understand the terms of the sale and did not realize he didn't own the land underneath the hotel and was tied to a lease that was increasing in proportion to land values in Manhattan. It was the part of the deal Donald loved, that touch of moral larceny. "This is one of the best deals I ever made in my life," he crowed. "I really, really whipped this guy, really took this sucker for some big money."

To make matters worse, Donald then refused to pay Jeff Patterson a commission on the sale for bringing the two parties together, which Donald had earlier agreed to pay. Needless to say, our reputation was severely damaged in Australia. Bond, whose businesses were in debt to the tune of $6 billion, ended up going bankrupt. Six months after he bought the hotel, he was trying to sell it. Of course, he never returned to our casino. In fact, we never got another major player from Australia. Which really rankled me. Donald certainly could have paid Jeff a respectable fee, still pocketed an enormous profit on the St. Moritz, and thereby protected the interests of his only consistently profitable operation, Trump Plaza. But he was as shortsighted as he was cunning. He had no regard for the future, so he chose not to do that. He aimed low. Consequently, he shot himself in the foot.

Our lunch at Trump Tower concluded with a discussion of personnel. Donald brought a unique approach to this as well. "Tell me about Steve Hyde," he said.

Of course, I had nothing but the highest regard for Steve and

I told Donald so. "Yeah, that's my man," he quickly added. "I have to tell you," he went on, "I feel real good about the quality of people he's brought in. It's been a real positive for us." Then just as quickly he changed course. "So who do you think is doing a shitty job?" he asked.

I told him no one. But he went down a list of names until we got to a finance employee of Trump Plaza, who happened to be black.

"What do you think of him?" Donald asked.

I said I was familiar with his abilities, and he had shortcomings. "To be honest, I don't think he's the best we can have," I said. "I'd like to see him either come up to speed, where he can help me a lot more, or maybe there's something else he can do."

Instantly, Donald was enthused. "Yeah, I never liked the guy. I don't think he knows what the fuck he's doing. My accountants up in New York are always complaining about him. He's not responsive. And isn't it funny, I've got black accountants at Trump Castle and at Trump Plaza. Black guys counting my money! I hate it. The only kind of people I want counting my money are short guys that wear yarmulkes every day. Those are the kind of people I want counting my money. Nobody else."

I couldn't believe I was hearing this. But Donald went on, "Besides that, I've got to tell you something else. I think that the guy is lazy. And it's probably not his fault because laziness is a trait in blacks. It really is, I believe that. It's not anything they can control. . . . Don't you agree?" He looked me square in the eye and waited for my reply.

"Donald, you really shouldn't say things like that to me or anybody else," I said. "That is not the kind of image you want to project. We shouldn't even be having this conversation, even if it's the way you feel."

"Yeah, you're right," he said. "If anybody ever heard me say that . . . holy shit . . . I'd be in a lot of trouble. But I have to tell you, that's the way I feel."

"Well, I have to tell you, I don't agree with you. We've got people at the Plaza doing good jobs, we've got people doing jobs that are not so good. It's got nothing to do with the color of anybody's skin."

He gave a short chop with his hand, as if to wave away my point of view. "Ah, it's a trait. Anyway I'm glad to hear you're going to get rid of the guy."

I hadn't said that. So I corrected him. "Donald, I'd like to see what the guy can do. Let's just wait and see. If we continue to have problems in the finance area, then yes, maybe he doesn't have the ability, and I'll think about a replacement."

Donald was satisfied with that. But for months afterward he continued to press me to fire the man. Ultimately the executive resigned to pursue other opportunities.

Donald talked expansively on a number of subjects that day, as he would when he was in a good mood. He spoke of the Taj Mahal in grand terms, insisting that it was going to be greater than the famed palaces of Europe, even the Hermitage in Leningrad, which he'd visited on his trip to the Soviet Union the summer before and considered to be the most fabulous building in the world. He told me again how fond he was of Steve Hyde, and how he liked what was happening at Trump Plaza. He liked my attitude, he said—"that competitive attitude," he called it. He said he was sure now that I was the "right guy" for the job as its president.

Then he stood up—there was no check, no tip—and we left. "C'mon, I want to show you this," he said, and we walked out into the crowded atrium for a brief tour. He was clearly proud of the planning that went into the building and the design of it. He wanted me to see these things for myself, he said.

At last we made our way back to the elevators. He stopped when we got to the doors. He shook my hand. "Thanks," he said. "This has been real good, a great meeting. I'll see you later." He turned and stepped onto the elevator with the two bodyguards and the doors slid shut behind them. I was embarrassed for a moment to be left so abruptly.

Outside on Fifth Avenue it was pouring harder than when I had arrived. The wind kicked bits of trash and wet paper along the sidewalk. With each gust I felt an icy spray of rain on my cheeks. But I felt good. I was certain I'd made a strong impression on the famous Donald Trump. To be honest, there could be nothing better in my world at that point. I was pleased to know that he had confidence in me, that he had no reservations that I could run this $300 million business for him.

I knew Steve and Mark would be eager to hear all about it when I got back. From the days when we worked together at the Golden Nugget, we had a goal: that someday Mark and I would be running casinos and Steve would be our boss. We talked about it all the time. Now it was happening. It was thrilling. A dream come true for three men still young and enjoying the best years of their lives.

"Well, it's all a game."
—DONALD J. TRUMP

As the new president of Trump Plaza, one of my responsibilities was to oversee arrangements for Marla Maples's visits. The demands she made on the facilities and the staff were increasing. More and more, she was arriving with friends in tow or with her parents, putting a greater strain on the luxury accommodations we tried to reserve for preferred customers. And it had to be VIP treatment all the way—helicopter transportation from New York, limousines, free run of the property, the salons, massages, restaurants, stores, whatever she desired. I handed over most of this responsibility to Jon Benanav, our executive vice-president, formerly the vice-president of hotel operations. It was a delicate balancing act for both of us. But I tried as much as possible to maintain Steve's rule, as I passed it down to Jon: make every effort to accommodate her, but not at the expense of betting customers.

Donald was understanding, for the most part. Sometimes he'd call ahead on her behalf, but if the hotel was filled, he'd say, "Hey, no problem. If you got it, you got it. If you can't keep her, fine. Don't worry about it. We'll stick her at the Castle. No big deal."

Generally, Marla accepted this. Aside from her complaints about the cleanliness of the beauty salon, where she spent a great deal of time, she was easygoing. But she wanted to drop the charade of registering in the hotel under "Fitzsimmons," the name of the former policeman and Trump bodyguard who still acted as her primary cover. "Why can't I sign in under my own name?" she asked.

"Donald wants you registered under 'Fitzsimmons,' " I'd say. Usually that was enough. But it was getting harder to talk her out of it. There was no doubt that Marla was pushing for a greater share of the control over her future. It was difficult to tell whether she was getting it, though. There were times when it seemed that Donald couldn't care less what happened to her, and he'd instruct us accordingly: "She's nothing. Don't go out of your way. Don't worry about it." Then a week later, it would be the opposite: "Jack, listen. Make sure she gets a real nice suite. Take real good care of her for me, will you?"

He'd be irritable whenever one of her parents was in town, though, since they usually shared a suite with Marla. So I was surprised when Donald had her mother flown into town for a weekend to celebrate her birthday at Trump Plaza. "Make sure she's taken real good care of," he instructed me. "Make it real nice, real special for her, okay? Do me the favor, Jack." I asked one of the women on the staff to select an assortment of clothes and jewelry and crystal from the retail shops, a few thousand dollars' worth in all. We had everything gift-wrapped and sent up to the suite in time for the arrival of mother and daughter. Donald was glad when I informed him. "Terrific, Jack. I appreciate it."

"What do you want the card to say?" I asked.

"I don't know. Happy Birthday, that's all," he said.

"How do you want it signed?"

He thought for a moment. "Sign it, 'Love, Donald.' "

Marla was quite comfortable with Trump Plaza by now, with the staff and with me. She was exuberant and sweet and unassuming, and it was hard not to like her. The one thing I refused to do, though, was act as the cover for her and Donald by escorting her to events or restaurants. Like Steve, I considered it a breach of professionalism. If necessary, I would assign one of our plainclothes security guards when she came in alone. But it was more difficult to avoid this sort of situation when Donald extended the invitation. He was sneaky in the way he'd maneuver me into providing the cover for them. I particularly remember one February evening.

Marla's father, Stan Maples, came to town with his daughter the last weekend of that month. They shared a two-bedroom suite. Mike Tyson was fighting in Las Vegas that Saturday night. We sponsored a closed-circuit telecast and fashioned around it a small invitation-only affair for some big players in the ballroom with drinks and a buffet.

Steve and I had just arrived for the telecast and were standing in the doorway of the ballroom. "Hold it, look," Steve interrupted. I turned and spotted Donald's bodyguards, then Donald, then Stan and Marla coming down the hallway toward us. Steve whispered, "Oh, boy. Here we go. Show time."

Donald and Marla greeted us at the entrance. Marla was even bouncier and smiling more than usual. She introduced "Daddy," as she called him, a smooth-faced Southerner of average height and build, who was quite youthful-looking—in fact, he looked to be about the same age as Donald. He wore a sportcoat and tie for the occasion, neat but not expensive. I later learned that Stan was an erstwhile country and western crooner whose act included an Elvis impersonation. He had divorced Marla's mother when his daughter was sixteen and later married a woman a year younger than Marla.

Steve quietly slipped away as Donald talked to me, inquiring vaguely about business in general that weekend. Suddenly, Donald stopped and said, "We can get a table down here. I was going to watch the fight upstairs. But I think we'll stay and watch it down here."

Carefully Donald positioned me and then himself at the table. Marla and Stan walked around and came in from the other side, Marla next to me, Stan at her other side. I was sitting in between Donald and Marla.

Stan said nothing to me or Donald for the rest of the evening. But he and his daughter spoke closely and affectionately the whole time. The way they held hands and he touched her shoulder from time to time, it looked like Marla was his date. Donald was extremely annoyed. He would have preferred to be alone with Marla upstairs in the hotel than down here entertaining her father. He fidgeted in his seat and barely said a word. It seemed to me that Stan was enjoying himself immensely.

We ordered soft drinks. Donald didn't touch his. The minutes dragged by as he sat glumly on my left and father and daughter giggled and cooed on my right. It was terribly uncomfortable. From the corner of my eye I spied Steve at a table in the back of the room. When I finally caught his eye he shook his head at me and chuckled, enjoying my predicament.

The round-card girl reappeared on the screen. At last, Donald spoke. "I got it! Marla, that's the perfect job for you. We finally found something you can handle," he said in a voice dripping with sarcasm.

"Oh? What?" Marla said.

"You can be a round-card girl at Trump Plaza. What do you think, Jack? Don't you think she'd make a terrific round-card girl for you?"

Stan didn't say a word. Marla looked at Donald sternly, then at me, waiting for my response. I was clearly on the spot. "Uh, I don't know. . . . I don't know, Donald. I think Marla can do better than that."

Donald sneered. "Ah, come on, what do you mean?"

Marla was overjoyed. She bounced in her seat and swung her arms around me and said in her sweetest Georgia lilt, "Oh, I knew you'd say something nice. Jack, you're just so sweet." She turned to Donald. "Jack knows I have more talent than a round-card girl. Right, Jack?"

Then she excused herself and left the table briefly. Stan also left. Donald watched Marla walk away, and as he and I sat there for a few minutes alone, he shook his head and said, "God, I wish you could see her body! She's got a dynamite fucking body, Jack. A body and a half. If you could take one look at it, just one look, you wouldn't believe it. It's unbelievable. Better than a ten."

In the spring of 1989, Pratt Hotel Corporation filed a multi-million-dollar lawsuit over Donald's interference, as they put it, with their option to purchase the old Penthouse site next door to Trump Plaza.

Unperturbed by this, Donald flew to Brazil. The occasion was the second "Trump Cup," a rich stakes race for thoroughbreds, the most prestigious event of its kind in South America. Trump Plaza was sponsoring the race in partnership with the Brazilian government. It was calculated to draw the wealthiest Latin gamblers, another link in our carefully mapped strategy to promote the casino worldwide.

In 1988, the first year we held the race, we won some big players. There had been only one obstacle: Donald refused to attend the race. He was fearful about security, he said, and had heard tales about runaway street crime. To avert a major embarrassment, we enlisted Robert Trump to go in his stead. Donald approved but insisted that his brother not give interviews or make any statements to the South American press. He didn't want any confusion as to who "the real Trump" was, he said.

Easygoing as he was, Robert only laughed about it. It was funny and a little sad at the same time to watch as autograph-seekers stopped him on the casino floor, because there was a fraternal resemblance, and he would have to say, "You want Donald. I'm not Donald, I'm Robert." The disappointed fan would say, "Oh," and walk away. Robert always shrugged it off with a smile.

Not only did he impress me as an unassuming man. He was evenhanded. He and his wife, Blaine Beard, a prominent New York socialite, were friendly and always delightful to be around. Robert was valuable to us because he had no illusions that one of his principal duties as executive vice-president of the Trump Organization was to stay out of Donald's spotlight. His unpretentious nature allowed him to accept such things. He required no deferential treatment, no bodyguards, no displays of power. He was content with a subsidiary role. The way I saw it, this made him a force for stability within the business. Plus, he and Steve Hyde had an excellent rapport. Robert was grateful that he didn't have the commitments on his time that his brother had. He preferred to enjoy his family and took great pleasure in bringing Blaine and their friends down to Trump Plaza once in a while for dinner and a show. There was a little hamburger shop across the street, where Robert ate regularly when he was in town. He loved the meatloaf special they served on Thursdays. If Robert was in town that day, that's where you'd find him, sitting at the counter.

Robert had such a good time in Brazil that he stayed an extra week. The Trump Cup, held in Rio de Janeiro that first year, was a tremendous success, despite Donald's absence. Rather than risk being upstaged by his brother again, Donald reluctantly agreed to attend the 1989 race, which was held in São Paulo. Ivana went along, with Steve Hyde and Mark and Lauren Etess.

On their return Steve told me that Donald and Ivana surprised him by how gracious they were, especially since it was extremely warm in Brazil that time of year, and he was certain they both would have lost their tempers over the wilting effects of the heat on clothing and hair. I don't think Donald enjoyed himself, however much he managed to restrain it for appearance' sake. He called me at home early on Sunday morning, the day of the race, from his hotel room in São Paulo. "Jack, thank God! I knew I could get in touch with you. I can't find the asshole running the other property." He was referring to Paul Henderson, the president of Trump Castle. "Fucking guy. What is it with him? He's never at work. . . ."

For a moment I felt a little strange. He had called me at home on a Sunday morning, yet he thought he had reached me at Trump Plaza.

"I'm going fucking crazy down here," he said. "What's going on up there? You got a newspaper there?"

"Yes," I said.

"Tell me what the main headline says."

I read it to him.

"What's under that?" So I read him the subheading.

"What are the other stories on the front page?"

I spent the next half hour taking Donald through the paper, headline by headline.

The trip did not conclude without one very touchy moment, when he was solicited to contribute to a fund-raising dinner to benefit a Brazilian hospital and he refused. He clearly resented what he considered the charity "game," and he said so in *The Art of the Deal:* "I don't kid myself about why I'm asked to speak at or chair so many events," he complained. "It's not because I'm such a great guy. The reason is that people who run charities know that I've got wealthy friends and can get them to buy tables. I understand the game, and while I don't like to play it, there is no graceful way out."

It was a sore point time and again at Trump Plaza, when Donald would get news of what we contributed in the interests of good community relations—relatively small things, maybe offering facilities for a local charity event or buying a $1,000 table at a hotel association dinner.

"Why do you do that stuff?" he'd ask. "We don't need to do that." Or he'd say, "It's not worth it. Don't give that money."

Obviously in the case of a foreign country, it could be a sensitive issue. And it was in Brazil. In fact, the importance our international marketing department placed on this hospital donation as a way to cement good relations raised it to a level of debate among Donald, Steve and myself before they left.

"Fuck it," Donald said. "Hey, I'm coming all the way down there. How much did they raise last year at this dinner?"

"Last year, they raised $200,000," the marketing staffer who was present said.

"Okay, well I'm coming to the dinner there this year. The whole country knows I'm coming to dinner. How much did they raise so far?"

"Five hundred thousand."

"Fine," he said, "that's my $300,000 donation."

Our South American marketing representatives argued that the public relations value was more than worth the price, indeed, it was almost vital. But Donald was adamant. "They got more money than they've ever gotten," he said. "That's because the whole world knew, all the socialites knew I was coming to dinner. That's my charitable contribution. I came to dinner."

Barely had Donald returned from Brazil when he turned to the financially crippled Elsinore's Atlantis Casino Hotel—the former Playboy Hotel Casino—just west of Convention Hall and Trump Plaza on the Boardwalk. Because of financial difficulties, the hotel was under the management of a state-appointed conservator until a buyer could be found. The deadline for what amounted to a state takeover was set for midnight April 14. As the day approached, Elsinore searched frantically for a buyer. What made the prospect interesting was the city's decision to put up for sale Convention Hall's western annex, known as "West Hall," which adjoined the Atlantis. Several possible buyers showed interest. Bass PLC, the British brewing company, was one. The other was Steve Wynn.

Marvin Roffman, the analyst with Janney Montgomery Scott in Philadelphia who was a specialist in casino securities, sized up the situation immediately: "Should a smart operator buy the Atlantis and buy West Hall, that would be a serious competitive threat to Trump."

Again, as with the Hilton and Resorts, it seemed to Donald that the rival he feared most was breathing down his neck. At 11:54 P.M. on April 14, six minutes before the state-appointed conservator was scheduled to take the keys to the property, Donald signed a deal with Elsinore to buy the casino for $63 million. He immediately announced his intention to turn it into a "super luxury" hotel.

The implications for the industry were staggering. In three months, with the purchases of the Penthouse site and the Atlantis, and again, as with the Resorts deal, without stepping over the state-imposed three-casino limit, Donald had added what could be as many as 1,400 hotel rooms to his resort empire. If the Penthouse deal was upheld in court—Pratt Hotel Corporation, as mentioned, was now suing Donald—he would own nearly half of the casino real estate in the city. Together with the Taj Mahal, he would own 31 percent of the gaming space, 39 percent of all first-class hotel rooms, 40 percent of the available convention space and 35 percent of the parking. A half-mile of Boardwalk frontage was his, and if a new multimillion-dollar convention center was ever built to replace the old one, he would control most of the land surrounding it.

"Donald Trump," said Roffman, "is playing Monopoly for real."

Like the rewards, the risks were high. By the spring of 1989, Donald's investment in Atlantic City approached $2 billion. There could be no doubt that his future wealth depended on what happened within the boundaries of the resort town. But Donald had discovered the ability of casinos to create cash. Once he tasted it, it was irresistible. Between 1986 and 1989, he had taken more than $90 million out of Trump Plaza and Trump Castle, according to one financial analyst's estimate. Gamblers had bank-rolled the decade's most extraordinary appetite.

The Castle, however, had been impoverished in the process. It was paying $41 million a year in interest on more than $350 million in debt. Its revenues were languishing in the bottom half of the industry's ranks, and by 1989 it was looking at a net loss even worse than the year before. Simply put, it was bleeding to death. By the end of 1989, it would exhaust a $15 million line of credit and another $2 million loaned by Donald himself.

Yet, to my amazement, Donald was still praising the Castle, even over Trump Plaza. Months earlier, during Christmas week in 1988, Trump Plaza had hosted a party for our top New York players at Regine's, an exclusive Manhattan nightspot. Donald took the opportunity of a Plaza-sponsored event to heap praise on the Castle, telling our customers it was "the best place in town." Ivana had done "a fabulous job" there, he said. "And now that Steve Hyde is there, it's still the best place in town. In fact, that's where a lot of our Plaza customers go."

It was beyond belief—until I figured out Donald's motives. He was trying to sell the place. He had had numerous groups in, primarily from the Orient, to tour it. He had been on the come the whole time, which explained why he wanted the Castle per-ceived publicly as the superior of the two properties. His interest in selling also explained his insistence on pumping up the gross revenue to create the illusion that the Castle was a viable, highly profitable operation.

You can't look at the skyline of Atlantic City without seeing the name Trump—more than once. Left to right are Trump Plaza, the Trump Regency Hotel, and the Trump Taj Mahal. (Thomas E. Briglia)

Donald Trump's other Atlantic City property, Trump Castle. (Thomas E. Briglia)

A closer view of Trump Plaza, showing Convention Hall on the left. This was my home for the three years I worked for Donald Trump. (Thomas E. Briglia)

Donald on the Boardwalk, surrounded by five security guards. Lynwood Smith is at far left, facing the camera. Jim Farr, Donald's other Atlantic City bodyguard, is visible over Donald's shoulder.

The press conference announcing the Tyson–Holmes title fight. At the podium are Don King and Steve Hyde, my boss at Trump Plaza and later the head of all the Trump Atlantic City casinos.

Another heavyweight title fight press conference. This time it's Tyson versus Spinks. That's Mark Etess with Donald.

A press conference at Trump Plaza. Mark Etess is on the far left and Donald on the far right. I'm seated on the left, next to Bill Cayton, who was then Mike Tyson's manager.

Robert and Blaine Trump. I came to respect Robert, and I always had the feeling that Robert found his brother as difficult to deal with as everyone else did.

The only time we ever saw Donald in anything other than a dark suit was on this occasion when Ivana had him wear a yellow blazer and white pants for a party they were throwing aboard the Trump Princess. I don't think Donald was too happy about the outfit.

This is DJ Trump, the ill-fated horse that Donald almost bought. You can see the bandages on his forelegs. (Lisa O'Donnell)

My daughter, Laura, with Mike Tyson. Out of the ring he was a sweet and gentle man, in my experience. (Bruce Boyajian)

The Taj Mahal under construction. This is the way residents of Atlantic City got used to seeing it during its dormant period until Donald bought it and finished the construction. (Thomas E. Briglia)

The grand opening ceremonies at the Taj. The small figure on the stage at center is Donald.

A close-up of Donald at the ceremony with an Aladdin's lamp. I'm willing to bet that now Donald wishes he could put the genie back in the bottle.

Merv Griffin was one of the very few celebrities who showed up for the Taj grand opening.

Two views of the lavish interior of the Taj: the hotel lobby and the casino floor.

Donald worked hard to ingratiate himself with Michael Jackson, and was convinced he would sign him to some appearances at the Atlantic City properties. It never happened.

Donald Trump, wearing his trademark scowl.

Some months later, as he was about to close on his purchase of the Atlantis, Donald found a consortium of Japanese banking interests willing to take the Castle and the *Trump Princess* off his hands as a package deal. Through connections on the West Coast, negotiations moved forward and a price was agreed on: $550 million for the casino and $60 million for the yacht. At that price, Donald could have walked away with a profit. Considering the Castle's indebtedness and its worsening financial plight, it might have been his greatest sleight of hand ever.

But then Donald hesitated. What about the licensing? These were foreign investors. There would be a lengthy investigation by the Division of Gaming Enforcement and then extensive hearings before the Casino Control Commission. There was the possibility of a denial, which would drop the Castle back into his lap significantly devalued. So at the last minute, he demanded a $150 million nonrefundable deposit. Surprisingly, the Japanese offered $50 million. Donald said no. Steve Hyde advised him to take the money. But he held firm, and the negotiations collapsed.

The purchase of the Taj would prove to be the deal Donald made that he shouldn't have. His failure to consummate the sale of the Castle would prove to be the deal he *should* have made.

*"I want great promotion because it's great pro-
motion."*
—DONALD J. TRUMP

Donald understood boxing; he was a fan as well as a patron.
He couldn't readily understand the prestige value of a
European-style bicycle race, though, when we proposed it
to him. It was the name that sold him, the "Tour de Trump."
And that was how the idea was first presented to him in his office
in New York one afternoon in the summer of 1988.

Billy Packer, a network television sports commentator, who
was a partner in the promotion, spoke first. The rest of us had
taken various chairs around the office while Billy made his pitch:
Mark Etess and myself, representing Trump Plaza, which would
be the principal sponsor of the race, Mike Plant of the United
States Cycling Federation, and Mike Burg of Jefferson Pilot Tele-
productions, Inc., our partner in the event.

"We want to do a race on the East Coast that's going to rival
the Tour de France," Billy explained. Donald sat at his desk and
listened. "It's going to go through New York City and wind down
the coast and end up in Atlantic City . . . or however we want to
do it. We can create the race however we want."

Donald said nothing.

Then Billy delivered the punch. "And we want to call it the Tour de Trump."

"Oh, my God, no!" Donald said, almost jumping out of his chair. "They're going to kill me in the press. They'll kill me. I can't do anything like that. The Tour de Trump?" He shook his head. "Nah, they'll destroy me." Then he leaned far back and thought for a minute. A grin appeared on his face. "But isn't that what it's all about? Yeah! They'll kill me. But I love it. I love it! I love the idea. Let's do this. This could be fun."

Mark and I glanced at each other and smiled. We had him sold.

"We have said all along that we are looking to bring major events of international significance to Atlantic City, and this is just another manifestation of that policy," Mark told the press when the race was announced at Trump Plaza on September 10, 1988. "This will present a monster opportunity to market the Trump name internationally."

Actually, I was skeptical at first. I was an avid cycler, but as an operator of a gambling hall, I would never have dreamed of sponsoring an outdoor spectacle of this nature and size. I wasn't hopeful when Mike Plant and some others first brought the proposal to us. First, there was the price tag. Second, there would be no immediate spinoff at the gambling tables. But it would market the Trump name. That was our product. What Donald liked about it was the play on the name of cycling's most prestigious race, the Tour de France. He relished the inevitable comparisons.

Because of my background—I had raced competitively and had owned a pro cycle shop on the West Coast some years before— I was the liaison between Trump Plaza and the race planners. The logistics were staggering. The race was to start May 5, 1989, and run through May 14. We mapped an 837-mile course that would begin in Albany, New York, and cover five states. The

finish line would be at the Boardwalk in front of Trump Plaza.
Eighty-seven cyclists from around the world signed on, split
about evenly between amateur and professional teams. Their
ranks numbered some of the best, including the American cyclist
and Tour de France champion, Greg LeMond. We hired a company
called Medalist Sports to prepare a budget and manage the race.
Medalist tallied Trump Plaza's costs for transportation, lodgings
and prize money at $1.5 million. The NBC television network
had been interested from the start and came up with a matching
share to buy the broadcast rights.

What was left was to find sponsors to offset our costs. Donald
was at the zenith of his fame then. Still, we encountered some
difficulties. Some potential sponsors, like the McDonald's restaurant chain, decided that the tycoon was too flashy and con-
troversial for their image. There were other large corporations
that didn't want to risk being overshadowed by him. Timing was
a problem, too. For instance, the Coors Brewing Company was
interested but representatives for the company said they required
more time and asked to be considered should we stage the race
again in 1990. One sponsor we set high hopes on was Chrysler,
whom we contacted and were waiting for a response from. Donald
and Lee Iacocca were partners in a luxury high-rise in Florida,
and Donald told me, "Don't worry about Chrysler. I got them.
I'll call Lee. He's a friend of mine. I'll take care of this."

Chrysler and Lee Iacocca passed on the event, Donald's friendship notwithstanding. Campbell Soup was interested, but only
for the following year. Our projections indicated that we stood
to lose $700,000 on the event. We discussed this with Donald. I
believed that it was well worth taking the loss now for a substantial gain later. Call it a promotional expense. Donald agreed.
The advertising value alone was calculated in excess of $1 mil-
lion.

On May 4, 1989, the eve of the race, reporters and television crews from around the nation and overseas descended on Albany, New York, for a lavish press conference. I sat next to Donald. Greg LeMond was on the dais with us. When it was over and we walked out together, Donald whispered, "How much money are we going to lose again?"

"About $700,000," I said.

He stopped. "What!"

"Donald, we discussed this already. I think we're going to lose $700,000."

But he stared at me in disbelief. "What the fuck is going on?"

"This is the number we've been talking about all along. We knew we weren't going to make any money on this from day one. You've seen the projections. We talked about it. I told you this is what is going to happen."

"Holy Christ! I never thought this would happen! Jack, why are we doing this thing?"

After nearly a year of work and considerable expense, it was disappointing to see that he had come this close only to back away. Here was an event of bona fide prestige, as the turnout at the press conference proved. Plus, there was going to be network television coverage. Admittedly, there was no direct gambling benefit. But as a promotion it dovetailed perfectly with our efforts to spread the Trump name among the international gaming elite, while the race route would traverse our primary markets along the East Coast. Actually, having watched for two years as the king of the sweet deal continually flung money at bad ones, either firing way over the heads of the marketplace (the Crystal Tower boondoggle is a good example) or shooting too low and hitting himself in the foot (the Japanese bashing he did in his newspaper advertisement, and the St. Moritz sale and its fallout in the Australian market), it was astounding. The value of the Tour de Trump extended past the bottom line. Properly nurtured, it might have been incalculable. Donald saw a glimmer of that in the beginning. Then, as was his way when the time came to count the money, he quickly forgot it.

I said, "Donald, look. Do you realize what just happened in there? We sat through a press conference that has never occurred in this country before. There were 150, 200 journalists in there! Think about it. Your picture, your name . . . they're going to be beamed all through Europe. You're going to be everywhere. Donald, this is incredible."

He listened, then he nodded slowly and said, "You know, you're right. It's great exposure." After that, he seemed to be fine.

Steve and I felt so strongly about the event that we decided to work it in as a colorful segment of a television commercial we had been trying for months to produce for Trump Plaza. Not surprisingly, it was the one area of our business in which Donald chose to involve himself. He was extremely sensitive to his image, and he was in awe of the power of television.

We had invited a man named Jeff Millman, from the Baltimore advertising agency of VanSant Dugdale, whom we'd contracted, to present to Donald the outlines of some television concepts that Steve, Mark and myself had essentially agreed on. It was the culmination of six weeks or so of intensive discussions and planning, working originally from some twenty different ideas to narrow it down to three. A meeting with Donald was arranged in Steve's office at Trump Plaza. Jeff had set up a series of "story boards," or illustrations, with which we'd walk Donald through the commercial frame by frame. We considered all three treatments acceptable. All we needed was for Donald to choose the one he preferred.

But as soon as he walked in, it was apparent that he was in a foul mood. He was curt; he mumbled something and made straight for the washroom to disinfect his hands from all the palms he complained about having to shake as he came through the property. He was annoyed to distraction about something else, too. We had prepared Jeff beforehand, reminding him to get right to the point, that he would have to take a thirty-minute presentation and do it in six or seven minutes because that's the way it must be done with Donald. Jeff was agreeable. When Donald came out of the washroom and sat down, Jeff stood up to start his presentation. But Donald wasn't paying attention. He fidgeted in the chair and looked around angrily. Thirty seconds into the first series of story boards, he held up his hand. "Stop. Stop. I don't want to hear any more of this horseshit." Jeff's mouth dropped. Donald turned to Steve, Mark and myself. "Who the fuck was that driving my limousine over?"

We looked at him.

"You heard me. I want to know where that guy that picked me up this morning . . . I want to know where he works. The Castle or the Plaza?"

"He works at the Plaza," I said, since I happened to know it was a Trump Plaza limo that had been sent to meet Donald at the airport.

"Goddamnit! I knew it!" he said. "The Castle would never. Never! How come every time I get a limo from the Castle the driver looks perfect? They've got their dark uniforms on, the cars are always spotless, they look like they've been spit-polished. Do you know the driver that came over today had gray shoes on? Yeah! The motherfucker had gray shoes! He looked like some goddamn Puerto Rican. He looked like somebody we picked up from Spanish Harlem. . . . Nobody! Fucking nobody wears gray shoes for me!"

Jeff was stunned. He stood motionless, still in midsentence. I casually looked down to see if any of us was wearing gray shoes. Then I excused myself and stepped outside and asked Steve's secretary, who'd overheard the hysterics, to arrange to have a different driver wait downstairs. She replied that the driver had been dressed down severely by Donald already, and fearful of getting fired, the poor man ran out to a store and bought a pair of black shoes. We tried to get the meeting back on track, but before Jeff could continue with the presentation, Donald stood up and said, "Fuck this. I don't want to hear about this. I don't want to see this bullshit. What you're showing me is crap anyhow." And he walked out.

After that, every idea we came up with failed to please him. Yet it was impossible to figure out what he wanted because he was either unwilling or unable to communicate it to us. Then we saw a commercial that had been produced in New York for Trump Tower. It was an atmospheric piece featuring a beautiful woman walking through the atrium and a handsome man stalking her, darting about and hiding behind pillars. It was a terrible piece, we thought, one that made a shopping and tourist destination look like a pickup joint. But at last we had an idea of what Donald liked.

Jeff and his agency developed a new concept. This time, though, we rejected the use of story boards in favor of a video presentation known as a "ripomatic"—a visual prototype made from clips taken from other commercials and spliced together with a soundtrack and various still photos of Trump Plaza. This was much slicker and faster and would allow us to deliver the presentation to Donald and make an impression before his mind strayed and he lost interest. We had this ripomatic produced with some fight sequences and still photos of Trump Plaza tossed in for effect. Then it was a matter of plotting how to get Donald to watch it. It was Steve's opinion that everything depended on choosing the ideal moment. "We're just going to hold onto this 'rip' until the right day," he said. "Jack, it may take us six weeks, but we're not going to give this to him until we think the timing is absolutely perfect. This is going to be one of those things where Donald happens to wander in on a Saturday night and we're here in the office and—"

"Right," I chimed in. "We'll tell him, 'Donald, listen, we're just horsing around with another commercial idea. Here, why don't you take a quick look.' "

"And we pop it in," Steve said. "We wait till he's got a smile on his face, when we know he's in a good mood . . ."

"After he's just come downstairs from having dinner with Marla," I said.

"Right. And no gray shoes," Steve added.

I laughed. "Yeah. No gray shoes."

Everything unfolded according to plan. Donald came down to my office on Saturday night when the casino upstairs was humming with gamblers and he was in a good mood. He wandered in and sat down. I gave him the pitch, nonchalantly, and at the same time, I quietly fed the tape into a videocassette recorder near my desk. "Okay, Donald, here is stylistically what we're trying to approach."

An indoor setting flashed onto the television screen.

"Visualize when you see the lobby that it's Trump Plaza's lobby."

Then a beautiful model walked across in the next scene.

"Now visualize this woman walking across the lobby of Trump Plaza. . . . That is actually what you're going to see happen."

Donald watched with great interest. A smile crept across his face. "I love it," he said.

I called Steve to come down and we viewed the tape again. Donald was enthused. "It's great. I love it. Go ahead, do the commercial."

Steve's face broke into a broad grin. If we could have in that moment, we would have slapped high fives. The production was launched. In the weeks that passed, Donald made only one request. If there were going to be male models in the spot, he wanted one of them to be Tom Fitzsimmons, the ex-cop and former Trump bodyguard, Marla's old boyfriend and unofficial escort. So a segment was filmed with him, and we paid him scale for the work, though the scene wound up on the cutting room floor.

The only thing missing in the production now was fresh footage of Donald himself. We knew it would be a mistake to try to stage anything with him. Inevitably he would lose his patience and stalk off the set. Instead, we suggested something else to him. Gary Selesner, our marketing vice-president, explained to him, "What we're going to do is, just in the normal course of events, we'll film you. You won't have to do anything. Just be yourself. We'll work on a date and let you know." Donald said that was fine with him. The date we decided on was May 14, the Tour de Trump finale, a day when the film crew would be in town anyway to shoot the race.

On May 14, the 87 Tour de Trump cyclists raced down the New Jersey coast to the finish line. Donald's black Super Puma touched down that morning at Bader Field on the outskirts of Atlantic City, within sight of Trump Plaza's giant red-and-gold logo and the finish line. A camera crew was positioned on the tarmac to film him, the moment he stepped out of the helicopter, for his segment of the television commercial. All he needed to do was step down and wave to the cameras. He had known about this for weeks, ever since that Saturday night in my office, when we had showed him the ripomatic. But to everyone's astonishment, he climbed out of the helicopter screaming, "What is this! What the fuck are all these people doing here?" There were about ten people from Bonner Films, camera operators and technicians, who were in town anyway to film the race finale.

But Donald was furious. "This must be costing a goddamn fortune!" he shouted. "What are you doing? What is going on here? All these people standing around. . . . How much is this costing me! I didn't say I wanted to produce a movie. I said I wanted a fucking commercial!"

This went on for several minutes before we managed to calm him down enough to go back into the helicopter and come out again, just to wave and get in his car. He swore and fretted all the way, and when he stepped back out again, he was wearing such a scowl on his face that the segment had to be edited down to a split-second glimpse.

Five thousand spectators converged on the Boardwalk at Trump Plaza that afternoon before a national television audience on NBC to cheer the Tour de Trump racers to the finish line. Donald congratulated the winners, along with Atlantic City Mayor James Usry and a host of political dignitaries. I felt vindicated. For publicity value there was no question that the event was a resounding success.

Donald's participation had exceeded our best hopes. He had flown to various cities on the race circuit, made numerous appearances, cheered the bikers and glad-handed it with the crowds. It was a pleasant surprise. As a rule, Donald took no personal interest in athletic competition, with the exception of boxing. In part it had to do with a theory Donald held about exercise and physical stress. He believed that the human body was like a battery: it stored only so much vitality, and when that was used up, it weakened and died. Exercise was foolish, he said, because it depleted the battery's energy. When he learned that I had competed in 1986 in the world triathlon championships in Nice, France, and was in training for the 1989 "Ironman" competition on the Kona Coast of Hawaii—a grueling event consisting of a 2.4-mile swim, a 112-mile bike race and a 26.2-mile marathon—he sternly disapproved and said, "You are going to die young because of this."

On the other hand, there was his selfish concern for his business. To his thinking, sports took time from work. He also resented the triathlons for the small amount of publicity I got from them personally. He approached me about it more than once. "Don't ever do this again," he'd say. "Don't do Ironman again. Stop this stuff."

Finally, I got fed up enough to confront him. "It doesn't interfere with my work. You know that. On that basis, I don't think it's appropriate for you to tell me how to live my life."

After that, he never mentioned it again.

But he never accepted it either. That May afternoon on the Boardwalk, as we watched the Tour de Trump finale, Steve mentioned casually, "Hey, Donald, you know Jack is kind of crazy like these guys, too. He's doing Ironman this year, a race in Hawaii."

Donald turned and snapped, "Steve, I don't give a shit about that." He looked straight at me.

Two weeks later, the commercial was finished. We gathered once more in my office with Donald to view the final product. I put the tape in the VCR. It was a series of quick segues: the fights, the luxury suites, the restaurants, a bevy of beautiful models, a glimpse of Donald stepping off the helicopter, the Tour de Trump, all set to a throbbing rock music score. He watched but the whole time he squirmed in his chair. When it was over, he looked around the room with disgust. "I hate the fucking thing," he says. "It's the worst piece of shit I've ever seen in my life."

"Donald," I said, "what do you want us to do? You've got to tell us. What do you want this to look like?"

He turned to Steve and said, "If they use more of me I'll take a look at it again."

The tape was reedited to lengthen his exposure. When the new tape was ready, he viewed it. This time he went berserk over the fact that one of the models, an incredibly beautiful brunette, had a tiny mole on her chin. "Did you see that? Did you see that?" he said, his anger rising. "I don't believe this. She's ugly! How could you do this? This is shit. This girl is a three, for chrissakes! How could you have a girl with a face that's flawed in my commercial?"

It was exasperating, especially since we knew how particular Donald was likely to be about the women in his commercial, and we examined hundreds of screen tests to select the ones we were certain he'd like. Now we had to scramble to try to repair the sequences using the model with the mole. But it was impossible because she had a prominent role in the entire production. Finally, Donald said, "Where's the commercial you showed me before? The one I liked so much in your office that night."

"The ripomatic?" I said.

"That's what I want. I don't want this shit that you've done here."

"Donald, that was the ripomatic. We didn't put that out. That was splices . . . splices from beer commercials, from this spot, that spot. . . ."

"I want that commercial," he insisted. "That's my commercial."

So we hastily reassembled usable footage from the original ripomatic plus footage we had shot. That aired as Trump Plaza's television commercial. We must have spent over $200,000 and ended up with what was, at most, a $25,000 production, a needless waste of time and money.

Publicly, Donald proclaimed the Tour de Trump "the most successful event ever." But a month later, after he got Trump Plaza's profit and loss statements for May, he exploded at me all over again, this time in Steve's office. "You see these numbers? What the hell is going on? How in the hell did we lose so much money in this month?"

"For chrissakes, Donald," I said. "You've heard these numbers before. Why are we going through this?"

"Don't give me that shit. I never knew I was going to lose all this fucking money on this! I don't believe what's going on here. What are you guys doing to me? I can't fucking believe this. I can't believe it. You're supposed to be watching this."

Steve listened and let me respond. "Donald, do me a favor. Just back the event out."

"What are you talking about?"

"The Tour de Trump. That's where the losses are. Say the event never happened. Then look at the numbers."

"Jack, that's the point. You know you have to watch every dollar. You have to negotiate every penny. You're not watching what you're doing. I don't think you're watching the business as close as you should be. You're not negotiating the toughest deals."

He ranted on for several more minutes before he finally calmed down. But he didn't relinquish his displeasure, even though he agreed the race was worth sponsoring a second year. "Well, I'm going to tell you something. We better get this squared away. I don't want to lose this kind of money next year."

11

"What I never anticipated was that we could win—and end up losing anyway."
—DONALD J. TRUMP

The heavyweight championship fight pitting Mike Tyson against Carl "The Truth" Williams on July 21, 1989, cost Trump Plaza $2.1 million for the site. It was the first major bout we negotiated with Don King, the flamboyant and combative promoter and manager who now had absolute control over Mike's career—thanks largely to Donald Trump. And not by coincidence it would also be our last heavyweight championship.

Only 11,000 people turned out at Convention Hall on fight night, a disappointing crowd compared with the Spinks and Holmes matches. The perception was universal that Mike was invincible. Williams was not of a caliber likely to shake that belief. He lasted two seconds longer than Michael Spinks. The first round was a minute and 33 seconds old when Mike crouched low, got inside on his tall, angular opponent, timed a left hook and sent it bouncing off his jaw like a jackhammer. Williams hit the canvas on his tailbone.

I remember it well because I missed it.

Fifteen minutes earlier, as we were taking our seats at ringside,

175

Steve Hyde asked me to go back to the casino and take $100,000 out of the cage for Don King. "We promised him we'd have $100,000 in cash available for him at the end of the fight to give to Mike," Steve said. "You're probably the only person in the building who can go into the cage and take out that kind of money. I hate to ask, but will you go over and get it for us?"

Of course I said yes. I left the arena through the enclosed walkway that links the hall to our building next door. At the cage the money was counted and stuffed into a gym bag. In the time it took to make my way across the casino floor and enter the walkway—the bag under my arm and one security guard at my side—I met 11,000 people coming the other way.

For the most part we had been able to bypass King in 1987 and 1988 as Mike battled his way to the top of the boxing world under the Trump Plaza marquee. Donald was in awe of Mike's skill in the ring. He enjoyed watching him work out. If Mike was sparring in our gym and Donald was in town, he'd be there. But it was more than respect for the boxer's fearsome strength that kept Donald so interested in Tyson. Donald wasn't satisfied with the success the fights were bringing him as a gaming operator. He was more interested in the $20 million purses Mike was commanding and the booty to be gained from endorsements and the highly lucrative pay-per-view market. Like Don King he had been angling for more than a year for a piece of all that. He thought he saw his opportunity when Mike's long-standing relationship with manager Bill Cayton collapsed in a bitter feud with the fighter's wife, actress Robin Givens, and her mother, Ruth Roper.

Mike had won his titles and made a lot of money under the guidance of Cayton and his partner, Jim Jacobs. They were a triumvirate with Kevin Rooney, Mike's trainer for eight years, whose mentor, boxing impresario Cus D'Amato, had raised Mike from the age of fourteen and developed his trademark side-to-side head movements and taught him to fire lightning jabs out of a low, bobbing crouch. Cayton had managerial and personal services contracts which gave him 30 percent of everything Mike earned. After Jacobs's death from cancer in March 1988, these were called into question by Roper and Givens. They claimed that Cayton's cut was too large. Mike had not had the benefit of legal counsel when he signed the contracts, they said, and he had signed them without knowing that Jacobs was terminally ill. They wanted to renegotiate them. Cayton refused. Don King, the promoter at the time and still on the sidelines, ingratiated himself with Mike by maligning Cayton at every opportunity. King, a brash and overt bigot, as I knew him, hammered away at Mike with one compelling message: "Don't trust the white man."

For a time, wife and mother-in-law appeared to have the influence and the upper hand and succeeded in tying up various Tyson bank accounts while Cayton's relationship with the champ disintegrated. At Trump Plaza the night of June 27, 1988, shortly before Mike climbed into the ring against Michael Spinks, Donald sought out Cayton to console him. The manager and his family had a table at the celebrity buffet. Donald went over and put his arm around him and said, "Bill, I'm with you one hundred percent."

Next door at Convention Hall, Mike proceeded to demolish Spinks. The same night, Cayton was served with papers notifying him of a lawsuit seeking to void his contracts. Eleven days later, Donald officially jumped into the three-way tangle. He took up the cause of Givens and Roper, calling Cayton's agreements "onerous and unfair," and he disclosed that he had been invited to step in as the champ's business adviser.

"Don't worry about it. I know what I'm doing," Donald told Steve Hyde when Steve expressed his concern over Donald's attempt to become involved in Tyson's management. Donald pursued his course against Steve's advice and that of Mark Etess. On July 11, 1988, Mike announced at a press conference at the Plaza

Hotel in New York the formation of "Mike Tyson Enterprises" with Donald as a member of the board.

"I am a friend of Mike's and I want to be sure that he has a substantial future," said Donald. "He respects me, so I am in a position to offer helpful advice." One area of that advice would inevitably concern the sites for the champ's future fights. Where did that leave Trump Plaza? Even if we were the highest bidder, it would be impossible to avoid the appearance of a conflict of interest. Suddenly all our delicate relationships with the promoters and managers of the sport, not to mention the boxing authorities, were placed in jeopardy. It was an absurd maneuver on Donald's part.

But his most serious miscalculation was to enmesh himself in Mike's private life. Scheming for a management contract of his own and a percentage of the fighter, Donald thought he saw a way to freeze out Don King as well. He befriended Robin Givens and her mother and even tried to cast himself as a mediator when the marriage collapsed amid allegations of physical abuse and infidelity. At Trump Plaza there was talk that he and the actress were involved romantically. Donald vehemently denied it. "Could you imagine me having an affair with her? Like I want to get caught in bed with Mike Tyson's wife," he said to me. But there was always a mischievous glint in his eye whenever the topic arose.

But Donald had backed the losing side. Givens and her mother fell from favor with the champ, and Donald found himself having alienated Mike through the support of the two women. With nowhere else to turn, Mike struck an alliance with Don King. Donald sued in a last-ditch attempt to recoup alleged management fees, but to no avail. By 1989 Don King was firmly in control, and Donald was scrambling to try to patch things up with the promoter.

Steve Hyde knew Don King better than anyone. Despite their

different personalities and ways of doing business, they got along. But Steve had no illusions about King, and always warned us: "He's a sneaky guy. Watch out. Because he'll take you if he can."

Donald was satisfied that he could string his own links onto King's chain and thereby reestablish his shattered relationship with Mike Tyson. His orders to us then were to give King whatever he wanted. If the flamboyant promoter demanded thirty rooms in the hotel for himself and his entourage for a fight weekend, and we refused, King called Donald and complained. Donald would call back and say, "Do me the favor, Jack. I told him you would take good care of him. I told him he would get whatever he wants."

"We can't do that," I protested. "Why do you tell him that stuff?"

"I know, but I want to take care of King on this. If you have to argue a little bit go ahead, but give him whatever he wants."

The worst part was that even after we signed a contract giving him the thirty rooms, he'd come back the next day and ask for forty, and he'd be furious if he didn't get them. I don't think written agreements meant anything to him. During the negotiations for one fight we were locked in a conference call with him for four and a half hours, and all the time he was clamoring for Donald to be brought in, which we desperately wanted to avoid because we knew Donald would give in to him. At one point he complained. "I don't like this; you're treating me niggardly," slyly using a term that played on the racial epithet. When Nick Moles, our in-house attorney, took offense, King replied, "Hey, I don't know what you boys are saying. You better get your *Webster's* out."

For all his stupendous successes in the ring, Mike's life was in disarray. His confusion was so pronounced that at the press conference after his pounding of Spinks, he announced his retirement. Like everyone, I saw the terrifying mean streak in Mike

Tyson that came out in the ring. But outside the ring I saw what people like Cayton insisted was the real Mike—a quiet, very shy and compassionate young man. One night he came to Trump Plaza to watch a fight. He took his seat in the front row and then opened a book to read. I took my daughter, Laura, to that fight, the only fight I ever took her to. She was eight years old at the time. The moment she met Mike, she took to him instantly, and Mike to her. He put his arm around her, very kind and gentle, and she sat with him happily. After the fight, we wandered down to the executive offices, where we happened to meet Donald, Steve, Don King and Jon Benanav. We were chatting for a few minutes before I realized that Mike wasn't with us. He and Laura were off by themselves, several feet away, talking and laughing.

Early in his career, Mike had shared the public's admiration for Donald's success—"Mr. Trump," he always called him—and he held a respect for Donald that bordered on awe. Donald was in a unique position, but he misused it, contributing instead to Mike's confusion about whom he could trust and whom he couldn't. This opened the door for King, who used his new-found leverage to inject race into the relationship. Donald Trump became a euphemism for the "white man." Donald's rear-guard action then was to try to buy King with costly site fees, rooms, complimentaries and the use of his private Boeing 727—the same one he denied to his $250,000 customers.

By the time Mike squared off against Carl Williams, the interest in him in Atlantic City was on the wane. In addition to the disappointing live gate, we played unlucky at the tables. We held a meager 3 percent of the cash, chips and markers circulated at the tables. Lesser costs, like contract expenses with King for rooms, food and beverages, were higher than for any of our previous heavyweight championships. In the end we lost $1.2 million on the event.

Donald blew his stack and it became an occasion for him to harangue us all over again about the loss on the Tour de Trump.

Yet, nine days later, on July 30, we had to buy a $200,000 fight for the Convention Center Ballroom, a ten-round junior welterweight bout between Julio César Chávez and Kenneth Vice, because Donald wanted to further appease Don King.

"We can't sell 4,000 seats to this kind of fight," I told him. "And to cover that kind of money, that's what we need to do."

"Charge them $100 a seat and put 2,000 in there," he said.

"We're not going to be able to do that, Donald. Not to see Chávez fight an unknown. We won't get 1,000 people. Nobody wants to see this fight."

I had been through this already with King on the phone. King called me to offer us the fight for $200,000, about $150,000 more than it was worth in terms of the tickets we could sell and the revenue we could expect to generate from it. Chávez, a Mexican, was an impressive fighter, holder of two world lightweight titles and a superlightweight title, though none of these were on the line in this fight. He was popular on the West Coast but a virtual unknown in the East. I told King as much. He threatened to take the fight to Caesars instead. "Great, go ahead," I said. As far as I was concerned that was the end of it. Two hours later, the phone rang again.

"Jack, it's Donald. Do me a favor. I want you to buy this Chávez fight."

"What? At King's price?" I said.

"Yeah."

"Donald, we'll lose $200,000."

"I know, but just buy it anyway."

For weeks prior to the fight, Donald and I went over and over this. His reply was, "What are you worried about? We'll make it up on the casino side."

I shook my head. "You know that's not going to happen. I promise you we are going to lose $200,000 on this fight," I said

"I know, but I want to take care of King," he said.

"You want to take care of King? Donald, you want to give him $200,000? Then just give him $200,000. Let me save you the expense and the aggravation of the whole event. Who needs it? Because that's how much you're going to lose."

"Okay, Jack. But I don't care. Let's just grease this one through for him. I want Don King to be real happy with us."

"It doesn't make any sense," I objected.

"Yeah, but I've got other motives, Jack. Just do it."

In fact, that summer, Donald made a significant move toward emulating King, graduating from mere promoter to producer, with the formation of Trump Sports and Entertainment, a Trump Organization subsidiary, headed by Mark Etess as president. (Mark remained president, as well, of the Taj Mahal, then well along in construction.) The fact that Trump Plaza had staged two of the richest pay-per-view events in history—"Wrestlemania IV," the nationwide pay-per-view television event we sponsored in March 1988 in conjunction with the World Wrestling Federation, and the Tyson-Spinks fight—had opened Donald's eyes to the enormous economic potential of cable television. The new group would use the marketing and promotional expertise of the casinos to extend his empire into the rich territory of cable television.

But before he could do that, Donald had to resolve a problem. That May Donald had bought Eastern Airlines' Northeast Shuttle on the belief that retitling it the "Trump Shuttle" would increase ridership dramatically and make him a tidy profit. Of course, that was doubtful from the start. But the bigger problem was that he had floated such enormous debt to finance the purchase that he couldn't wait to find out whether business would improve. It was under considerable pressure that summer that he turned for help to his only operations with marketing expertise, his casinos.

The slash-and-burn business style of Frank Lorenzo, chairman of Texas Air, which had acquired Eastern in a hostile takeover, had left the sixty-year-old airline in a showdown with its unions and wrestling with bankruptcy. In October 1988, Donald appeared on the scene with an offer to buy its only profitable operation, the Washington-to-New York-to-Boston shuttle. Opportunist that he was, Donald thought he smelled a steal. He bought the shuttle from Lorenzo for $365 million.

"We are very pleased that Mr. Trump has been awarded the shuttle," Lorenzo told a press conference in New York on May 24, 1989, the day the sale was approved by a bankruptcy judge. "We always felt he was the most logical buyer, and we're delighted to see this important step taken by Eastern Airlines on its road to rebuilding."

Lorenzo must have been laughing all the way to the bank. What Donald bought were the most rundown and expensive jets in the Eastern fleet, all more than 20 years old: 21 vintage, fuel-guzzling 727s for which he signed a personal unsecured line of credit from Citibank for $135 million and borrowed another $245 million with the jets as collateral. Citibank, in turn, farmed out the loans to 20 other domestic and foreign banks. Assessed at $80 million at the time of the sale, within six months the value of the jets fell $30 million. During that time, Donald spent a fortune to repair them and refurbish the interiors with amenities like telephones at every seat, and to repaint them with the Trump name. With that on the sides of the fuselages, he believed that ridership would magically double. Ridership did increase—some passengers had avoided the shuttle under Eastern's ownership because the airline was in the midst of a bitter strike—but nowhere near the 40 percent improvement he needed to meet its staggering debt level.

Originally, Trump Castle executives were brought in to help with the marketing, but nothing substantial came of that. Finally I was invited to New York to meet with Bruce Nobles, the shuttle president. We discussed various newspaper advertising campaigns promising subsidies and frequent-flyer discounts, but it was all conceptual. What they needed was a specific package they could advertise. They got it that afternoon. We hammered out a combination "two-for-one dinner" coupon and coin subsidy redeemable at Trump Plaza that amounted to the price of the plane fare, essentially a "fly for free" promotion.

But without being an expert in the airline business, I had some doubts about the efficacy of the advertising effort. It seemed to me that people choose one airline over another largely out of habit. For example, the Pan Am Shuttle, Donald's principal competitor, enjoyed a niche in the market simply because a significant percentage of the people flying it have always flown Pan Am. From a marketing standpoint I believed the focus should be on altering those habits. As an executive who flies myself, I knew that I never chose my airline. My business flight bookings were handled by my secretary. In the shuttle business, where flights cover short distances and are often booked on the spur of the moment, it seemed reasonable that secretaries probably have an even greater influence. I came up with an idea for discounts or prizes aimed at them, a package of incentives for choosing the Trump Shuttle over, say, Pan Am. I introduced this at one meeting with the airline braintrust, but it fell on deaf ears. But in addition to the incentive programs, we did come up with some gambling charters, junket runs, mostly during the fleet's down time from 7 P.M. to 4 A.M.

The shuttle was a clear example of how the exaggerated value accorded his name led him into a purchase whose foolishness was apparent almost immediately. But he was acting more impulsively than ever, giving less and less thought to the consequences of everything he did. His affair with Marla Maples was moving into the open. In the spring we hosted a second Wrestlemania, "Wrestlemania V," at Convention Hall. Marla sat in the row directly behind Donald with Robert and Blaine Trump.

Shortly after, I was surprised one morning when Donald and Marla came down into the hotel lobby together and walked through side by side. Waiting for them at the curb outside was the white Mercedes-Benz convertible with the IVANA license plates. They climbed in, Donald took the wheel and they drove off.

By now Ivana knew all about the affair, as I was told by friends, and Marla harbored a great fear of confrontation with her lover's wife. Just the mention of her name made her anxious. This spilled over at a birthday party we held for a top customer in one of our ballrooms. A couple of hundred people were there. Somehow Marla got word in the middle of the festivities that Ivana was on her way. She turned pale, ran out of the room and fled upstairs to her suite. Marla refused to come down for the rest of the night, even after we confirmed that Ivana was not on her way.

With Ivana safely gone from Atlantic City and Donald spending more time at his apartment at Trump Castle, Marla moved across town. It made better business sense for her to leave Trump Plaza, since the Castle was not as busy as we were and could easily find an empty suite for her with little trouble. Marla usually stayed on the 26th floor, the floor where Donald's apartment was located and where his bodyguards held two rooms down the hall. She continued to register under an alias or under the cover of a girlfriend. They'd arrive together, take two suites or a suite and a room, and they'd leave together. If she came with one or both of her parents, it would be three suites. Sometimes, though, she arrived at the property in the company of Donald's bodyguards. If Donald was in town, he'd typically visit her in her suite, though she might end up in his apartment. The routine was basically unchanged. If they were attending a show, they would not enter together and would not sit together, though they were always close. If he called, he took to using a code name, leaving messages at the front desk for her from "the Baron."

Marla's favorite suites at the Castle were even larger than Donald's apartment, with living and dining areas, two bedrooms, three baths, a wet bar, refrigerator and butler. Her favorite, though, was a suite on the 6th floor of the new Crystal Tower. It had one bedroom done in soft pastels and peach-colored marble with thick, snowy carpets and a pink marble hot tub. Under these conditions she quickly learned to feel at home. She partied into the wee hours at Viva's Lounge with her friends or with Donald's bodyguards, while "the Baron" slept upstairs. But fitful sleeper that he was, he'd frequently wander downstairs for a milkshake or bags of his favorite popcorn.

The Castle arrangements were supposed to be temporary. We had been told that summer to prepare a permanent residence for Marla at the old Elsinore's Atlantis on the Boardwalk, which Donald had purchased that spring and renamed the Trump Regency. Then Donald called and abruptly canceled the plans. Later in the summer Steve Hyde told me that Donald confided that he was "finished with her."

Early in September, at the time of the U.S. Open tennis championships, Donald came to Trump Plaza with another woman on his arm. The night of the women's semifinals, he flew down to Atlantic City unannounced, and pulled up to the porte cochere at Trump Plaza shortly after midnight in a silver limousine. He entered by the hotel lobby with his customary security retinue and a group of several friends. Ivana was not among them, although they had attended the tennis matches together. But one woman stood out. She was lovely, dark-haired, and Donald kept her close by his side. They made their way to the casino and from there to the black marble and chandeliers of the baccarat pit. Baccarat is the most expensive game on the floor, and in every property the pit is secluded somewhat from the aisles of slot machines and craps and blackjack tables. It was Donald's favorite place on the floor, an island where he could escape the crowds. That night he lingered in the pit for an hour or more with the dark-haired young woman while some of his friends tried their hand at the high-priced card game.

Of course, Donald's presence was noted by the observers from the state Casino Control Commission who are posted in every casino. One of them happened to be a tennis fan and recognized that the young woman on the billionaire's arm was tennis star Gabriela Sabatini. The regulator also knew a bit more about the leading tennis players than Donald, and a subsequent check confirmed his fears. Sabatini, the brilliant Argentine pro, was only nineteen years old, a minor under New Jersey law and forbidden by statute from being on the casino floor. Both the minor and the casino could be liable for fines of not less than $1,000.

On Monday morning, the state regulator called me at my office. "Jack, your boss was in there Saturday night and guess who he was with?"

"Should I know?" I said.

"Gabriela Sabatini, the tennis player."

"Oh yeah? That's nice," I said.

"Jack, the girl is nineteen years old."

"Uh oh."

"Nah, it's all right. Forget it," he said. "At this point, it's not worth the aggravation, not for me, not for you. But I'll tell you one thing, if he does it again I'm going to throw the book so hard his ears are going to ring. This sort of thing could be real embarrassing for me, not to mention for him."

Immediately afterward, I notified Steve, and we called Donald in New York on the conference line in my office.

"Holy shit!" Donald cried. "I never even thought. . . . Hey, I didn't realize. I never would've done that. . . . So what's the story? What happens now?"

"We got a break," Steve said. "The regulator is upset, but he's going to let it go this time."

"Phew! I can't believe this guy's giving me a break. Why?

What's his name? I've got to talk to him. Because nobody ever gives me a break."

Steve gave him the regulator's name. Donald then said, "Get this guy. I want to see him. Next time I'm in town I want to meet this guy personally. . . . Phew! Thank God! But, man, I'll tell you what. She is one hell of a woman. She is really something else. God, what a body she has!"

Steve and I looked at each other and rolled our eyes.

He went on, "She's a beautiful girl. Just a beautiful girl. Fucking gorgeous. An incredible body, just an incredible body. The girl is so physically fit. Beautiful face. A beautiful, beautiful girl."

But even as Donald's interest in tennis, or certain tennis stars, anyway, seemed to blossom, he appeared to be losing some of his interest in boxing.

We had scheduled a press conference in New York for October 10 to announce a World Boxing Organization bout planned for next February at Convention Hall between two colorful fighters, Hector "Macho Man" Camacho and Vinny Pazienza.

This press conference loomed large for several reasons. Though my property, Trump Plaza, was paying $2.3 million for the live rights to the fight and underwriting Camacho's $800,000 purse and $400,000 for Pazienza, it was the first boxing event promoted under the umbrella of Trump Sports and Entertainment. Through the new subsidiary formed that July we would own the rights to the match in their entirety, the first of all the fights we had sponsored over the past two years in which we would own the closed-circuit and pay-per-view in addition to the receipts at the gate.

Strangely enough, it was Donald who opposed our involvement in this. He was fearful the investment would prove a money-loser. Admittedly, the fight itself was not an especially significant one from the standpoint of the sport. Camacho was a former featherweight and lightweight champion with an impressive record, 37-0 with 17 knockouts, but he hadn't had a major title bout in a few years. In some boxing circles he was considered past his prime and a troublesome client. By the same token, Pazienza, a former lightweight champ, had seen better days. Trump Sports and Entertainment, as Mark Etess's organization was known, had signed agreements with United Artists Entertainment Company and PACE Management for the live telecast and the pay-per-view, and Mark, especially, and Steve, too, believed the event would be an important test of the subsidiary's television muscle.

But Donald, at first, refused even to attend the press conference. "It's not going to be a big fight," he insisted. "The public doesn't care about this. I'm not coming. I can't be attending every shitty little press conference. It's not dignified."

To impress upon Donald the importance of the press conference, Steve offered to go as well. "It's ridiculous," Steve complained to me days before the show. "I have to be there because we're trying to convince Donald that this is a big-time, legitimate event. . . . And he's making me go to New York, and you know how much I look forward to that."

By then, Steve was starting to weary of the news conferences. The fact that this one was in New York made it even more bothersome to him. He disliked big cities, New York most of all, simply because it was larger and more congested. But Steve was also concerned about the amount of time Mark was spending on Trump Sports and Entertainment rather than working to open the Taj Mahal. As a result, more of the burden of preparing for the opening of the Taj—scheduled then for December—was falling on Steve.

"If the game plan is for Mark to run the new company instead of a casino, that will be great when that happens," he said. "But for now we have to get the Taj Mahal open. Let's do one or the other."

Shortly after 8 A.M. on Tuesday, October 10, under a sparkling, sunny sky, Steve and Mark met at Bader Field to catch a chartered helicopter to the East 34th Street heliport in Manhattan for the 10 A.M. press conference. The helicopter waiting for them was a large twin-engine Sikorsky S76, Steve's favorite. As often as we flew, and as much as helicopters were part of our business, we had all become familiar with the various craft, their capabilities and the air services that flew them. Steve especially, because he did not like to fly, studied the flight histories and safety records of every aircraft we used. He felt secure in a Sikorsky.

Jon Benanav, my executive vice-president and second-in-command, was also on board because I specifically asked that he stand in for me as the representative of Trump Plaza at the press conference. I was then in Hawaii about to compete in the grueling "Ironman" triathlon. Jon, 33 years old, a relative newcomer to the business, was enthusiastic and gifted with a sharp mind and bright good looks. He was excited by the prospect of going to Manhattan and facing the national press alongside Donald, Steve and Mark. His whole career lay before him and was on the ascendant. He had recently become engaged to be married. He had just bought a ring for his fiancée and planned to give it to her when he returned from New York.

As it happened, Steve Hyde and I had our longest conversation in some time just before I left for Hawaii. The previous week Steve had returned from a two-week vacation bow-hunting on horseback in the wilds of British Columbia. The day after he got back, he and I must have spent an hour in my office talking about the trip. He returned hale and healthier than I'd ever seen him. He had lost some weight before he left, getting himself in shape, riding his bicycle every morning. We lived in the same suburb so I'd see him on his bike when I was running. He had lost even more weight in the wilderness, and he looked fantastic.

His thoughts that day were still in the Rocky Mountains.

These were the times when he seemed out of place in a casino. He loved the outdoors. On Saturdays he'd leave his house at 3 A.M., drive three hours to the eastern shore of Maryland, hunt ducks until 11 or 12, and drive back in time to be at Trump Plaza for the busy evening.

That day he talked about the things that meant more to him than work and career—his dreams. At that point in his life, he was 43, Steve was looking ahead to leaving Donald Trump in the next couple of years and retiring, getting away from the casinos altogether, buying some land. He enjoyed talking about his dream to one day start a horse farm. "The only thing, Jack," he said that day, "is I just hope I'm still young enough and healthy enough to enjoy the outdoors."

The vacations in the mountains always refreshed his thinking on that. They were the times when his religious devotion came out. He described to me how he never felt closer to God than when he was in the mountains.

"Oh, look at the time," he said, glancing at his wristwatch. "We've been shooting the breeze here for a while. I better go. I have to get over to the Castle and see what's going on."

I saw him again just briefly later in the week. He asked me if I was coming to work on Saturday. I said no. "Great," he said. "Good idea."

"Well if you need me for anything, give me a call Saturday," I said.

He smiled. "No, I don't think so. Take the day and relax. Have fun out there in Hawaii. And good luck."

I wished him the same at the press conference in New York.

191

12

*"Life is very fragile. Anything can change, with-
out warning, and that's why I try not to take any
of what's happened too seriously."*
—DONALD J. TRUMP

arrived in Hawaii early Sunday evening, and took the next
day off. Tuesday morning, I was up early. I swam a mile in
the surf and rode out with my wife, Lisa, to inspect the bicycle
course, a two-lane highway that runs along the coast, preparing
to log fifty or sixty miles on my bike.

The fight press conference in New York occupied my thoughts
the whole morning. I planned to call Jon at Trump Plaza when
I returned to the hotel to find out how it had gone.

We had rented a van for my bicycles and equipment. Lisa and
I designated a spot on the course as our rendezvous point. From
there I was to bike about thirty miles out, turn around, and ride
back to meet her at the rendezvous. It was a sunny, hot day,
almost tropical, relieved only a little by a steady breeze blowing
in off the Pacific Ocean. When I returned to our rendezvous, Lisa
was waiting for me with fresh water and towels. "You know, we
had that press conference today," I said. "Don't let me forget to
call the hotel as soon as I get back."

"I won't," she said. Then she drove back to the hotel in the van, and I followed the remaining ten miles or so on my bike.

In New York, Steve and the others had encountered problems with their flight back to Atlantic City. They had planned on leaving by noon, but the press conference ran late, there were interviews afterward, then a meeting with Donald at Trump Tower, so they missed the noon departure of the Sikorsky helicopter they'd flown up in. Steve called Trump Plaza to arrange a later flight and was told that there was a Bell 222 helicopter available at 1:30 P.M. Steve wasn't personally comfortable with the Bell's safety record, although we used them frequently to fly customers and executives and had never had an accident. So he checked with the others. They all expressed concern about getting back to Atlantic City in time to meet their afternoon schedules. Jon for one had a 2 P.M. appointment back in Atlantic City and asked if an earlier flight couldn't be arranged, maybe with another air service. That was enough for Steve. He instructed Trump Plaza to try to locate another aircraft for an earlier departure. Through our New York office one was found. Paramount Aviation, a company Trump Plaza had never used before, had an Agusta A109 helicopter available to leave Manhattan's East 60th Street heliport at 1 P.M.

The Agustas, manufactured in Italy since 1976, were 42 feet long, with twin engines and rotors, a crew of two and stylish cabins that seated six. Most important, as far as Steve was concerned, there had never been a fatality on the Agustas, which had logged 250,000 flight hours without a single problem in the air. The 16 Agustas in Paramount's fleet underwent maintenance inspections after every 100 hours in the air. The one that Trump Plaza had located for Steve, Mark and Jon was a model built in 1984 that still had 36 hours to go until its next inspection.

"We'll take it," Steve said.

It was still morning in Hawaii, about 11 A.M., and I was pedaling hard, less than a mile from the hotel, when I saw a van just like ours up ahead on the highway. It sped toward me, the horn honking wildly. As it whizzed past I saw enough of it to realize that it *was* ours. I waved and continued on. But I noticed that Lisa wasn't behind the wheel. And I hadn't gone far when it came racing back behind me. It caught up with me as I was approaching the hotel driveway and pulled up alongside me at the curb. Lisa was in the passenger's seat. She had an expression on her face I had never seen, a look of horror, and she was crying. Instantly I thought of our daughter, Laura, thousands of miles away in New Jersey.

But before I could ask, she choked back her tears and said, "Laura is okay. Nothing's happened to her. She's fine."

"Lisa, what's happened?" I felt my limbs weaken and begin to shake.

"There's been a helicopter crash . . . and Steve and Mark and Jon have been killed."

In the next few seconds every thought and sensation disappeared. "No, that's not true. That's impossible," I said. But I saw the terror in Lisa's eyes, the tears streaming down her cheeks, and I knew it was true. I sat down at the curb and cried.

It was after 5 P.M. on the East Coast when I called Donald from the hotel. Just hearing his voice confirmed it. He sounded almost panicked. "Jack, this is awful. . . . This is the most awful thing. We've been sitting here praying it wasn't true. I still can't believe it. . . . I can't believe it. . . . This is awful . . . awful. . . ."

He didn't have many details, he said. His office was in touch with the New Jersey State Police, but not much information had been released. "I'm going down to Atlantic City tonight," he said. "Jack, I hate to ask you this because I know how important this race is to you, but I need you to come back."

"What do you mean, Donald? Of course I'm coming back."

"Oh good . . . great, Jack," he said. "I'm going to need you here."

Next I called my administrative assistant, Joellen Seville, who switched me to Trump Plaza, where I left instructions to gather the vice-presidents and get them rooms in the hotel. I wanted them visible to the employees. I wanted it known that management was intact.

But I couldn't get a flight out of Hawaii. So I called Donald for permission to book a private charter. He said yes. Then he added, "Yeah, I can't believe this. It's crazy. Don't tell anybody, but I'm getting on a helicopter in an hour and I'm going down to see the families. A helicopter. Isn't this crazy?" He went on, rambling a bit, or so it sounded to me. "I guess life goes on, huh? You have to keep your life going. You've got to keep getting on the planes, getting on the helicopters. You've got to keep living the way you have to live." But he put it almost as a question. He wanted reassurance. For the first time since I had known him, I heard fear and uncertainty in his voice.

The charter took me as far as Los Angeles. We had to switch luggage to a second plane waiting at the airport there, which flew us nonstop to Atlantic City International Airport in Pomona, some ten miles inland from the coast. It was Wednesday morning. At Pomona a van and a limousine were waiting to take us and the bicycles and equipment and baggage to our house. I showered at home, then took the limo straight to Trump Plaza. I got to my office around noon. I had gone halfway around the world and hadn't slept in twenty-four hours. Now I learned the awful details.

The helicopter had gone down over Lacey Township in Ocean City near the coast about twenty miles north of Atlantic City. The only eyewitness, a camper, reported hearing "a big bang," which made him look to the sky. According to a preliminary investigation by the National Transportation Safety Board, one or both of the Agusta's two engines apparently seized in midair, which caused the four-blade main rotor to break off. The 16-foot blades splintered, pieces shot off into the sky, smashing into the tail rotor and slicing into the cockpit, probably killing the pilot and copilot instantly. The Agusta shot upward, spun out of control and plunged 2,800 feet into the pine woods. The wreckage was found just inside the northbound lanes of the Garden State Parkway, the superhighway linking New York City and the New Jersey coastal resorts. The first local emergency and rescue crews to arrive found the bodies of Steve, Mark and Jon on the ground outside the cabin, within ten feet of it. The bodies of the pilot, Captain Robert Kent of Ronkonkoma, N.Y., and copilot Lawrence Diener of Westbury, N.Y., were still inside the crushed cockpit. Most of the detached main rotor was discovered in the woods a quarter mile away. The tail rotor was found a half mile away across the highway's southbound lanes.

The state police had arrived almost immediately, followed later by federal investigators. From what they could determine from interviews with the camper and workers at the Oyster Creek Nuclear Generating Station three-quarters of a mile away, the crash occurred at approximately 1:40 P.M., a half hour out of Manhattan and only ten minutes from Atlantic City. By 4 P.M., Donald was given the news.

The *Atlantic City Press* reached him by phone that afternoon in New York. His voice, according to the report, was "cracking with emotion."

"I'm sick, just sick. It's unbelievable," he said. "When I first heard about it, I prayed it wasn't true. There were different reports coming out, and I just kept on praying. I thought, 'Please, please, let it be a mistake. Let them be all right.' Then I found out what happened. I can't find the words." His voice "trailed off" at that point, the newspaper said. Later, the Trump Organization released a formal statement: "These were three fabulous young men in the prime of their lives. No better human beings ever existed. We are deeply saddened by this devastating tragedy. Our hearts go out to the families."

Donald arrived at Bader Field in Atlantic City at about eight o'clock Tuesday night. He flew down in his private Super Puma helicopter. He was whisked past a horde of reporters and television cameras, led into a waiting limousine and driven directly to Mark's home in Margate, a resort town a couple of miles away on the island. When he saw Lauren Etess, Mark's widow, he hugged her, and his first words were, "Can you believe that they rode back in a rented helicopter?" Donald was under stress, but it sounded as though he was emphasizing the fact that it was not *his* helicopter. Could it be that even amid such emotional devastation he was thinking to protect himself against a potential lawsuit?

The following afternoon in one of our conference rooms, Donald opened a meeting of the management staff, about 100 people in all. He stepped up to a small podium at the front of the room. "This has been a horrible experience . . . a terrible, terrible thing. I'm still in shock," he said. "These were three incredibly vibrant guys. And great friends. To see quality like that go for no reason, it's just a tragic waste. . . . But we're going to do something marvelous for them, a statue here in the building, a monument, something just incredible. I don't know what yet, but it will be incredible." Then he turned to me and said, "Now that I'm faced with this . . . I feel like I hardly know Jack. But I know he's been doing a great job down here. I know he's been running the show. And I know how much confidence Steve had in him. And that was always good enough for me. If Steve had confidence in somebody, I had confidence in them. I know Jack and I will work together closer than we ever have to make sure everything is squared away here."

Afterward, and privately, Donald brought up the possibility of sabotage. "Boy, wouldn't the competition love to hurt me in this way," he said. But knowing how the flight was booked belied the suspicion. The charter, after all, was not prearranged. The authorities came to the same conclusion, as NTSB Regional Director Frank Ghiorsi said, "There is no evidence to reveal there was foul play." But until the preliminary report on the crash came back, I don't think anyone was prepared to dismiss the thought completely. Certainly not Donald. "Did someone tamper with it, yes or no? Who knows? We don't know," he said at the time.

Donald did receive death threats on what I would characterize as a routine basis. We received them in Atlantic City and they were received in New York. We followed certain procedures in screening them, working in close concert with Donald's security in Manhattan. Only one of those threats, a phone call, was considered legitimate enough for us to put our casino security on special alert. But the threat never materialized.

Donald's elaborate personal security was a source of great pride for him. He felt good about the private maintenance staff he kept for his jet, which he considered a good insurance policy, and he never flew on anything but his private helicopter or one of the commercial helicopters of the Trump Air fleet, which he purchased in the Resorts deal and formerly known as Resorts International Airways. Only once that I know of did he come to Atlantic City on a chartered helicopter, and then only because the Super Puma was not available. When he landed at Bader Field, he climbed out furious, swearing and complaining that the flight was rough, the pilot incompetent and the cabin dirty. So when the word got out after the crash that the accident was being portrayed as Donald Trump's brush with death, I was outraged. The Trump Organization in New York released a statement two days after the crash saying that Donald had planned to accompany Steve, Mark and Jon on the fatal flight. "He really doesn't want to talk about it, but he was going to go to Atlantic City and he did change his mind," a spokesman said. That was flatly untrue. If Donald had planned to go to Atlantic City that day, he would have instructed Steve to cancel the charter and wait until the

Super Puma could be made ready. As it turned out, the statement was nothing but a cover for Norma Foederer, Donald's administrative aide, who upon learning of the crash blurted out in the initial shock something to the effect that "it could have been Donald." Then when Donald realized the public relations value of the story, it was allowed to play itself out for weeks afterward. In many later interviews, Donald himself spoke of how he had been "this close" to making the fateful trip.

Funeral services for Mark were held Thursday morning at Temple Beth Israel synagogue in the mainland suburb of Northfield. Donald was a pallbearer. Ivana attended. Marla was there as well, standing back in the crowd, hobbling about on crutches with one foot bandaged. I heard she injured her foot kicking the outside of a limousine after she had been hustled off the *Trump Princess* in anticipation of an arrival by Ivana. Later I was told by one of Donald's close associates that she had thrown a tantrum in her suite at Trump Castle for similar reasons, overturning furniture and kicking in the television screen.

When she appeared again the next morning at Jon's funeral in Mount Vernon, New York, an ugly scene with Ivana was barely averted. As Ivana was coming out of the chapel, she turned to one side and she and her younger rival found themselves face to face. Ivana glared at Marla with such anger that I was sure she was going to throw a punch at any moment. Marla stood there petrified, no more than six inches away. Quickly Donald stepped in, took his wife's arm and pulled her away.

More than 1,000 people came to pay their respects at Mark's funeral. His younger brother, Mitchell, gave a sad and moving eulogy, his voice breaking throughout until finally he lost his composure and broke into tears. Mark was buried that afternoon in Cedar Park Cemetery in Paramus, New Jersey.

Afterward, Donald met us back at Trump Plaza. Along with Robert Trump and Harvey Freeman, we spent some time in my office that afternoon talking, sharing memories, and trying to set priorities to shepherd the properties through the loss. Not being the reflective type, Donald never dwells in the past or speculates too much about the future in a meaningful way. "Life goes on," he said, and he repeated it often in those next few days. In a very short time it was business as usual.

Donald did talk about the eulogy. "God, that was an incredible thing that Mitchell did! This is really some kid. I could just never get up in front of people and look like such an asshole. I could never let that happen to myself."

First I was dumbfounded. Then I realized that, poorly as he phrased it, he meant it in admiration.

I replied, "Well, there was a lot of love in that eulogy. You know, that's what that was."

"Yeah, I know," he said. "But I would never want to look like an asshole. I'd never let myself be put in that position. I could never . . . I'd never ever want anyone to see me like that."

It was clear to me then that Donald would not be reaching for a handkerchief at any point through this ordeal. Certainly he understood the financial consequences, especially what the loss of Steve Hyde meant to the billion-plus dollars he had sunk into Atlantic City. And I think that Donald regretted the loss of a friendship he had with Steve and with Mark. In that respect this was a personal tragedy unlike any Donald had ever experienced, greater than the loss of his older brother some years earlier. Donald did not have many friends, and Steve and Mark Etess were two men whom I think he believed sincerely liked him.

That week, Donald was in the thick of a purported takeover of American Airlines, one of the nation's largest air carriers and at that time its most financially stable. It was one of the most farfetched schemes he ever hatched, and it wasn't going his way at all. On Wednesday, the day after the helicopter crash, trading had been furious on the New York Stock Exchange. More than 2 million shares of AMR Corporation, American's parent company, were dumped on the market. Donald, who had bid $120 each for 58 million outstanding shares, a $7 billion assault, lost millions before the stock finally closed at 97⅛.

Donald was playing a favorite game, a carbon copy of his raids on the gaming industry three years before. The plan, as I saw it, was to spotlight the airline's value, force its board of directors to restructure, thus inflating the price of the stock, or make them run up the white flag and submit to a greenmailing. Either way he was hoping to stuff millions of dollars into his pocket.

"When can we get out of this?" he asked on the phone at one point. "Now? No? Should we wait? I'm thinking we should wait. . . . Yeah, because the longer we wait, the more they'll be convinced that I want to do something."

But Donald had chosen the wrong time to strike. There was chaos in the junk bond market, triggered by Campeau Corporation's announcement in September that it would not make the interest payments on the high-risk securities it had floated to pay for its purchase of Allied Stores Corporation and Federated Department Stores, Inc., the most expensive leveraged buyout in history. On that news, the financing for a $6.7 billion leveraged buyout of United Airlines began to unravel. The big banks pulled the rug out from under the United Airlines deal. The alarm was sounding: the long-feared collapse of the junk bond business was under way. Like a siren, it clamored throughout that tragic week in October, signaling the end of the tumultuous 1980s—Donald's decade—the wham-bam era of fast bucks, paper capital and the raping of corporate America.

When Donald announced his offer for American's stock on October 5, instead of knuckling under, AMR's chairman, Robert Crandall, one of the airline industry's toughest and most respected bosses, stood firm. Wary investors, stung by the Campeau and United Airlines fiascos, sat on the sidelines. Within days, Donald found himself under attack in Congress, which feared the consequences for air safety with another airline saddled with debt, looking to sell off assets and maybe scrap union contracts. The unions joined the chorus. In major airports around the country, American's baggage handlers were scrawling anti-Trump slogans on cargo carriers.

As the days passed, the value of AMR stock fell. On Thursday, October 12, the day of Mark's funeral, it was trading at $22 below what Donald had paid for his chunk of it. On Friday, the Dow Jones plunged 190 points in frenzied trading, sparked by the panic in the bond market. Some $200 billion was wiped from the paper value of stocks. "Total emotional and psychological chaos" was how one analyst described the trading floor at the New York Stock Exchange.

AMR's stock continued its slide the next week. In a mere two weeks, Donald's chunk of stock lost $45 off the price of every share. The day that AMR's board of directors was scheduled to meet to consider his offer, he wrote a letter to Crandall withdrawing his bid. The talk on Wall Street was that he had never secured the bank financing.

That may have been the sort of bad business decision that anyone could make. But I started to see other signs of flawed judgment.

Jon Benanav's secretary was a dedicated, hardworking woman who was devoted to him. She was devastated by his death. When I saw her on Wednesday afternoon, my first day back at Trump Plaza, she was in Jon's office, sitting behind his desk. She jumped up when she saw me, grabbed me, buried her head in my chest and held on for several minutes, crying uncontrollably. She had been up the entire night, and as people will do in times of grief, she had become obviously inebriated. I understood, and since no business was being conducted from the office that day, I ignored it. My only fear was how Donald would react if he saw her. It wasn't long before I had my answer. He and I had just finished talking in my office when, after a half hour or so, he popped his head back in. "I just saw Charlotte," he said, referring to Jon's secretary. I sat up and prepared myself for an outburst of temper.

"I got an answer to one of your problems," he said.

"What do you mean?" I asked.

"Who's going to be the next executive vice-president."

"Oh?" I was taken by surprise. It was the last thing on my mind at that moment.

"Jon's secretary, Charlotte. She'd be perfect," he said.

"What? Donald, you can't be serious."

"Jack, listen to me. I do this with people. I take people with no background and I put them in a position, and they perform for me."

"Donald, she's a secretary. . . . Look, this is a difficult time for everybody. Please let's not get into this now," I said.

"Jack, I just talked to her. You know what she said? She said, 'Mr. Trump, don't worry. We're still going to run this hotel the Benanav way.' "

"That's great, Donald. Fine."

"Listen to me, Jack. This girl will perform for you. You put her in this job and she'll perform for you. I just know it. I have feelings when it comes to people. She can do this."

"Well, thanks," I said. "I'll think about it."

"Oh, yeah, absolutely, it's your decision," he replied. "But I really think you ought to give this serious consideration."

I wrote it off to the stress of the ordeal, even though Donald seemed genuinely excited about his suggestion. A week later, he called from New York. "Did you think about my idea?" he said.

"What idea, Donald?" I said.

"Jon's secretary, Charlotte. Are you going to make her the executive vice-president?"

Then I had to tell him point-blank: "No."

Donald was simply unable to cope with the emotional demands that the crash placed on him. I wondered whether he cared about anyone other than himself, or if he harbored a sincere emotion.

I learned from those who made the rounds with him the night of the crash that Donald was terribly uncomfortable and emotionally detached when he visited the families at their homes. But the whole night he had a look of fear in his eyes. He kept saying over and over, "I can't believe these guys are dead. This is impossible. It can't be." The fear was for himself. He had lost his two key players: Mark, the one who showcased the Trump name so well, the promoter who was instrumental in enhancing the Trump image; and Steve, the manager and operator, the one who kept all the pieces together and protected Donald from his own worst excesses.

Steve was buried on Monday, October 16, in Kaysville Memorial Cemetery in his hometown in Utah. It was where he belonged, under the big Western sky. Three days before, on Friday night, throngs of people had converged on a funeral home in Northfield, New Jersey, for the viewing. The line of mourners spilled out the door and stretched for two blocks. Ivana, no friend of Steve's during his life, was true enough to her feelings to stay away. Donald mingled among the crowd that night. But there was one moment when he broke away by himself and walked over to the closed casket with the portrait of Steve beside it. He stood there alone for a time, gazing at the photograph with his head bowed. From where I stood I could see his face. For the first time I saw sadness in it, profound sadness. I was certain he was about to cry. I think he did; I think he shed a tear. I knew that

Donald would be a lonelier man from then on, lonelier even than before.

But then in an instant he composed himself, stepped back from the casket, and eased back among the knots of people, unflappable as ever. He rejoined our circle at one point—Lisa, myself, Robert, Blaine, Harvey—and he turned to Lisa and said, "Well, we've got a lot riding on your husband now. Now it's his turn. He's really got to step up to bat now."

"I have the greatest hotel managers in the world who want to work for me."
—DONALD J. TRUMP

Donald continued to get on planes and helicopters as necessary (though he was a little more apprehensive about it and took to asking his pilots often if they were afraid), but in the aftermath of the tragedy of October 10, extra steps were taken to ensure his personal safety. Under the supervision of his favorite bodyguard, Lynwood Smith, who would be elevated to the post of director of corporate security, surveillance cameras were installed in the hallway outside the Trump apartment on the 26th floor of the Castle. In one of the two rooms nearby where his bodyguards normally stayed, a rifle rack was mounted on one wall and enclosed in a locked cabinet to secure it for those occasions when the rooms were rented to players.

The attention focused on Donald and Atlantic City as a result of the crash suddenly made it necessary to hide Marla Maples. Her presence at Mark's funeral had been discomfiting enough, but apparently Marla was insisting on attending Steve's viewing and service, over Donald's objections. He had barely averted a confrontation between her and Ivana outside the chapel after

Jon's funeral. He couldn't risk wife and mistress meeting again.

To make matters worse, the state Division of Gaming Enforcement routinely examined listings of guests who were issued complimentaries, and I heard there was concern at the Castle that Marla's name would turn up on it.

Of all the condolence calls Donald received soon after the tragedy, the one from Pat McGahn, his powerful local attorney and friend, really upset him. As Donald told me, McGahn, who was an ex-Marine, phoned him within an hour of the news, and said, "Well, Donald, you know, they're casualties of war, that's what they are. That's just life. That's the way it goes. Sometimes you lose good soldiers in a battle. . . . But there's new troops coming in and life goes on. It's time to get moving and it's time to rethink, to regroup. Figure out who's going to do what and how we're going to go forward."

Donald was angry when he recounted the conversation to me. "Can you believe this fucking guy? Within an hour! I'm sitting here thinking about the friendships I lost and this guy is saying stuff like this to me."

Yet Donald proved to be even colder. He exploited the tragedy to tighten the net he had cast over "center Boardwalk" with the purchase of the Atlantis and Penthouse properties.

On the heels of the disclosure of his deal with Penthouse in March 1989, it was announced that he had reached an agreement with a local businessman to buy the latter's small restaurant supply store on Missouri Avenue in front of the Trump Plaza parking garage, concluding negotiations that had dragged on for a year. Donald claimed initially that he didn't need the property, trying to devalue the prime location and snap it up for less than $100 a square foot. But the store owner had held firm for $150. The standoff even made the cover of *Newsweek* magazine. In the end, Donald reluctantly agreed to the higher price and forked over $2.2 million for the property. Actually, it was Steve Hyde who succeeded in bringing off the purchase, and in the process won the store owner's trust. The final sale contract included a provision that gave him three years to vacate. Donald agreed to this. But he was growing impatient and he asked me to persuade the owner to get out earlier so he could tear the store down. The emotional confusion left in the aftermath of the crash gave him his chance.

It wasn't long after the funerals that Donald and I were sitting in his office in Trump Tower one day, and he mentioned it again. "Did you get in touch with him?" he asked.

"No, not yet," I said. "I've been trying, but I missed a couple of phone calls."

Donald picked up the phone and switched on the conference line. "Let's call him, now," he said.

After a few rings, the owner answered.

"Bob, how are you? Donald Trump."

They exchanged pleasantries, then Donald cut to the point. "I know Steve Hyde spoke highly of you and what a great guy you are and how much he enjoyed negotiating with you on this deal."

"Oh, yes, I loved Steve. What a great man he was. Ah, so tragic! Such a loss!"

They talked about Steve for a few minutes. Then to my surprise Donald said, "Yes, well, you know, a couple of days before Steve died, we happened to be talking about this, and Steve told me you promised him that you would be out in six months."

The man was surprised and confused. At first, he hesitated. He had to be wondering: Had Steve Hyde deceived him and made this false promise? Knowing Steve, he said, he couldn't believe Steve would have said that. But here he had been placed in a position of having to call Steve a liar. It was obvious how uncomfortable he was from his voice. "Well, Mr. Trump, I . . . I don't remember ever saying that," he replied.

Now it was Donald's turn to be surprised. "Gosh, I hope you're not going to make Steve look bad in this situation. He promised me this and he said that you and he had this worked out."

"Steve would ask me how I was doing with it, but I never made a commitment, and he never asked for it," the store owner said.

Donald replied, "But Steve gave me a specific promise. He promised me this."

I realized then that it couldn't have been true, just from the way Donald hammered away at this over and over again. The conversation went on like that for a minute or two longer, then they hung up without anything firmly agreed on beyond the store owner's promise to think over the possibility of moving earlier.

After Donald hung up he said, "Hey, I don't know if it was ever said or not. What the hell. Whether it's true or not . . . Steve wouldn't care. One thing, I know it puts more heat on the guy. What difference does it make? Steve is gone."

But where were the "new troops" McGahn assured Donald would be coming in to replace him? "Warriors," he called them, a term Donald adopted as well and began to use frequently. Donald liked to boast to the press that "Everybody wants to work for Trump." The fact is, his efforts that fall to fill Steve's position from the top executive ranks of the competition failed. The night of Steve's viewing he approached Peter G. Boynton, the president of Caesars' Atlantic City property. The details of the offer are unknown, but it seems Donald failed to elicit the interest he expected because later that evening, when the talk turned to the future, he was overheard complaining to one of his Castle executives, "I don't know what I'm going to do."

In a move that smacked of desperation, he even made an overture to William Weidner, the president of the Sands, his adversary in the Penthouse suit. He asked my opinion. "I'm talking to some people," he said. "Steve would roll over in his grave, but what do you think of Bill Weidner?"

"I don't know, Donald," I replied, trying to be objective. "Weidner's got a reputation as a strong marketing type. But you've got to look at the performance of the Sands. Mainly, you've got to decide whether you and Bill can get along."

Donald thought for a moment, then said, "Good point. You're right. I'll think about it."

As I learned later, Weidner spurned his offer, saying, "I could never work for someone I couldn't trust and couldn't respect. In fact, never is too short a time."

At that point, nobody wanted to get too close to Donald. The tales of his erratic behavior, his lack of operational knowledge and his explosive temper were all too prevalent in the industry by now. Without Steve Hyde to act as the buffer, there were few executives with the requisite talent and seasoning willing to wager their careers on him. It didn't help matters that in the weeks after the crash, the first reports surfaced that all was not well financially with the Trump empire. There were rumors of a cash crunch on the fringes.

Despite Donald's assertions of loyalty and confidence in me, it wasn't long before I became the subject of some earnest private inquiries on his part. In the middle of one telephone discussion with a Trump Plaza executive over plans to sue Agusta (the families ultimately settled out of court for an undisclosed sum), he asked, "What about Jack O'Donnell? What's the story on him? Do the employees like him?" When the executive asked why Donald was asking, Donald replied, "You know, I really don't know Jack that well. He was Steve's man."

But if Donald was uncertain about my future in his organization, so was I. The men to whom I'd entrusted my future were gone. The brightest bulbs had gone out behind the Trump marquee.

At the end of October, the first of the "Hyde people" was gone. Donald announced that Edward M. Tracy, Trump Castle's executive vice-president, was replacing Paul Henderson as the property's president and chief operating officer. Tracy, 36, had been vice-president and general manager of the Sands Hotel and Casino in San Juan, Puerto Rico, before coming to the Castle in July. Henderson disappeared in the international marketing department for a time before quietly resigning from the organization.

In Tracy, it appeared that Donald had found someone whose style matched his own. At his first quarterly meeting of Castle employees after taking over the job, Tracy took the dais, introduced himself, and proceeded with the kind of motivational speech expected at such a gathering—only his was laced with four-letter expletives which, as one witness recalls, shocked his audience, many of them older employees not accustomed to such language. There were some complaints, and after that, subsequent meetings took a milder tone. But the incident was expressive of a style of managerial vigor that impressed Donald; just as in Tracy's seemingly total absorption in the business, Donald saw the likeness of himself.

When Tracy was hired, he moved into a suite on the eighth floor at the Castle, 18 floors down from where Donald kept his apartment. This helped him to develop a close relationship with Donald. Regardless of the hour, Tracy made it a point to be waiting on the roof of the parking garage when the Super Puma touched down. This impressed Donald, and he spoke highly of Tracy in those first weeks—a "hard worker" is how he described him to one of his competitors.

In the restructuring of the Castle's upper management following Tracy's hiring, there was a clear and conscious effort, as I saw it, to get rid of anybody known as a "Hyde person." This would only hasten the property's decline in the marketplace. But what concerned me more was the dismantling of Steve's efforts to position the two properties to complement rather than compete with each other.

In the weeks after the crash, the Castle decided to lease space for its casino marketing office directly above the same office we maintained in a Connecticut office building. Tracy went up to Connecticut at that time with one of the Castle's executives and offered our staff pay raises as high as 30 percent to desert Trump Plaza and move upstairs. It was a return to the heavy-handed tactics of Ivana, a move that could only drive up the cost of doing business for both properties. It was unbelievable, coming in a year in which profits industrywide, though higher than in 1988, were less than 1 percent of gross revenues, a clear signal that the cost of doing business in a relatively stagnant market was increasing at an alarming rate.

Donald was increasingly relying on his attorney-adviser Pat McGahn. Because of my responsibility for Trump Plaza's finances, I had been watching McGahn's fees rise steadily for almost two years. By the summer of 1989 he was routinely billing us for $150,000 to $200,000 a month. Donald's phenomenal legal bills were and still are something of a legend. In those days it was a running joke among us at the Plaza. But I had told Steve Hyde that I thought McGahn's bills were out of control. For example, with no evident legal purpose, McGahn attended Trump Plaza's regular construction meetings. He always brought a second attorney from his firm with him, with the result that those meetings were costing us thousands of dollars in legal fees. After Jon Benanav's death, I began chairing those meetings. I questioned members of my staff about the reason for the two lawyers' presence. When I couldn't get a satisfactory answer, I directed them to tell McGahn his attendance would no longer be necessary. As I later heard, he was furious.

In November, some weeks after the crash, Donald and I were having dinner at Maximilian's. I brought up the subject of our enormous legal bills.

"So who's screwing me?" Donald asked with some concern.

I replied that I thought McGahn's bills were excessively high.

"Jack, I'm 13 and 0 with this guy," he said. "What do you want me to do? He gets things done in this town."

And as a measure of his esteem, Donald named a cocktail lounge at the Taj Mahal for his attorney and friend—"Paddy's Saloon" it is called.

Then a brand-new problem popped up in the Connecticut marketing office. One of our representatives there came to me with a proposition for Donald on behalf of a group of real estate investors who had visited the Plaza and done a little gambling. "Jack," he said, "I think we can get this group of customers to really dedicate a lot more of their play to us if we invest in some of their limited partnerships."

The proposal was for Donald to invest in some units in one of their properties. Our Connecticut man was hoping for an initial buy-in of $100,000. "And, Jack, if you're interested, too, it would really be great because these guys will look at this and look to your property as the place to go."

I was suspicious immediately. This was a representative whose performance had left us less than satisfied. When I refused to recommend the investment to Donald, our Connecticut representative became frustrated and he quit. Soon after, he was hired at the Castle at a huge increase in salary.

Donald then called me to say he was thinking of making the investment anyway. I later learned that he invested a huge sum in one of these developers' limited partnerships. Ed Tracy also invested, as did one of the hosts at the Castle—a total in excess of $175,000 of their own money, all in an effort to attract the play of this group to Trump Castle. I later heard that the developers went belly-up, and they stuck the Castle and several other Atlantic City casinos with large unpaid gambling markers.

But I soon witnessed a situation that told me much more than I had ever expected to learn about the realignment of power and authority in the Trump Atlantic City operations.

Mark had been the lead man in a series of negotiations that summer which would have gathered some of the best-known performers under the Trump umbrella. He had been close to signing a deal with a man named Elliot Weisman of Premiere Artists Management to commit a package of stars to exclusive Atlantic City contracts, among them Frank Sinatra, Liza Minnelli, Sammy Davis, Jr., Paul Anka, and Steve Lawrence and Eydie Gormé. These were to be two- and three-year deals setting a specific number of performances a year with guaranteed money per show. The costs and the performances would be shared among the Plaza, the Castle and the Taj Mahal.

In order to afford these stars it was crucial for us to be able to put a significant number of the right kinds of players in the casinos. We had had success at the Golden Nugget with Sinatra, Liza and Paul Anka. But since then, they had all hit a certain level of overexposure in the Atlantic City market. With fifteen to twenty-two shows a year, year after year, it was becoming difficult to motivate the wealthier gaming customers to come in to see them.

In addition, some of these performers made excessive demands on the property. Liza, for example, wanted a beach house rented for her. (Once, at the Golden Nugget, we had to buy her entire crew new clothes and dole out gift packages to them to keep her happy.) Steve and Eydie demanded special suites and furnishings, hotel staff on call twenty-four hours, even a particular brand of drinking water. Such costs became harder and harder to justify. We were not making money on them in the showroom, they weren't attracting enough affluent players, and they weren't helping us break into new markets. Add to that the fact that they were booked in the first place to draw high-end players and then took suites from those same players, it simply didn't make sense anymore. (Steve Wynn got so frustrated with Steve and Eydie at one point when I was at the Nugget that he let them walk out on their contract and go to Resorts International.)

Happily, Sinatra and Anka were the exceptions. At $37,000 per show, Paul was affordable, and he had maintained considerable appeal among our high-end bettors. Paul was agreeable as well. All he required was a one-bedroom suite with a small office area so he could conduct business during the day. (And we did actually remodel a two-bedroom suite, converting one bedroom into an office, and calling it the "Anka Suite," which proved very popular with our customers.) Frank had an understanding of our business from his many years working in Las Vegas. He loved to perform and would appear any night of the year, including holidays and New Year's Eve, if he had no prior engagement. He didn't need the best suite in the hotel, just a nice room with a couple of additional rooms so he could have access to his attorneys and business people. What was a consideration in sponsoring a Sinatra performance, though, was having to reconstruct the stage to install TelePrompTers at various locations because he no longer remembered all the lyrics to his songs. It was a considerable expense and permanently altered the stage with holes cut through the floor.

What complicated the negotiations was Elliot's insistence on tying up all the contracts in a single package. I was opposed to this. Steve had had some reservations, but he agreed with Mark that it would enhance the Trump image to have entertainers of this caliber under exclusive contract. Mark was also looking ahead to the opening of the Taj Mahal. Having half his key dates filled for two or three years before the place ever opened was a tremendous benefit to him. Mark sold the idea to Steve and myself with the argument that while no single property could afford all these stars, if spread among the three properties, it could be cost-effective. This was how the deal was brought to Donald that summer, and he approved it.

Mark concluded the bulk of the negotiations with Elliot in September. No contracts were signed yet, but a letter of intent was drawn up and Mark signed it.

Then after the crash, Ed Tracy backed the Castle out imme-diately. The Taj backed out as well. Donald called me and said, "Tracy doesn't want these people. He thinks they're worthless and so do I. What do you think?"

I explained how I thought we might be able to negotiate for the stars we really wanted, but Donald didn't want to know the details. He just said, "Jack, just get me out of this. Get me out of this mess."

"Donald, I think we can salvage some of this," I replied. "Lis-ten, the way Mark negotiated this, we—"

He interrupted, "Hey, Jack, let me tell you something. Mark was never good at negotiating these things. I don't know what he was thinking. I never liked this deal." And he added, rather testily, "Let me tell you something else. Mark spent way too much of my money. And I blame Steve. He wasn't watching the business the way he was supposed to. Mark . . . you know, nice guy and all that . . . but he spent too much money. And that's because it wasn't his."

That was the first time I had heard Donald speak this way about Mark and Steve, and I was shocked.

Elliot made it more difficult by refusing to negotiate on in-dividual contracts and insisting we abide by the original agree-ment and pick them all up. If we did not, he threatened a lawsuit. This became increasingly uncomfortable to handle because Don-ald refused to get involved for fear of dirtying his name in show business circles. When Elliot called Donald to complain, Donald reassured him that the deal could be salvaged. He told Elliot to call me and work out something suitable. Then Donald called me. He was quite open about the subterfuge he had planned: "Look, Jack, I just talked to Elliot. I said he had to work it out with you. But, Jack, don't listen to him. I don't want this fucking deal. Get me out of it. I agreed with everything he said. I told him the deal was all contingent on working it out with you. So don't work it out with him. Whatever you do, don't work it out. Because I don't want any part of it. But I told him I did because I don't want to be the rat here. I don't want to be the guy to say no. So you've got to be the one."

It was typical of how you never knew what you'd have to protect Donald against. In this case, he wanted to be the hard-nosed deal-maker but he didn't want the celebrities he so admired to think of him that way and be angry at him.

This had to be exasperating for Elliot Weisman, who on the one hand was talking to the boss, Trump himself, and getting the go-ahead, then dealing with me, Donald's subordinate in At-lantic City, who was refusing to negotiate. And it made me angry, not least because it all impugned Mark's name. Mark not only had a long-standing relationship with Elliot going back to his days at Grossinger's but had made some pretty strong commit-ments to him on this deal.

The phone calls flew back and forth that October and Novem-ber. Finally, Elliot sent legal papers to us saying he considered Mark's signed letter of intent a valid contract. If we did not honor it, we faced a lawsuit.

"Fine, Elliot," I said. "Sue us."

Paul Anka got wind of all the wrangling and called me per-sonally. "Hey, Jack, what's the story? I'm hearing all this stuff. Does this mean I don't perform at Trump anymore?"

"Paul, I've tried to explain this to Elliot a hundred times," I said. "This doesn't affect you. I still want to do this deal with you. The only thing this affects is the original promise to perform at all three properties. We've got to revert back. If it works out that you'll just perform at Trump Plaza for the next two or three years, that's fine with me."

"You know me, Jack. I don't care if I perform at your place, at the Taj, wherever," Paul said. "We've worked together too long," he said. "We go back to the Golden Nugget. I love working at

Trump Plaza. I don't need Elliot Weisman. I got my attorney right here. Let's do this deal. . . . Unless you have a problem with me?"

"None at all, you know that," I said.

"Okay, then, we'll do it just like last year."

"Fine," I said.

"How's a $2,500 raise per show? Is that a problem?" he asked.

"No."

"Great, let's get the contracts going."

That was it and I was glad. Not only was Paul an impressive performer and a favorite of many of our top players, but he did some significant gambling himself. In fact, he was a rated player in our files and received amenities few stars got—like private helicopter transportation to and from New York—based on his value as a player. Paul was what we called a "triple threat" as a performer: he sells tickets, attracts the high-end customers and lays down some chips himself. He was the only triple threat of that entire group. (Frank Sinatra, contrary to what his reputation may suggest, was never more than a recreational gambler.)

Elliot eventually took the rest of the package—with the sad exception of Sammy Davis, Jr., who was ill with cancer and passed away the following year—up the Boardwalk to the Sands, where, I understand, they were booked for substantially less money than what we might have paid them.

But what sickened me about the entire episode was Donald's anger at Mark and the bitterness of his attack on Mark's memory. I wondered whether this was going to continue.

14

*"Sometimes your best investments are the ones
you don't make."*
—DONALD J. TRUMP

That *fall of 1989* saw growing signs that there were serious
financial problems in the Trump Organization. At first I
didn't realize how bad things were. Over at the Castle,
Trump's counselor Al Glasgow was calling for deep cuts in busing
and marketing programs. Ed Tracy took up the cry and did it one
better, indicating that he was willing to swing the blunt ax to
cut payroll. In 1989, the Trump properties individually spent
more on complimentaries than any other casino in Atlantic
City—$47.5 million at Trump Plaza, a $6.7 million increase over
the year before; and $49 million at Trump Castle, an $11 million
increase. The Plaza could justify this in a year that would see it
win $306 million in the casino, more than any other property in
town, and have almost $400 million in total revenue from all its
operations, including the restaurants and hotel. Operating income after costs and depreciation would reach $60 million, third
best in the city and more than enough to handle $32 million in
interest on its debt and still turn a $24.5 million profit. The Castle
would win $264 million in the casino, and generate $343 million

from all operations. But with interest payments of $41.9 million against operating income after costs of only $35.2 million, the Castle would suffer a net loss of $6.7 million, its second money-losing year in a row and more than twice the previous year's loss.

And it looked as if the economy was in for some heavy weather. From one end of the Boardwalk to the other, the signs should have been obvious. The junk bond market collapsed that autumn. There was an enormous debt level in corporate America, and there was a decline in real estate values. All these struck at the heart of Donald's wealth.

Merv Griffin's Resorts International, buried under a mountain of long-term debt, suspended interest payments to its bondholders and filed for protection in U.S. Bankruptcy Court. Atlantic City's first casino had succumbed to an ailment that was afflicting the entire industry. Midway through 1989, the industry's long-term debt exceeded $2 billion, not counting the Taj Mahal—$6 of debt for every $1 of equity. The combined interest on it had reached $293.5 million the year before, 9.5 percent of total revenues and 20 times profits. Debt was so pervasive that it had become customary to ignore the net profit line as long as there was sufficient cash flow to meet interest payments. The situation was so perilous that Marvin Roffman, Philadelphia brokerage firm Janney Montgomery Scott's gaming securities specialist, derided the casinos as "Houses of Cards" in a report issued in June of that year.

In 1989 gross revenues for the gaming industry reached $3.16 billion, a meager 2.7 percent increase over 1988. The previous year's growth had been 9 percent. The Casino Association of New Jersey projected unofficial average net profits industrywide of $28 million for the year, a return of less than 1 percent on gross earnings. For the fourth quarter of 1989, nine of the eleven casinos (Elsinore's Atlantis, now the Trump Regency, had shut down in the spring) would report a decrease in profits. And with all the signs pointing to an economic recession in the Northeast in 1990, debt was an explosion waiting to be touched off.

Based on private documents filed by the Trump Organization in May 1989, Donald claimed a net worth of $1.5 billion. Based as it was on his own valuation of his assets, it was presumably a generous estimate. Still it was substantially lower than a 1987 estimate by *Business Week* magazine, which placed his net worth at $3 billion.

But Donald pulled off a public relations coup in October when the *Forbes* list of the 400 wealthiest Americans was published and he was sitting comfortably at No. 19 with a net worth of $1.7 billion. Donald had been pestering the *Forbes* editors for years for a higher place on the list. Earlier in the year, he volunteered a list of his assets and their estimated values to the magazine's researchers. Prominent on the list were the West Side Yards in Manhattan, 76 acres of old railroad yards along the Hudson River. Donald told *Forbes* the land was worth $650 million, the amount he claimed developer William Zeckendorf offered him for it. That sum represented the largest single part of what Donald considered to be his net worth. By way of confirmation, Donald sent one of the magazine's researchers to someone the researcher believed was Zeckendorf's lawyer but was in fact a Trump attorney. *Forbes* got suspicious and set off on Donald's financial trail. *Fortune* magazine appeared on the scene at the same time, soliciting Donald for an interview for its December issue. These investigations into his real net worth would soon return to haunt Trump.

In mid-November, the mood was somber at Trump Tower, where I was summoned to present Trump Plaza's 1990 budget. A private audit completed by Arthur Andersen & Company that month suggested that in acquiring a stupendous array of real estate assets, the Trump Organization may have borrowed hundreds of millions of dollars more than they were worth.

221

Donald had been able to score his great triumphs in the late 1970s and early 1980s by buying in lean years. Then when the economy revived and overheated, he was sitting on assets worth three and four times what he had paid for them. Riding the boom cycle to the top, Donald was able to pile on a massive bank debt to finance more acquisitions—ten years of installment buying at stratospheric levels. The key assumption was that his assets would continue to appreciate in value. Donald prevailed in this assumption for a long time because, like many before him, he ignored the lessons of his own rise to power. He had deluded himself into believing that the Trump name on a building or a property guaranteed its value. He believed he was immune from a downturn in the economy because his properties were "trophies" and therefore someone—perhaps another Alan Bond—could always be found to offer a higher price for them.

The Arthur Andersen audit was an unpleasant awakening. It showed deficient operating income at the Plaza Hotel in New York and at the Trump Shuttle. Meanwhile Donald was incurring tremendous expenses through his estates in Palm Beach and Greenwich, Connecticut, plus his private plane, helicopter and, of course, the *Trump Princess*.

Add it all up, and by the end of 1989, a conservative estimate would have suggested that Donald's empire was bleeding at a rate approaching $100 million a year, $8 million a month, $280,000 a day. Against this, his accountants stacked some $700 million in cash and marketable securities, not counting the debt associated with their acquisition.

Had I known all this at the time, I might have been more apprehensive about my budget meeting. But I was upbeat because I was bringing the only good news in the organization. Trump Plaza was having a banner year. We would be one of only four gaming houses to increase our market share over the year before, which for us represented about $4 million knocked off Caesars' high-end business. Not only would we beat Caesars in total revenue for the second year in a row, $396 million to $375 million, but for the first time we would topple them as the number-one producer of gaming revenue. We would win $3 million more than our rival. But even that wasn't enough for Donald. Al Glasgow had convinced him that we were a cinch to break Caesars' record win of $308 million in 1988.

Our 1990 budget reflected the concern over a coming recession. My outlook was for a flat year, but one in which we'd hold steady. This was an optimistic assessment. The fact was, we'd be very lucky to hold steady, and with the Taj opening, our casino revenue was likely to decrease.

I took these numbers up to Trump Tower in New York in November and discussed them first with Robert Trump and Harvey Freeman, the executive vice-presidents of the Trump Organization, in Harvey's office. They wanted to know only two things: what we were projecting in revenue, the top-line or "image" number, and what we were projecting in operating income, the "cash-flow" number, always of intense interest to Donald and which represented our ability to turn a profit after costs and servicing the interest on our debt.

I told them we projected operating income of $64 million. It represented a decrease from our 1989 projections, and for that reason Harvey and Robert were upset. It was a realistic goal and an attainable one, counting on the moderate increase the Taj would bring to the market. We expected to be at or near the top of the list in town. Robert said nothing. Harvey cast his eyes down and shook his head and said, "That's not good."

I said, "Harvey, these are the real numbers. This is the trend right now. This is what's going to happen in town."

He sighed. "I'm telling you," he said, "this is never going to fly. We've got to be up; we're always up. We have to paint a picture that we're on the move, we are on the rise."

"We *are* on the move," I said. "We're still on the rise. We are *still* going to be very profitable. But the market is changing. There are going to be some significant changes this year and there is nothing anybody can do about that. This is reality. Do you want us to live in a fantasy world?"

"Well, let's go talk to Donald," he said.

As we walked in, Donald was sitting back in his chair at his desk, framed by the great wall of glass behind him and the stately turrets of the Plaza Hotel beyond. We each took a chair. Harvey said grimly, "Jack has some bad news on the budget."

I looked at Harvey and then at Donald, who suddenly sat up and leaned forward with his elbows planted like a bipod on the rim of his desk. He pursed his lips between his broad, baby-faced jowls. I shifted a little uncomfortably in my chair. This was not at all what I had been expecting.

"Well," I said, "I don't know if you'd call it bad news. We're projecting $310 million in casino revenue, with $64 million in operating income."

Donald grimaced. "Holy shit!" he cried. "No fucking way, Jack! No way. You are *wrong*. The business *can't* be down. There is *no way* that business is going to be down. I expect $95, $100 million in operating income next year. How can you bring us numbers like that?"

"Donald, I'll be honest with you," I said. "We've been working on these numbers for a long time. This is not something I'm just pulling off the top of my head. You know, I'm not trying to turn 1990 into an easy year for us. I'm not fluffing the numbers here. This is realistic."

"What is this, Jack? Is there going to be a problem down there?"

"The market is not going to be there next year. The market is changing."

He shook his head. "No, it's not. You've miscalculated. There is not going to be a problem."

"Well, Donald, there is the Taj Mahal, that expansion right there . . ."

"The Taj Mahal isn't going to hurt your business," he insisted. "It's going to help your business. The Taj is going to be a monster. This is the greatest thing that's ever happened to business down there, Jack. You're going to do numbers you never fucking dreamed of."

"Donald . . . yeah, in the long term the Taj Mahal, the Trump recognition factor, all that, has the potential to help our business. But it's going to hurt it in the short term. For chrissakes, we're basically flat this year, particularly in the last half. And we're going to be hurting until the Taj comes on line."

Donald was shaking his head. But I continued. "More important, 1989 was the most competitive year ever," I said. "Everybody spent more to get the business to come in. The market is going to be jockeying for position in the first quarter, spending money to solidify the customer base in preparation for the Taj onslaught. You know that, Donald. It's going to cost more money just to bring the same customers back in."

He shrugged and replied sourly, "There is no way that is going fly. You guys better get your fucking numbers squared away."

I glanced at Harvey, who gave me a look of "I told you so."

Now I was angry. "I don't know, Donald," I said, trying to contain the seething inside me. "I don't know what the hell you want from me."

"I want you to go back and do your budget and get it up to where it should be," he said.

That was the end of the discussion.

I left with no intention of trying to rewrite a budget to reflect Donald's delusions. Two weeks later, early in December, in a conciliatory gesture, Harvey and Robert came down to Atlantic City in an attempt to persuade me.

We met for lunch that day at Roberto's at Trump Plaza. I

brought my chief financial officer, Tim Maland, with me. It was an unseasonably warm afternoon and the sun beat down on us from a nearby window overlooking the ocean.

Harvey started the conversation. "Jack, the facts of the Trump Organization are this: we'll never put a number out that is not better than the prior year. We can't. We always have to be showing a positive; we can't show a decrease."

Robert added, "Hey, we think we want to go public."

At that time, Donald was speaking warmly of the idea himself. "I've never had partners, and I don't want them now," he told a *Fortune* magazine reporter. "But I could make a lot of money just by offering a small piece of what I own. It's a great opportunity."

"We're thinking of taking all three of these casino properties public," Robert continued. "You understand, Jack, that we can't have you telling us that the numbers aren't going to be as good as last year."

So Tim asked, "What is acceptable? What do you want?"

Harvey said, "Ninety-five million in operating income would be acceptable."

Tim looked at me. I looked at Harvey and Robert. "Unh, unh . . . that can't be, it's impossible."

"Well, make it happen," Robert said. "You can do it."

So we went back to our financial department and informed them that the budget as written was simply not good enough, and we'd have to work and rework the numbers until we got the operating income into the $90 million range. What we ended up with was a plan that gave us $92 million. Correspondingly, the projected casino revenue was inflated to $327 million. Donald accepted that. But how were we going to generate the business to make it happen? The number was so unrealistic that it was demoralizing. Of course, I could never let on to the staff that this figure was a fiction created to satisfy Donald's ego and his need to raise cash in the public arena. The greatest challenge was to make them believe it was attainable. To their credit, our marketing staff wrote a comprehensive plan that gave us our best shot. Our plans for 1990 projected even more aggressive expansion into the international high end, those ten or fifteen gamblers who play in a world of $100,000 stakes and above.

But more and more Donald's future was riding on the Taj Mahal. After Donald acquired the controlling share of Resorts' voting stock in 1987, he talked about having the Taj up and running by the fall of 1988. That date was tossed aside when Merv Griffin entered the picture early that year to thwart Donald's attempt to take the company private. In the deal by which Donald and Merv carved up Resorts, Donald bought the Taj back for $273 million. He floated $675 million in 14 percent first-mortgage bonds and kicked in another $75 million capital contribution and a $25 million line of credit to complete construction, finish the property and get it open. He signed his name to a March 1, 1990, opening deadline as a condition of the bond offering. Donald announced confidently that the Taj would open its doors in December 1989, three months ahead of schedule. But building so massive a facility in a sandy coastal environment proved to be a frighteningly expensive undertaking, as Resorts International had found out to its undoing. The Taj had to be underlaid with so much steel that Donald used to joke that in the event of nuclear war he'd want to be in the Taj basement because it would be the safest place in the world. The cold weather and salt air took their toll during the years the Taj stood unfinished, something that Donald, the construction expert and developer, should have foreseen. Millions had to be spent in rehabilitation. Design changes ordered by Donald and his architects cost millions more: a year's output of Carrara marble from Italy, mammoth Austrian cut-crystal chandeliers, carpets handwoven in England. Originally pegged at $250 million to complete, the project cost ballooned to over $550 million, including a $10 million management fee Donald paid to himself. By early autumn, the project was awash in millions in cost overruns. Worse yet, it was doubtful whether he was going to meet his timetable, and this immediately raised the issue of whether the Taj would be able to meet $94 million in interest obligations due the following year.

The first alarm had been sounded as early as June in a prospectus for casino investors published by Janney Montgomery Scott and written by Marvin Roffman, the securities analyst who was bearish about the highly leveraged casino industry: "While we love the aesthetics, what scares us about this project is our concern over its financial success," he wrote. "The Taj is going to be a very expensive property to operate. . . . Its casino will have to win more money per year than any casino in the world in order to operate in the black. While we are not concerned about filling the property during the busy season of 1990, we are concerned about Atlantic City's slow period, from October through January. Adding to our concern is the possible state of the economy in mid to late 1990. A recession could be a big short-term negative for so leveraged a property. . . . Holders of its first-mortgage bonds have little to fall back on should the Taj not work. Certainly it can't be made into a K Mart."

After the helicopter crash, Donald hastily reshuffled Trump Taj Mahal Associates with Robert Trump as chief executive officer. It was the first time Robert had actually had his hands on a casino operation, however, and Donald couldn't have planned for the search to end there. Robert supported Walter J. Haybert as Mark's replacement in the president's office. Haybert had been plucked from ignominy after disaster in the slot machine areas during Trump Plaza's opening five years before. He was rehired as a financial executive at Resorts during Donald's management of that property. Mark later made him senior vice-president of finance and administration of Trump Taj Mahal Associates.

Donald, however, had someone else in mind for the president's job. He wanted John Groom, the vice-president of casino operations at Caesars, an experienced and highly respected operations man. Donald turned to his attorney, Pat McGahn, to commence negotiations for him. Through McGahn a meeting was arranged between Groom and Donald aboard the *Trump Princess*. As I was later told, Donald offered Groom the Taj presidency on the spot and held out the possibility of promotion to Steve Hyde's post as overseer of the entire Atlantic City operation. On October 25 at Pat McGahn's office, with Al Glasgow and Donald's lead casino attorney, Nick Ribis, both present, McGahn and Groom hammered out a deal, which reportedly carried a guaranteed cash advance of $800,000 and a three-year contract worth almost $3 million in all. Robert, the Taj's chief executive officer, was not present.

The next day, the contract was completed in Donald's office at Trump Tower, again with Glasgow sitting in. When the deal was closed, Donald called his brother in Atlantic City and said, "Robert, I want you to meet your new successor."

Robert fought the appointment and demanded the right to name his own president. He backed it with a threat to resign. The deal with Groom was scrapped, and within a week it was announced that Walt Haybert would be the Taj Mahal's president.

Aside from the question of who would be the president of the Taj, there were serious operational concerns. Steve Hyde had brought in a slot operations expert from outside the organization as a consultant. Upon inspection, the consultant confirmed that the cash cage and coin holding areas were too small. Another problem was a shortage of manned coin booths on the gaming floor, only two, to accommodate 3,000 slot machines. Trump Plaza, by comparison, with half the floor space and 1,600 machines, had eight. The consultant warned against relying too heavily on automated changemakers that had been installed at every machine. The changemakers had suffered mechanical problems in test runs at Trump Plaza, but they were considered state of the art. The image appealed to Donald, though; they represented the cutting edge of gaming technology and would catapult the Taj to the forefront of the industry as an innovator. Plus they would save him on payroll by replacing crews of change attendants. The consultant, however, advised that more change booths be constructed. Steve had agreed, and the slot areas were being redesigned. Donald no longer had the patience or the financial wherewithal to withstand more design changes and delays, so after Steve's death, the slot areas were reevaluated and pronounced satisfactory.

Staffing, especially at the management level, was another major problem. Mark and I had had intense discussions about this throughout the summer. As my predecessor at Trump Plaza, Mark was certainly aware of the talent we had, and he was prepared to take key people with him. Indeed, he felt he was entitled to. At one point, the Taj was offering significantly more money, in some cases as much as 25 percent more, to induce qualified managers and directors to move over.

I resisted. We had a top-notch management team, the best in the industry, as far as I was concerned. I didn't want to lose them; I couldn't afford to. The Atlantic City labor pool isn't very large to begin with, and it is limited even further by the state's strict licensing requirements. Qualified people are really hard to come by at all levels, especially in the mid ranges.

Steve was involved in these discussions as a mediator. In the end, I had to concede some valuable help. In those cases where the pay raises or promotions were substantial, it would have been unfair to the employees to try to stand in their way. So among the three of us compromises were worked out. Mark and I concluded a gentlemen's agreement to discuss key transfers beforehand. We agreed on a 10 percent limit within each of Trump Plaza's departments.

Another issue, and perhaps even more significant, involved discussions over the transfer of player lists, any casino's most preciously guarded asset: the names, addresses, ratings and other pertinent personal information on our customers, which were built up through years of marketing and promotional work and comprised the very essence of our success. Mark was under the impression that the Taj would have full access to our lists. I was opposed. First, there was the issue of legality. Did our bondholder agreement prohibit the surrender of so crucial an asset? Second, how would it affect our profitability? Our lists were developed through some very painstaking, very creative efforts of our marketing department and our player development representatives, nationwide and around the world. How many of these customers would we lose for good? How long would it take to cultivate new ones before our revenues were crippled? Finally, how was I to explain this to the people we paid to bring in this business, who have tremendous pride in their work and over the years developed close relationships with their players? This was how they made their living. Many were paid on a commission basis.

I took the issue to Steve.

"I have some serious concerns over the legality of this," I said. "I don't know about the bondholders."

Steve acknowledged that he'd discussed it with Mark. At the same time, he had no answers yet. "I don't know, Jack," he said. "What about compensation?"

"That's just it," I said. "I don't know what would be adequate to compensate the company for turning over the work of three and a half years."

Steve promised to have it researched, and he did. He came back to me in early September. "Don't worry," he said. "The files are not going to be transferred. Yes, I've had some conversations with Mark about it, as you know. But I've made the determination that it can't be done."

"So what happens now?" I said.

"I don't know, Jack. They're going to have to obtain them some other way than a blatant transfer. That can't happen. I think you're right. We do that and there are going to be legal problems down the road."

Donald and I never discussed this, but I assumed that Steve was keeping him informed.

As the year drew to a close, the Taj's opening was pushed from December to February 1990. Then it appeared that the March 1 deadline was in serious jeopardy. To avoid violating the conditions of his financing, Donald obtained an extension from Bankers Trust, the trustee for the bondholders. Opening day was moved to April 1. The delays only fueled the speculation over Donald's ability to make all of the first interest payment due in May. Donald insisted he had the money.

He was encouraged by the performance of Steve Wynn's fabulous Mirage on the Las Vegas Strip when it opened in December. The Mirage won $40 million its first month. But trying to achieve that in Atlantic City's seasonal market was frightening even to think about. And every delay in opening the Taj increased the danger. In addition, the Taj was adding 20 percent more capacity to a market that the smartest analysts were certain was growing by less than half that. Nevertheless, Al Glasgow predicted in the December issue of *Atlantic City Action* that the Taj would dramatically expand the market merely "by virtue of its theme and opulence." The theme, he wrote, "is magnificent and surreal. It will be a breathtaking sight to behold."

Steve and Mark and myself used to have long conversations about that. Would the Taj truly be a spectacle of the magnitude of the Mirage, with its 50-foot volcano, its indoor rain forest, the live sharks and white tigers? Or was it just a big building with lots of marble and chandeliers? The inevitable question remained: Could it drive enough business through the doors in a flat Atlantic City market to justify a final price tag of more than $800 million and meet $94 million in annual interest payments?

Glasgow insisted that the Taj would do $400 million its first year—a tidy number, just enough to service the debt with a remainder very close to Trump Plaza's prodigious earnings for the year. The Taj "is like spitting on the floor," Glasgow said. "It can't miss." He conceded that in a weak market, the Taj Mahal was certain to push its more vulnerable competitors over the edge. Merv Griffin's Resorts Casino Hotel and the Claridge Hotel & Casino were identified as the two most likely to fold. He would never have dreamed of suggesting that it was Donald's two existing casinos that were the most dangerously exposed.

"The worst thing you can possibly do in a deal is seem desperate to make it."

—DONALD J. TRUMP

T he *Rolling Stones* concerts of December 17, 19 and 20, 1989, at Convention Hall were easily the costliest and most sense-less casino entertainment events Donald Trump ever sponsored. Ironically, of all the Trump Atlantic City events, they were the ones he was most responsible for.

The band first approached Trump Plaza in 1988 with an offer to share in corporate sponsorship of their upcoming sixty-city North American "Steel Wheels" tour. We declined. It would have been expensive, and we weren't certain the promotion suited our identity. Our market, generally speaking, did not fit the demographics of a rock concert. However, if we could get a group such as the Stones for a slow period, like December, and for the right price, staging a rock concert might be an interesting thing to try.

On that basis, Mark Etess, as president of Trump Sports and Entertainment, had begun negotiations in the summer of 1989 with the Stones' tour management, the Toronto-based BCL Entertainment Group. Our leverage was Convention Hall. The Stones had been looking throughout the tour to perform in a national pay-per-view television broadcast, but had been unable to find a location that combined the excitement of a large concert and the intimacy necessary for a television production. Convention Hall offered both. We agreed that the Stones would own the pay-per-view rights and Trump Plaza would own the live concerts rights. But the talks broke down over the site fee. The Stones and BCL originally wanted $3 million each for three shows, which was far too expensive for an event from which we stood to gain little action in the casino relative to a major prizefight.

Some weeks after Mark's death in October, negotiations resumed, at the wishes of the Stones and BCL. With the "Steel Wheels" tour winding down, they were anxious for a lucrative pay-per-view broadcast. They came back to us with an offer of $4.2 million for three shows. I felt certain that we could negotiate a more reasonable site fee and maybe break even on the event. But Donald suddenly stepped in with orders to "Do the deal. Whatever it takes, just do it." As president of Trump Plaza, I asked for the latitude to negotiate a site fee that wouldn't saddle my casino with a huge loss. Donald wouldn't let that happen. His ego took over, as it so often did with celebrity events. And so I lost control of the negotiations. Mick Jagger & Co., hot off a tour in which they raked in some $44 million from concerts, record sales and merchandising, came chugging into Atlantic City for the biggest payday of their lives, compliments of Donald Trump.

I explained to Donald why BCL's $4.2 million asking price was still too high. "There's no way we can get that out of 22,000 seats."

"Why not?" Donald said.

"Because here's how we have it scaled: We have tickets starting at $25 and going up to $250."

Donald was surprised. "We only got $250? What do you mean? Scale it from $250 to $1,000. Then you'll get the revenue."

I couldn't believe what I was hearing. "Donald, this isn't boxing. If we scale it that way, we're not going to sell the tickets."

"Hell, Jack, I sell them boxing, I'll sell them rock and roll."

"Not at $1,000 a seat."

"Yeah, you will," he insisted. "C'mon. Don't underestimate the Rolling Stones. Don't underestimate Trump. You know, you guys don't know what . . . I'm the promoter here. This is what makes me famous. This is why I know more about making deals than you do."

"Donald, here's how we have to scale it," I said. "You can afford to pay a million dollars for this."

He refused to consider that if it meant losing the event. "Fuck it," he said. "Pay them $4 million and we'll just scale it differently." Then he had Bernie Dillon, Trump Plaza's former director of special projects, who succeeded Mark at the helm of Trump Sports and Entertainment, work up a cost and revenue analysis to show that if we sold a certain number of tickets at $1,000 each we could afford to pay the Stones' price. It was fictitious revenue, an illusion. The way I figured it, we were certain to lose about $2 million at that price. I refused to negotiate on that basis, and as the Thanksgiving holiday approached, there was still no contract. Then BCL returned with an offer to buy 25 percent of the tickets for promotional use, including most of the $1,000 and $500 seats. With that offer, the event suddenly appeared feasible; we might even break even. I authorized the deal, the contracts were signed and the dates set. But in the first week of December, ten days before the first concert, BCL refused to take more than 100 seats per show. They returned the $1,000 and $500 seats, the same ones we couldn't sell. All of a sudden we were looking at a huge loss again. I called Michael Cohl, of BCL, the Stones' tour manager, who was with the band in Montreal at the time. I told him I wasn't taking back the seats and I considered BCL and the Stones to be in violation of the contract.

"Well, fine, we're not performing," he said.

"Great. Don't perform," I replied. "Do us a favor and save us a lot of money."

But Donald was adamant that we not walk away. "I want the fucking Rolling Stones," he told me. "I told everybody the Rolling Stones are going to be playing at Trump Plaza. I'm coming down to watch them. My friends are coming down. Don't lose this deal, Jack."

I knew then that either I tried to renegotiate on my own or Trump Plaza was going to be stuck for a loss of $2 million. That week I was on the phone with Cohl in Montreal every day, but we were getting nowhere. Finally I called him one night from my home. "What's the exact address of your hotel?" I asked.

"Why?"

"Because I'm chartering a plane right now. I'm coming up to see you, and you better be prepared to see me."

Then I called Donald in New York. "I'm going up there to try to renegotiate this thing," I said. "Just so you know, I may come back with nothing. I might blow this whole damned thing out."

"Jack, I've got to have this event," he said. "Don't lose this event."

"Donald, I'm not going to go into this and lose $2 million because every time I go into an event and we lose money, I get my ass kicked by you and everyone else. Now I'm telling you again right up front, we're going to lose $2 million."

"Just don't lose the event, Jack," he said. "Go up there and do your best, but don't lose the event."

At six o'clock the next morning, Bernie Dillon, Trump Plaza's chief attorney, Roger Claus, and myself were on a chartered flight to Montreal. We spent the entire day locked in negotiations in Cohl's hotel room. Without his knowing that my boss was prepared to pay his price, I was able to use the leverage afforded by the band's desire for the pay-per-view broadcast. On the strength of that, we flew home to Atlantic City that night with a new contract that sliced $1.2 million off the site fee. We closed a deal for $3 million. On paper I had reduced Trump Plaza's risk to about $800,000. Donald was matter-of-fact when I told him. Now he believed he had a profitable event. Congratulations were never forthcoming in the Trump Organization. I felt like a hero anyway.

The Rolling Stones turned out to be more demanding and cranky and contentious than any entertainers I'd ever encountered. They were worse than Liza Minnelli, Steve and Eydie, and Don King all thrown in together. Mick Jagger demanded that Trump Plaza's name not appear on any advertising. We insisted on it, as was our right.

Before the first show on Sunday, December 17, Donald strode backstage for the lone press conference the band agreed to grant. Then to my surprise, Marla Maples walked in with Tom Fitzsimmons. They entered separately. Marla was wearing a plush, full-length fur coat (finally, Donald sprung for an expensive gift for her). It was the first time I'd seen her in months. She came rushing over when she spotted me, and she gave me a kiss and a hug, the warmest greeting I'd ever gotten from her.

We sat and waited for the Stones to appear, but they refused. Instead, one of their representatives demanded that Donald leave. They were angry over what they felt was an attempt to upstage them.

"What do you mean? What the hell's going on?" Donald said when he heard. "It's my press conference."

"This isn't your press conference, this is for the pay-per-view," the representative replied peevishly. "You have no business being here."

"Fuck that," Donald said angrily. "I'm paying $3 million for this. It's my press conference. I'll fucking be anywhere I want to be."

But the band was adamant. They were not coming out. Finally Donald stormed out of the ballroom.

The press conference was astonishing for its brevity—the band set eight minutes as the limit, as everyone was instructed beforehand. One reporter asked them, "How do you justify ticket prices of $250 when they were selling for $34 everywhere else on the tour?"

"We can't," Keith Richards answered smugly.

Donald and Marla attended the first show together. Donald led the way through the skywalk that joined the casino to Convention Hall. A few yards behind his phalanx of bodyguards followed. Behind them strode Marla's familiar hourglass figure, long legs propelling a black leather mini-dress, just the way Donald liked it. Robert and Blaine Trump brought up the rear, along with Tom Fitzsimmons, his date and another young couple. It was surprising to me to see Donald and Marla together so openly. I wondered if the stakes were not suddenly being escalated. For two years the pretty young model had lived in fear of discovery by Ivana.

Donald and his entourage took the first row balcony. Donald didn't stay in his seat long. He fidgeted and shifted about, and finally he and Marla and their circle left the concert early.

As I feared, the Trump–Rolling Stones partnership was not as strong a draw as Donald believed. None of the three concerts sold out, not even the base-priced $38.50 seats. The third and final night, the pay-per-view broadcast, was especially disappointing. Unlike the boxing matches, where even with a poor turnout at the gate we could get lucky if we held well at the gaming tables and slot machines, this event had nothing to redeem it. At month's end, we realized we would not recoup any of the $800,000 we risked with the Rolling Stones. At the time, Donald was concentrating on the revenue war with Caesars, where we were well out in front despite the loss we took in December. He was on the phone with me every day, asking for the 24-hour tallies right through the last week of the year. When the year ended and we sat in first place with $396 million in gross revenue, he was overjoyed. "Fucking tremendous year," he said.

On December 27, Donald took off for Aspen on his annual family vacation. Ivana took a separate flight with the children. Donald dispatched his private jet to pick up Marla in Chattanooga, Tennessee, to take her to separate lodgings at the posh ski resort. But before he left he congratulated me again on the great year we had, and he promised, "Jack, I'm going to take care of you. You're going to get the biggest bonus ever."

I was happy about that, though I would have been satisfied with the same $150,000 bonus that Steve and Mark had gotten during their tenures as president of Trump Plaza. I certainly felt that I deserved it. We were the one bright spot in the Arthur Andersen audit. And we brought in our results in a year that was flat by industry standards, in which we were one of only four gaming houses, along with Caesars, Harrah's and Bally's Park Place, to record net profits higher than 5 percent of gross revenue, the acknowledged standard of financial health in the business.

After Donald returned from Aspen, I heard nothing more about my bonus. In January 1990, we led Atlantic City with revenues of $23.6 million. Finally, I brought up the subject of the bonus with Donald. Immediately he shifted the subject to the poor December we'd had. "You're talking about a bonus? Jack, those numbers are shit! What are you guys doing down there?"

I should have seen it coming. "Donald, why are we going over this?" I mentioned the $800,000 loss we took in December on the Rolling Stones.

"Yeah, well I knew that," he interrupted. "That was a bad fucking deal from day one."

"What are you saying? You were warned about that deal up front. *You* wanted them."

He sounded surprised. "Are you telling me I let that deal happen? I don't believe I'm hearing this. That was Mark's deal. And I should have known better."

I could feel my anger rising, but I stayed calm. "You wanted to do this deal. We told you not to do it. You did it anyway. But who's going to get beat up now? Me! Because it's my bottom line."

He was silent for a moment. Then he said, "Well, sue the bastards."

"Sue who? The Rolling Stones?" I asked.

"Yeah."

"What?"

"Sue them," he said.

"Donald, we're getting off the subject here. Let's get back to . . . let's just . . ."

"Fucking sue them, Jack. I want to sue them. It's their fault we took the loss."

"Look, I want to talk about the bonus."

"That? Oh, I can't talk about that right now. We can't have that conversation right now. I've got to go. We'll get together down there next week."

I was certain we had no basis for a lawsuit against the Rolling Stones, but I reviewed the situation anyway with Trump Plaza's general counsel, Roger Claus. On the basis of that I was convinced we had no grounds. Donald flew down one afternoon the next week and arrived unannounced at Trump Plaza. I looked up from my desk to see Donald standing in the doorway. He made directly for the executive washroom, complaining about all the hands he'd had to shake upstairs. He came out, took a quick stride to the conference table and sat down. The January cold clung to his dark overcoat, which he kept on the whole time. I realized right away that I was going to have to negotiate for my bonus.

"I want you to give me your thoughts on my bonus," I said.

"That reminds me," he said. "I tried to reach you last night."

"What time?"

"I don't know. About ten o'clock."

"Did you try me at home? That's where I was."

"You know, that's funny," he said. "I called over to the Castle. Tracy was in his building. Why weren't you?"

"He lives there, Donald."

He went on, "Are you looking at the Castle's numbers this month? I think they're turning around. They're doing phenomenal numbers."

"Yeah, well, they've got nowhere to go but up," I said.

He took no note of my sarcasm. "Steve never had a January like they're having over there now," he continued. "You know why? You know what Steve's problem was? He was too soft on people. I loved the guy, but I have to tell you, I wasn't happy with some of his people he had in there. You know, everybody said Trump's going to take a fall with that property. But I've said it all along, it's a winner. And I'm going to prove it."

This was all a tactic to put me on the defensive about my bonus. I refused to take the challenge. I redirected the conversation back and I said, "I think my record last year speaks for itself."

Donald shifted to one side in the chair and grimaced. "Jack, December was the worst fucking month ever. When I saw those numbers I couldn't believe it. I said to myself, 'What the fuck is going on down there? Is the place falling apart or what?' "

"Do we have to go over this again?" I said.

"Jack, what do you want from me? The numbers don't lie."

"We've been through this before, Donald."

"That reminds me," he said. "Who's suing the Rolling Stones?"

"Nobody's suing the Rolling Stones. We've got no grounds for a suit."

"Yeah? Who says?"

When I gave him Roger's opinion, he replied, "Oh, fuck him. That guy doesn't know what he's talking about. He's an asshole." Donald said he was going to turn over the case to his brother-in-law, attorney John Barry. I found out later that he had already contacted Barry's office and told him to proceed with a lawsuit.

I was still waiting to discuss the bonus, but Donald stood and made for the door. "C'mon, walk with me, walk with me downstairs to my car," he said. Downstairs in the hotel lobby, he turned to me just before he opened the door to leave. "So what do you want as your bonus?" he said.

"Well, Donald, I really think it's appropriate that you tell me. You know the results. I've explained everything to you."

"No," he said. "I want to know from you what you think you should get."

"I obviously have access to all the financial records of the past. I don't think I should get any more or any less than what Trump Plaza's presidents got the last four years."

"And what was that?" he asked.

"One hundred fifty thousand."

His face twisted into an expression of disgust. "Oh, no! Uh, uh . . . no way! Absolutely not. December was the worst month ever."

"Donald, why are you going through this again?"

"Well, I'll tell you what. I must be the biggest sucker in the world. I'll give you . . . Tell your people to cut you a check for $75,000."

He pushed the doors open and walked outside to his waiting limousine.

Trump Plaza's top financial people, who knew what our bonus pool was, were surprised when they heard. The irony is that it was the largest bonus I'd ever been awarded in my life. If Donald had simply said in the beginning, "I'm going to give you $75,000," I would have accepted it and been grateful. Instead I had to negotiate with Donald for the bonus he promised me. He wrung the sweetness out of it, the sense of pride and accomplishment. I returned to my office, walked behind my desk for a moment and stood there. I could only shake my head.

*"What separates the winners from the losers is
how a person reacts to each new twist of fate."*
—DONALD J. TRUMP

In *January* 1990, after the Castle reported its second consecutive losing year, Salomon Brothers, one of Wall Street's most influential brokerage houses, advised its clients to sell their Castle bonds. The issues, which were trading at 92 cents on the dollar, immediately dropped by 10 cents. Everywhere, investors were taking a hard look at the cumbersome debt level of corporate America, especially in the casino industry. In the case of Donald Trump, whose holdings alone accounted for over $3 billion of corporate debt, his mystique was fading fast within the financial community.

Meanwhile, the 14 percent first-mortgage bonds Donald had floated to complete the Taj Mahal were trading at less than 75 cents per dollar of face value. Wall Street was not optimistic about the casino's chances. With payroll and debt service exceeding $200 million a year, the cost of operating the Taj per room would be the highest of any hotel in the world. As one analyst told the *New York Times* that January: "In the next couple of months, the downside risk of these bonds is greater than the upside. . . .

244

There won't be any news in the next few months to provide any reason for these bonds to go up."

The first alarm had been sounded a month earlier when the December 18 issue of *Fortune* magazine hit the stands, the day after the first Rolling Stones concert, with a three-page story titled "Trump's Troubles." The main topic was the Taj. And the prime question was: "Has Donald Trump finally dealt himself a bad hand?" Casino analyst Marvin Roffman, who had become something of a Cassandra on the issue of casino debt, figured centrally in the story, warning again that the Taj would need $1 million a day in casino revenue just to break even; while to turn a profit, it would need $1.3 million a day, an average daily win nearly 50 percent greater than Trump Plaza's in 1989, which was our best year ever.

The new year opened grimly for Donald on other fronts.

Reports had appeared in the press of an ugly confrontation between Ivana and Marla in Aspen during the Trumps' holiday vacation. It seems that Marla had made it a point to place herself close to the Trumps wherever they went, at one point even squeezing between them at a ski lift. It was more than Ivana could stand, and she confronted her pretty young rival—"Moolah," she called her derisively—during lunch at a mountaintop restaurant. "You bitch!" she said. "Leave my husband alone!" An angry shouting match followed, all within earshot of Donald, who was putting on his skis and trying to escape down the slopes. But the screaming continued down the mountainside as Ivana, the former Olympic skier, easily caught up with her husband, whizzed past him, then angled in front of him and spun on her poles, shouting and wagging her finger in his face.

Back home, husband and wife were barely observing the formalities now. A night out in a restaurant, as one close friend told me, would pass without a single word between them. But Donald lumbered about indecisively for a few more weeks. Like an adolescent, he was lunging at freedom then backing away, posing in *Playboy* magazine in black tie and shirtsleeves next to a Play-mate who appeared to be wearing nothing but his tuxedo jacket.

"What is marriage to you?" he was asked in the interview inside. "Is it monogamous?"

"I don't have to answer that," he lamely replied.

Ivana hired a lawyer.

It was plain to me that Donald's two great gambles, Marla and the Taj Mahal, were taking their toll on him. He looked pale; his trademark scowl seemed to be permanently on his face. And the glint in his eyes had given way to a dull glaze. Wrinkles had crept around his eyes like tiny vines. He was gaining weight. He spent the greater part of his visits to Atlantic City sequestered with Marla in the Castle's hotel tower, sometimes for entire weekends. He canceled meetings.

His judgment seemed to worsen. A small example was his insistence on adding an unprofitable oyster bar to Trump Plaza. Marla loved seafood and ordered it constantly from room service whenever she was in the hotel. It must have been to gratify her that Donald asked us to consider installing an oyster bar at our Boardwalk entrance at a vacant spot where we had planned to open an upscale women's clothing store, which our marketing studies indicated would do well there. But Donald pushed for the oyster bar. So we worked up profit and loss projections which showed that the oyster bar would likely take years to break even at best, while the retail store stood a good chance of making us $100,000 to $200,000 a year in profits. Not to mention that the location hadn't been designed for a food operation and wasn't equipped with the necessary refrigeration, kitchen and storage space. I showed the projections to Donald and I tried to talk him out of the restaurant. Finally he said, "Okay, fine. You say it's not going to make money? Go ahead and do the retail space you want." But a week later, he changed his mind. "No, I want an oyster bar in there," he said.

"But, Donald, did you forget the numbers?" I protested. "We're going to lose money if we put that thing in. Maybe if we're lucky, over a ten-year period, we break even."

"Nah, I have to tell you, I think the oyster bar is a good idea. It'll be a real positive for the building. That's what I want in there," he said.

Construction of the restaurant was a major undertaking, as I knew it would be. We had to install refrigerator and pantry facilities in the basement parking garage and then break a hole through the first floor to connect them to the restaurant via a special elevator system. The work cost Trump Plaza more than $1 million.

Our advertising agency came up with three or four names for the restaurant (someone jokingly suggested calling it "Marla's"), one of them being "Oysters Trump." I instantly selected that name and gave it to the contractor for the signage. There was no need to run it by Donald; I knew he'd approve, and of course he did. The contractor was so happy with the name he saved it for a future meeting to spring on Donald to put him in a good mood. It worked. "I love it. It's great," he said when he heard it.

Intuitively, Marla knew by now that not to push ahead meant falling behind. She arrived at Trump Plaza the last weekend in January for the festivities we planned for the Super Bowl. It was the last time I would ever see the woman who first came to attention as one of the billionaire's "trophies" but who had built for herself a position of such surprising strength. It was clear to me that weekend that she was the most important woman in Donald's life now. It was a fitting coda to the time that I would know her. She had proven herself to be the most difficult trophy of all to unload. She was stepping forward, unashamed, to claim her share of Trump's future.

Marla had the run of the entire property; all she needed to do was sign her name. She brought several girlfriends with her that busy weekend and took two of the three two-bedroom luxury "super suites" we had. She and her entourage dined expensively in the restaurants, ordered huge amounts of room service and dominated the health club, spa and masseuses. They came to several of the player parties we hosted, never bothering to make reservations, which placed a tremendous burden on table space that was tight to begin with. It was a distraction for the entire staff that weekend when she'd suddenly appear and demand access, saying simply, "My name is Maples." Knowing she was Donald Trump's mistress, no one wanted to risk making her angry.

She spoke often that weekend of how much she missed her "little honey." In the women's locker room adjoining the spa she lounged about for more than an hour one afternoon, completely naked, as I was later told, while she talked to her friends about Donald. "I wish my little sweetie was here," she said with a giggle. "I miss him so much, and I love him so much. But maybe it's for the best that we spend this weekend apart from each other."

Donald was down at his 118-room estate, Mar-a-lago, in Palm Beach, Florida. He returned to Trump Plaza the next weekend for the fight that indirectly led to the deaths of my friends, Steve Hyde, Mark Etess and Jon Benanav. On Saturday night, February 3, Hector "Macho Man" Camacho squared off against Vinny Pazienza before 11,000 fans at Convention Hall. "A Fight to Match the Hype?" one headline wondered. The two boxers went the entire twelve rounds. Camacho outlasted his opponent, though, and retained his welterweight crown with a unanimous decision. The fight spurred a $3 million drop at the tables that night, a fabulous performance for a winter weekend. Trump Sports and Entertainment, Mark's brainchild, earned $1.6 million in its first foray into the pay-per-view television market. But the mood was somber at ringside. I sat with some executives and friends. We couldn't help but think about Steve, Mark and Jon. Everyone wanted the event to end that evening and to put this terrible chapter behind us. Donald sat at ringside that night as usual. He never once mentioned his three fallen executives.

He flew to Tokyo the following week to see Mike Tyson defend his title against James "Buster" Douglas. It promised to be another Tyson walkover, and the fight was really a cover for efforts to try to sell some of Donald's luxury condos at the new Trump Parc in New York. The Trump Organization had launched an expensive marketing effort in the Orient, but as one of our Far Eastern representatives confided to me, the expensive residences were not selling at all. Donald was also hoping to raise badly needed cash, and he was meeting with Japanese investors in hopes of unloading his most prized trophy, the Plaza Hotel.

I made sure to call him in New York before he left.

"Donald, you've got to do me a favor. We've been working on this guy Kashiwagi. If you can give me fifteen minutes while you're over there, I want to have him brought up to your suite." He agreed.

Trump Plaza's efforts to court Akio Kashiwagi, a billionaire Japanese real estate baron and the biggest of the international high rollers, dated back to 1988. But it wasn't until December 1989 that things started to move fast in our favor. Kashiwagi had gone to Las Vegas for the opening of Steve Wynn's Mirage and had lost $6 million there playing baccarat at $200,000 a hand. Temperamental and superstitious, like many high-stakes players, he left Nevada unhappy with his treatment there, and though he'd never been to Atlantic City, he told our Far Eastern representative Ernie Cheung that he was eager to match stakes with the famous Donald Trump. "I think we've got Kashiwagi," Ernie said. "He's ready to play."

When I heard Donald was going to Japan, I had Ernie on standby in Tokyo to arrange a possible meeting between the two tycoons. Shortly after Donald arrived, I reached him at his hotel in Tokyo.

Again, he agreed to meet Kashiwagi. "Jack, I'll do anything while I'm here, anything you want."

"Great," I said. "I'm going to have Ernie give you a call and set it up. But you've got to do me this favor. You've got to meet this guy. If you meet him and spend a little time with him, I think we'll get him in."

As Ernie told me, their meeting came off splendidly. The following Monday, the day after Donald's return, Ernie called again to say Kashiwagi wanted to come in that week.

"Okay. What do we have to do?" I said.

"He wants to wire $6 million to our cage, and he would like another $6 million in credit."

I didn't hesitate for a moment. I said, "Let's do it."

It was never my intention to consult with Donald over whether we should deal Kashiwagi's action. Concerned that he might get nervous or try to interfere, I didn't mention it to him until Kashiwagi's visit was all but certain, and then I put it to him in passing, "By the way, Donald, I want you to know we are finally going to see the fruits of a long hard effort in the Oriental market. We are bringing in a guy who is going to be the largest customer that's ever come to Trump Plaza, this guy from Tokyo who is betting $200,000 a hand."

"Wow! Two hundred thousand a hand!" he exclaimed.

"Just be prepared," I said. "There are going to be tremendous swings between now and the time he stops playing. But I'll keep you posted."

"Right. What do you think of this guy?"

"Well, Donald, what do you think of any guy that brings $6 million in cash and sticks it in your cage. I want that $6 million."

"Yeah, yeah . . . you're right." But he quickly added, "Do you think we're going to get it?"

"Donald, the guy definitely has a history of losing that kind of money. But he's got some big wins, too. But we'll see. I've got a real good feeling about this guy."

All Donald understood was that a gambler was bringing $12 million to wager in our casino, therefore we stood to win $12 million. Yet it was such a frighteningly large sum. He sounded a little nervous on the phone but he managed to suppress it. "Yeah, whatever you say. It's your call, Jack."

Ed Tracy, I learned, was active behind the scenes, trying to talk Donald out of dealing the game on the belief that it was too risky to be good play. That position struck me as curious, since our competition elsewhere would have been thrilled to get Kashiwagi. John Groom, the vice-president Donald had failed to woo from Caesars, called us expressly to offer his advice. He concurred with the element of risk, but he agreed that the potential win for the casino outweighed that.

Baccarat is an extremely volatile game. The house advantage over time is lower than in practically any other bet in the casino (along with the "pass line" bet in craps, where the bettor wagers that the thrower will roll his number before he rolls a "7" and loses the dice).

The game is based on the European card game *chemin de fer* of James Bond and Monte Carlo fame. Baccarat is a test of nerves, a game of great theatrical and psychological intensity because the odds of winning or losing are dead even. Each hand pits "banker" against "player." Both draw two cards, with the winning hand the one that comes closest to nine. Bettors at the table may wager on either "banker" or "player." A third bet, the "tie," is the least likely and pays at 8 to 1 odds.

Baccarat employs eight decks of cards, and as in blackjack, they are shuffled and stacked inside a "shoe," an enclosed dispenser, usually made of clear plastic. The shoe is passed in counterclockwise order among the bettors at the table, who deal the hands to "banker" and "player" until the "banker" loses, at which time they must pass the shoe either to the highest "player" bettor or, in the absence of any wagers on "player," the next bettor. The bettor holding the shoe sees the "banker's" cards and passes them face down to the croupier, who announces the total. The "player" hand belongs to the highest bettor there, who follows the same procedure.

Baccarat is chancy from the casino's standpoint because the house covers all winning bets, which can far exceed the losing bets on a hand-by-hand basis. Plus, as noted above, the casino's advantage is relatively slight compared with other games. In the case of "player," the house advantage is 1.36 percent—that is, the portion of the total wager theoretically sacrificed to the house over time. (By comparison, blackjack affords the house a variable edge of 2 percent to 7 percent; roulette, 5.6 percent; the slot machines, from 5 percent to 17 percent; and craps, as high as 20 percent.) The "banker" bet is even lower, 1.17 percent, and for that the casino is compensated with a 5 percent commission on those winning bets.

Kashiwagi always bet $200,000, never more, never less, though he shifted his wagers from "banker" to "player" with no apparent pattern. Covering those stakes in what is essentially an even-money proposition was a bold move for the house, but a mathematically correct one. The key element was time. The longer the play continued, the more likely it was that the slim house advantage would assert itself.

Kashiwagi was the largest gambler ever to come to Atlantic City. That he chose Trump Plaza was an enormous coup for us. It capped years of effort in the international market; it was the perfect complement to the world-class image we were marketing, and enhanced the Trump image of elegance and excitement. Developed properly, Kashiwagi's play could propel Trump Plaza into an entirely new realm of action. Two trips a year from a player of this magnitude, joined by the three to five others like him in the world, and Trump Plaza would know the difference between the great revenue months we were already experiencing and spectacular ones. The Mirage won $40 million its first month in business. The best we'd ever done was $31 million in August 1989. With Kashiwagi and a handful of other top international players, $40 million months could be a reality for us, too.

We knew Kashiwagi had lost $6 million to Steve Wynn in Las Vegas in December. But only days before he arrived at Trump Plaza he brutalized the Diamond Beach Casino, a small establishment in Darwin, Australia, for $19 million. That sum represented the casino's entire average win for the year. He had broken their bank. Oddly enough, they had him beat for $10 million at one point. He was down to his last bet—$200,000, one more hand—when his luck changed and he swung back and in four hours won it all. If you believed in streaks, Kashiwagi was riding a searing hot one. But I never questioned for a moment whether we should deal his action. We had the bankroll to weather the stakes. The key, as I've said, was how long he stayed at the table. He promised us at least four days of steady play.

We had done our homework and were prepared when, one morning early in the second week of February, a limousine deposited Akio Kashiwagi and his partner, a Japanese man we knew only as Darryl, at the porte cochere. Our best suite, the "Chairman Suite" at the top of the hotel, a bi-level with two bedrooms, hot tubs, a grand piano, butlered service and spectacular ocean views, was ready. A translator was waiting. Security was coordinated round the clock to ensure his protection. An elevator remained on standby to take him upstairs to his suite and down again to the casino to play. We hired a Japanese chef whom we put up temporarily at the hotel. Cocktail servers were on call to serve only Kashiwagi in the baccarat pit.

As it turned out, his needs were simple. He ate tuna fish sandwiches and drank tea. During breaks between shoes, he requested a hot towel and lemon to wash his face and hands.

His one overriding concern was privacy. He dreaded notoriety and wanted no publicity associated with his visit. I made it clear in our strategy sessions in preparation for his arrival that we were to act as though it was business as usual in the baccarat pit: no pacing the floors, no crowds, no spectators, above all, no press.

Following his modus operandi, he did not come down from his suite until evening. He was dressed simply in suit pants and a sport shirt. He was escorted into the baccarat pit and shown to his table. A tray stacked with $5,000 chips was brought to him. He sat down to gamble. I entered the pit during a break in the first shoe to greet him. He smiled and nodded and returned the greeting in Japanese. I told him I hoped that at some point we might have dinner together. He said he would like that. Then I went upstairs alone to Roberto's, our Italian restaurant, for dinner. Afterward, as I finished my coffee, I called down to the pit for a report. Kashiwagi was ahead $2 million. I left the restaurant, stopped at my office and then returned to the casino floor. At most a half hour had passed. We were up $2 million—a $4 million swing in 30 minutes.

So it went the rest of the night, $200,000 a hand, every hand, hour after hour. The swings were wild.

Late that night, I called Donald with an update. "We're up two and a half million."

"Terrific, Jack, terrific. This is great, isn't it?" he said.

"Yeah, this is great, because as time goes on, the better the odds of beating this guy for big money. . . . Donald, I feel like we're going to tattoo this guy for $6 to $10 million." And I was certain we would. I was not cocky about it. But I felt lucky. Our dealers at the table told me they felt lucky. We all had a good feeling about it.

"Well, look, Jack. Keep me posted. Call me. Just keep me posted."

"Donald, that's really pointless because I'm telling you the swings are going to be incredible. I will let you know, okay?"

"Yeah, that's good, Jack. Just keep me posted."

At 2 A.M., with only two hours left before closing, we were

still ahead of him by about $2 million. He had played for nearly eight hours straight, exactly as we were told he would. But by three o'clock, we were up only $600,000. Then Kashiwagi won 23 hands in a row. When the casino closed at 4 A.M., we were in the hole for $4 million.

Donald called me the next morning for an update. I told him where we stood. I was concerned but I wasn't worried. All that mattered was keeping Kashiwagi at the table.

But Donald was clearly agitated on the phone. "How could that happen?" he asked.

"What do you mean, Donald? That's the game."

"But do we keep playing to this guy? Should we throw him out?"

"Absolutely not," I said. "That's crazy."

"Well, have you considered when you're going to cut this guy off?"

"No, I haven't even thought about that yet."

"Christ, what are you going to do if he wins another $4 million?"

"Well, he will win another $4 million then," I said. "Donald, the key is, the guy is going to stay here and play. I still think we're okay. Everything's fine."

But everything was not. Word leaked to the *Atlantic City Press* of the presence in town of the highest-stakes player in the world. Soon a reporter was on the scene. When Kashiwagi heard, he became anxious. But he returned to the pit that night to play. His streak continued. In two hours he won another $2 million.

Media exposure was the last thing we needed. In Las Vegas these kinds of things are treated more or less routinely, especially since press coverage tends to scare this type of player away, but in Atlantic City the reporters were buzzing around, asking for interviews. We tried to explain the delicate position we were in, but to no avail.

Then to make matters worse, there was a blowup in the pit

between Kashiwagi and Darryl. Darryl had been sitting with him the whole time he played, betting the "banker" and "player" hands along with him and occasionally taking the shoe during a losing streak. Word reached me that he'd made a passing remark about Kashiwagi being up $6 million and in great shape. In a huff, Kashiwagi stood and reprimanded his partner in Japanese. "What is this?" he shouted. "Why are you counting my money? Who is counting every hand? Are they counting every hand?"

We were very sensitive to Kashiwagi's superstitions in this regard, and we had made every effort to avoid giving that impression.

"No, no," Darryl replied, suddenly realizing his mistake. "No, it was me. I was counting. I thought you would want to know."

But Kashiwagi was furious. "Why is everybody so worried about where I am? What is going on?" He refused to play, left the table and returned to his suite.

Ed Tracy had been calling the pit and regularly asking Ernie Cheung for updates. He was told of this latest development. Of course, so was I. But before I had a chance to inform Donald myself, he'd already heard from Tracy.

"What's going on, Jack? I told you this was bad play. See? The guy quit. He's not playing anymore," Donald said.

"Donald, I don't know for certain that he quit. Yes, he's off the table and he's up in his room. But he may be down in an hour; he may not come down at all tonight, I don't know."

At 11 P.M., he did, in fact, come back down to play again. He was at the cage making preparations when he got a call from a friend in Tokyo. The friend read him an article in a Japanese newspaper about his phenomenal win in Australia. A similar story in the *Press* was then brought to him. That was enough for Kashiwagi. He returned to his suite and instructed us to make airline reservations: he was leaving.

I had gone home in the interim and was sitting down to a late supper when Donald called me. "He quit, Jack. What the fuck? See? I told you this guy was bad play."

"He quit?" I said. "Well, okay, that's news to me. No one told me he quit. I just came home for dinner and I'm going to go back there tonight. Don't worry about it. The guy will probably start to play again. I know he's not scheduled to leave for two more days."

Donald said harshly, "Well, I'm telling you he quit . . . and he's up $6 million."

I called Ernie and got the story. When I called Donald back and told him, he wasn't angry; it was more like disgust. "Oh, God, six million dollars! What's the story? You told me he was going to play for four days. . . ."

Needless to say, I was just as disappointed as Donald.

Kashiwagi left the next morning at five. He assured us he would return, though, and we talked briefly about setting something up in the near future. I made sure we had staff to see him out, and we presented him with a small gift. We provided a limousine to the airport. But no sooner had he left the building than I told Ernie, "The faster you get this guy back, the better off we're going to be."

Ernie was optimistic. "No question, Jack. We'll get him back. It's just a matter of time."

Kashiwagi's win was a record for Atlantic City. It was a painful note for Trump Plaza so early in the year. The hit contributed to knocking $3 million off our first-quarter results. While our "drop," all the cash and markers placed in circulation, was $84 million in February and the highest in town, our win for the month fell to $19.6 million. Naturally the loss to Kashiwagi wreaked havoc with our hold percentage, which plummeted to 7.6 percent, the worst in town by far, less than half the next lowest house. So now the second-guessers emerged, Donald in the forefront. He was gracious in front of the press, telling them philosophically, "He played the game, and he won."

But to me he said, "What the hell are you doing? You know, Tracy told me this guy was bad play from the beginning. He told me he talked to some people at Caesars. Do you know what they said? They said they would never have dealt to him; as a matter of fact, they stopped dealing to him. I don't understand why we did this."

I assured Donald that given the same opportunity I would deal to Kashiwagi again. My biggest concern was knowing how difficult it would be to overcome the loss, given the unrealistic budget that had been imposed on us for 1990. We had hoped a player like Kashiwagi would help us realize a ridiculous goal like $92 million in operating income. I hid my concern from the staff, but I did not sleep well for days after he left. All I knew was that I wanted him back at Trump Plaza and our $6 million with him.

17

"Good publicity is preferable to bad, but from a bottom-line perspective, bad publicity is some-times better than no publicity at all."

—DONALD J. TRUMP

t would have been impossible to predict the magnitude of the media coverage of the separation of Donald and Ivana Trump in February 1990. At first, Donald was baffled by the sheer size of what even the *New York Times* called "the most talked about and written about divorce proceeding in years." But then it was clear that he was having a ball with it. "The show is Trump," he proclaimed, "and the show is sold out."

The tabloids were in the front-row seats—"They Met in Church" . . . "Don Juan" . . . "Separate Beds" . . . "Best Sex I've Ever Had" . . . "Oh, Baby! Is She Mommy Marla?" It was all so deliciously steamy in the spotlight, and the papers gorged themselves on the wily, flamboyant billionaire, the loveless marriage, the glamorous wife, scorned and wretched, secret love nests with a buxom 26-year-old model and aspiring actress. The headlines chased Donald for five straight days. He was surprised but delighted about it all. "Geez, Jack, did you read the papers today? It's just incredible. It's incredible. It's unbelievable what they're printing."

I said, "I think you better do what you can to lay low."

But I knew my suggestion made no impact at all. Publicity was Donald's element. But what concerned me was that he had convinced himself that the media frenzy was good for business. It was additional evidence that his judgment was dangerously skewed.

"What are you talking about, Jack?" he said. "This is great for business. I think this is great for business. Don't you? Don't you think this is great for business?"

"Donald, I'm being honest with you. I think this is going to hurt us."

"C'mon, Jack. It's the best thing that ever happened to us."

"This is different," I said.

"Nah, I disagree."

"I'm only saying this, Donald, because a lot of our customers are married too."

He replied, "The way this works is, this'll bring all the men in. They're going to want to be with Trump. Jack, this is good for business. Trust me. I know."

That taught me, if I didn't know already, that Donald was so self-centered and unfeeling that he put his business ahead of everything else. His children, especially his eldest son, Donny, Jr., were devastated. But there was a business advantage to be gained, or so he thought, and he continued to publicly promote his affair. His family, it seemed, was expendable. He went on record describing Marla as "better than a 10." "Denigating the competition," as he described the deal-maker's art, he attacked his wife as "arrogant" and "another Leona Helmsley" (the hotel queen he'd previously described as "a vicious, horrible woman" and "a disgrace to humanity"), even as his mother and his sisters and sister-in-law turned out to comfort Ivana at a tearful birthday reunion at La Grenouille in New York on Valentine's Day.

For her part, Ivana played the role of the wronged wife and mother to the hilt. "I am afraid," she told her friend Liz Smith.

"I know the children and I will be Donald's next 'project.' I know how he is. He will simply zero in on us."

Sloshed around in the press as it was, the spectacle severely damaged Donald's image. Suddenly he looked like an ogre, emotionally abusive, self-centered, a money-grubber squabbling over a $25 million settlement with his wife, a mere 1 or 2 percent of his perceived billions.

What was of concern to me was the blow it struck at our business. An integral part of our marketing strategy had always been directed at fostering relationships with our high rollers and with their spouses through a variety of entertainment and social events. It was a conscious strategy designed to dispel the seamy cigar-smoke image of the gambling junket and the age-old association between gaming halls and prostitution. In one week, Donald was tearing that down, leaving an impression that Atlantic City and the Trump casinos were places where the billionaire cheated on his wife with a much younger model. The wives of some of our biggest players expressed disgust over the whole affair. It soured many of the male customers as well. One of my executives at Trump Plaza always said that the key to working for Donald was finding a way somehow to like him. Donald was making that harder than ever.

One evening early in March, as the tabloid frenzy had begun to quiet down, Donald called me at about seven o'clock. I was still in my office. He was in his car, he said, on the way to his parents' house in Jamaica Estates in Queens.

"So what's up?" he asked rather aimlessly.

"Not much, Donald. What's going on? What are you doing?"

"I'm with the kids. We're going to eat dinner," he said.

I could hear them in the background, jumping and playing and having a good time, as children will in the back seat of a car, even if it is a limousine. I told him, "That's good. That's real good."

"Yeah," he said with a small chuckle. Then he must have

moved away from the phone because I heard him holler, "Ivancka! Stop that!" But whatever she was doing, the little girl continued laughing and shouting merrily.

He mentioned a billboard he'd passed on the highway, a Trump Castle billboard. He was unhappy with the message and the colors, he said. "You know how this billboard should look, right?" he asked.

"Yes," I said.

"Then you'll fix it for me."

"Sure, Donald."

That's how it was with him. Whenever he wanted the Castle to do what he wanted, he invariably called someone at the Plaza because he knew we understood what he wanted.

"Jack, do me a favor. Call the people at the Castle. Tell them to get their shit together. . . . Donny! Sit down! Don't do that. . . . Tell them what I want on this board. You guys know what I want on a billboard."

"I'll take care of it," I said.

"Ivancka . . . I want you to sit down right now. Get away from there . . . Donny! Shut that window!"

I laughed to myself as I listened. I felt happy for him. I said, "Hey, Donald, I'm glad to see you're spending some time with the kids."

"Yeah, this is good for them. . . . Donny, don't do that, I said! . . . Yeah, and it's good for me, too; it's good for me to be with them."

When I hung up the phone, I shook my head. Well, what do you know, I thought. He *is* a human being.

Although Donald refused to believe it, the criticism of his personal conduct was affecting business. In Japan, Donald had represented an almost godly image of wealth and power. Now suddenly he was more than human. With the news of his separation, investors with whom he had negotiated a tentative sale of the Plaza Hotel shied away from the scandal.

The first week of March, *Newsweek* brought it all home with the headline: "Divorce Isn't His Only Worry . . . Souring markets and a soiled corporate image could spell trouble for Donald Trump's empire." The securities analyst Marvin Roffman of Janney Montgomery Scott was quoted again, still skeptical about the Taj Mahal's and Donald's chances. "He will have to do on a steady basis something that no other casino in the world has ever been able to do," Roffman said.

Donald countered with the announcement that Marla was coming to the grand opening of the Taj Mahal on April 5. Donald calculated that the news of Marla's appearance would guarantee that an army of journalists from around the world would descend on Atlantic City for his newest and grandest venture. His family was outraged, as I was told, and it was only Fred Trump's blunt warning that he would not attend the opening that forced his son to keep her away.

By then Donald had seen our poor revenue figures for February. He called me in an angry mood. "Look at your shitty results," he said.

"Donald, did you forget about Kashiwagi?" I said.

"Yeah, but you're not number one in town anymore."

"Yes, it was a wash with Kashiwagi. But back Kashiwagi out and we are still number one by a landslide."

"Oh, yeah," he said, "yeah, okay."

Then he mentioned the Rolling Stones again, and asked for a progress report on our lawsuit against the rock group. He had already called his brother-in-law John Barry's law firm and spoken to one of the attorneys there, who, in turn, had called me. The attorney and I had discussed it. I didn't believe we had sufficient grounds to undertake the large expense of a lawsuit, and I heard nothing to indicate otherwise.

This was the message I delivered to Donald that day. But again he refused to accept it. "I'm taking it to McGahn," he said.

Sure enough, I got a call one day from a member of Pat

McGahn's law firm, who asked me for the paperwork on the deal and informed me that they were taking the case.

Meanwhile, the Taj Mahal lumbered toward opening day.

On February 29, the casino passed a physical inspection and the New Jersey Casino Control Commission declared the building in compliance with state regulations.

After Mark's death there had been considerably less enthusiasm among Trump Plaza's employees to be part of the Taj. The Taj personnel department was swamped with tens of thousands of job applications from elsewhere. Neither Robert nor Donald had any management expertise, and neither understood how important even one midlevel manager could be to a casino operation. As opening day approached, Taj officials were simply picking up the phone and ordering us to send them whomever they required.

Responding to Wall Street's concern about the $47 million interest payment due in May, Walt Haybert told the *Atlantic City Press*, "Our project is on time, on budget, and there is no question that interest will be paid." He added, "For us to do a million a day is not a concern whatsoever. Last year, Trump Plaza generated $836,000 a day. For us to generate an additional $160,000 a day with twice the capacity, we don't view that as a problem at all."

Walt had called me in January to renew the request for our customer lists. The Taj brain trust had been scratching for months for potential players—all kinds, high-end, middle and low—and in desperation was turning again to the only sources it could think of, Trump Castle and Trump Plaza.

I said, "Walt, it can certainly be done if that's the decision that has been made. But I think it's an issue I need to discuss with Robert to make sure all the t's are crossed and i's dotted."

Really, I hoped to stall. Politically, it was a delicate issue. Legally, it could be explosive. I did not want to turn over the lists until I could get a conclusive legal opinion I trusted. And so we let the matter rest until a meeting of all three presidents in February at Robert's temporary headquarters in a trailer on the island of Brigantine, just across Absecon Channel north of Atlantic City.

Robert opened the meeting by saying, "I'm aware of all the talk about this. But we need the transfer of the lists."

Of particular interest were Trump Plaza's middle- to upper-middle markets, the $10,000 to $15,000 players with whom we'd enjoyed great success. The Taj needed more of that type of customer than any place in town. But they were looking for anything they could get, top end to low end, qualified lists or unqualified—even the lists pulled from the entry forms of a million-dollar promotional giveaway Trump Castle was sponsoring.

I took up the same argument Steve and I had mulled over the previous summer. "I've got some concerns from the standpoint of the bondholders," I said. "It just doesn't sound right on the surface that we can do this. I'll be honest with you, my people internally are very uncomfortable with it. We need some assurance that they're not going to be liable for this, particularly at the lower levels, because they're very concerned."

Actually, I had already looked into it, and I was satisfied that, if we received compensation, we were on safe legal ground. But how much compensation was adequate? That remained an open question.

So what happened even before the opening was exactly what Donald promised would never occur: the Taj was building a customer base at the expense of the other Trump casinos. To satisfy our bondholders, Robert did promise that six months after the opening, the Taj would transfer expanded lists back to the Plaza and the Castle, which theoretically would allow us to tap into the huge mass of people we all assumed would flow through the Taj in its early months. In the meantime, we were going to have to make the sacrifice.

Shortly after the disks were prepared and transferred, I stumbled on a bound copy of all our customer names and phone numbers. It had been transcribed from the disks. If it circulated, its contents would be revealed to anyone, without the safeguard of having to gain access to our computer code. I was curious, since there could be no legitimate reason for the existence of the book. And at the same time, I was furious. I confiscated it and placed it in a drawer in my desk.

On March 20, licensing hearings for the Taj Mahal were scheduled to begin before the Casino Control Commission. That morning, the *Wall Street Journal* quoted Marvin Roffman again. Asked about the Taj, he said, "When this property opens, [Trump] will have had so much free publicity he will break every record in the books. . . . But once the cold winds blow from October to February, it won't make it. The market just isn't there."

Donald fired off a letter to Janney Montgomery Scott threatening "a major lawsuit" unless their analyst retracted his statement. "Unprofessional," Donald called him, a "bad analyst," an "unguided missile."

Astonishingly, Janney caved in. Roffman, 50 years old, a securities analyst for 25 years, with 12 years covering the casinos for a host of clients, was ordered to sign a letter of apology to Donald Trump, which said in part: "Contrary to the presentation in the [*Wall Street Journal*] article, I have every hope that the Taj will ultimately be very profitable. . . . I do hope that you will forgive what has turned out to be a very unfortunate interview on my part."

Roffman signed the letter.

Satisfied, Donald let the matter drop. Roffman didn't. The next day he reconsidered and wrote a second letter retracting his apology. Janney fired him instantly, confiscated his files and escorted him out of their high-rise office building in downtown Philadelphia. The episode sent a chill through the securities industry. A

Michigan congressman called on the SEC to investigate. Donald was unmoved. I was in Hong Kong at the time aboard the *Trump Princess*, entertaining some prospective Chinese high-rollers and trying to elicit a buyer for Donald's high-priced floating mansion, which he was anxiously trying to unload. We didn't find a buyer. My wife, Lisa, called me and told me what happened. Donald called shortly after, and I asked him about Roffman. "Ah, that little shit," he said. "He doesn't know what he's talking about. He said some bad things. He's been out for me for years."

I said, "But with everything that's happened, Donald, do you think we want this kind of publicity?"

"Jack, this guy's always been bad. He's bad for the industry. They obviously got sick of him at his company because they got rid of him."

He never mentioned another word about it.

On March 29, the Taj Mahal was granted a license by the Casino Control Commission subject to completing a successful test run and receiving its certificate of operation. Within hours, Donald showed up in Atlantic City to host a rollicking pep rally for his 6,000 new Taj employees, complete with a laser light show, rock music blaring through speakers and a giant video projection of the property's "mascot," a Max Headroom-style genie named "Fabu"—short for "Fabulous"—who led the packed ballroom in choreographed cheers and exhorted the crowd to live up to the "Eighth Wonder of the World." The ballroom shook with cries of "Donald! Donald! Donald!" as he strode up the center aisle, waving and clasping hands, and took his place on the stage with Robert and Blaine, Harvey Freeman, Walt Haybert and Bucky Howard. The Trump mystique was still a force in the public's eyes. Donald looked pale and visibly tired under the lights. He turned to someone next to him and wondered aloud, "Am I paying all these people already?"

As long promised, "Trump Taj Mahal Casino Resort" was

ready to open its doors the following Sunday, April 1. But then Donald said no; it was April Fool's Day. Instead, on Monday, April 2, at 10 A.M., the casino staged its first test run, a state-mandated "play money" day. Players at its 167 blackjack, craps and baccarat tables were allowed to make a one-time exchange of $10 in cash for $100 in gambling scrip, with the win going to charity. The exception was the 3,000 slot machines, which were open for cash play. As customers poured in by the thousands to pull the handles and try their luck, problems were apparent almost immediately. Millions of dollars changed hands, bills for coin and tokens. The automated changemakers installed at the machines, upon which Donald had chosen to rely, were emptied in minutes. Hundreds more broke down. So many of the "trouble" lights were tripped atop the slot machines that Robert described the casino floor as resembling "a forest of candles." Slot attendants were overwhelmed by the demand for change and couldn't deliver it fast enough to the players, who were forced to abandon their machines and queue up in long lines at the only two manned change booths on the floor. But at 6 P.M., when the casino closed, the Taj's public relations office claimed the test run had gone flawlessly, and confidently predicted that the casino would be granted its certificate of operation ahead of schedule.

Earlier that afternoon, Donald had led a horde of reporters and TV crews on a tour of the mammoth property. He appeared relaxed and thoroughly pleased with his accomplishment. Effusive as always for the press, he pointed all around them to the year's output of marble from the quarries of Carrara in Italy and to the $400,000 in carpets imported from England and the $14 million in lavish cut-crystal chandeliers from Austria that hung above their heads.

The tour concluded on the Boardwalk, beneath the giant minarets atop the casino's long candy-colored facade. It was a gloomy, overcast day. Donald stepped outside and into the flashbulbs with his dark topcoat opened against a biting ocean wind. The cameras clicked away. He broke a stiff smile that always looks like a sneer, that crocodile's grin. If he was worried about his billion-dollar investment he didn't show it. But, of course, Donald never would. Or was it that his ears were still ringing with the din of millions of nickels and quarters and silver dollars feeding the hungry slot machines inside?

If the Taj Mahal would never make the annals of architectural wonders, it would survive as nothing short of a miracle of large-scale construction. Donald truly believed the world would hold its breath in the face of what he had done. He had silenced the critics, he had succeeded where Crosby and Resorts had failed, he had beaten Merv and frozen out Pratt. Now he had to believe he would finally vanquish Wynn. It's no wonder that the Taj Mahal captivated him, just as it was now drawing to itself tens of thousands of gamblers and sightseers and journalists at that very moment to witness its birth. If it was only an investment, it might have been indistinguishable from Donald's other towers of glass and steel. But the Taj Mahal was more. It was an extension of his personality. As surely as it drained every last ounce of his wealth to come into being, so the restless parvenu from Queens needed the Taj Mahal, as though to verify for himself and the world that his wealth existed for that time and for always. It was a creature of his unbridled ambition, its very personification. As he once confided to a doubting friend, "I have to have it. It's the biggest hotel in Atlantic City. I can't let anyone else have it but me."

The casino industry's revenues for March confirmed every-one's worst fears. The recession was making itself felt. The At-lantic City gaming market had peaked, at least for the time being, and was settling into stagnation. The win for all eleven casinos was $234 million, a meager 0.2 percent increase over the same month in the previous year—"as flat as yesterday's glass of beer," observed Al Glasgow. The figures for the first quarter showed total win at all the properties of $654.4 million, a $2 million decrease from 1989. The industry as a whole reported a $4.3 million net loss, a $10 million decline from the previous year's $6 million first-quarter profit.

"It becomes even more obvious that the Trump Taj Mahal's entrance into the Atlantic City marketplace this month is critical to citywide gaming revenue growth," Glasgow said in *Atlantic City Action*. He predicted the Taj would break all records with $42 million in win its first month. "For those who say the Taj Mahal and Donald Trump will never make it. . . . Guess what? He already has. . . . Trump Taj Mahal is now holding the dice."

18

 "In my life, there are two things I've found I'm very good at: overcoming obstacles and motivating good people to do their best work."
—DONALD J. TRUMP

At ten o'clock the next morning, Tuesday, April 3, the Taj was scheduled to reopen for a second test run. At the tables, the "play money" day had gone well, and the state cleared those games for gambling with cash and chips.

I awoke that morning before dawn as I usually do and ran six miles. I couldn't help but think of Steve and Mark and Jon that morning. It was going to be a perfect spring day, sunny and warm. Mark would have loved it. This was to have been his day. Donald had made a significant public display after the crash. The Taj's sparkling new Trump Arena was renamed the "Mark G. Etess Arena." (Later, during the grand opening, Mark's ten-year-old son, Scott, lingered in the arena almost the whole night. He told me, "I feel Daddy here.")

Lisa and I were still undecided about attending the grand opening. But the opening of the Taj seemed insignificant to me, professionally speaking. I was an outsider and so was my staff at Trump Plaza, and we were made to know it. Steve and Mark and I had talked every day, filling each other in, discussing ideas, seeking

271

advice. But since October my knowledge of what was going on at the Taj was limited to that of an outsider.

I mentioned it to Lisa that morning over coffee in the kitchen. "This is really funny," I said as I folded the morning paper and put it on the counter. *TAJ: OPEN SESAME!* the *Atlantic City Press* proclaimed, lifting one of Donald's own billboard slogans. *Huge Crowds Flood Casino on 1st Day*, it said. *Donald the Biggest Attraction.* His name possessed the power of myth. Maybe he was right in presuming that the public wanted to believe in it.

Lisa looked up at me over her coffee. "What's that?" she asked.

"I think the papers can be misleading," I said. "Opening a property is a nightmare. Whether things are going good or not. Everybody's working long, hard hours. You've got problems. Even if the state is saying everything's fine, you just know they're giving you a bad time."

"Well, thank God you're not involved," she said.

"Yeah, I really don't need the headaches right now."

I was in the middle of a meeting with some members of my executive staff at Trump Plaza, about three hours into the day, when my secretary, Joellen Seville, poked her head into the conference room and looked at me. "Donald's on the phone," she said. "He wants to talk to you right now."

That's odd, I thought as I walked briskly back to my office. It must be important. Usually he'd wait for a call-back if I was in a meeting.

"Jack, I'm at the Taj. . . . I got big fucking problems over here." He spoke rapidly and harshly. I was familiar with that tone; I knew he was furious. "I've been in meetings with the state all morning. They're not going to let me open. I've got a bunch of fucking idiots down here."

"Okay . . . Donald. Wait a second . . ."

"You have to come down here and straighten this out. I mentioned your name. I told them I'm bringing you in and you're going to get this squared away. Jack, you're my ace in the hole. I've got people waiting to get into the casino. This is embarrassing."

"Donald, what's the problem?"

"Nobody knows what they're doing. . . . I'm going to fire all these assholes."

"What is it? Is it accounting?"

"I don't know. There are problems in the cage." He was referring to the coin bank.

"Donald, listen . . ."

"No, Jack. Just get down here now." He hung up.

I put the phone down not knowing what to think. But if there were problems in the cage, I knew I needed Tony Rodio, our casino controller, an expert in casino accounting procedures.

Joellen intercepted him on his way to lunch. I told him about Donald's call. He didn't want to go. "Will this take long? I've got a meeting at four o'clock," he said.

I considered his question. "Nah, it can't be a big deal. We'll lend them a hand and be back in an hour."

At 12:30, security called up to say our limousine was waiting. Downstairs, Tony pressed me for details. "I don't know, Tony. An hour or two," was all I could say as we climbed into the back of the stretch Lincoln and sped north on Pacific Avenue.

We were there in ten minutes. We turned right onto Virginia Avenue, past tall white colonnades guarded by nine-ton faux marble elephants. It was the first time I had seen the Taj Mahal this close. The hotel tower was so high the top was hidden in mist. It was magnificent, gleaming in the sunlight. Its long glass shafts were a dazzling blue, as if the sea and sky had been poured inside.

From the hotel to the Boardwalk, a fabulous neon avenue unfolded, wrapping around lavish fountains and disappearing under a broad archway that proclaimed "Trump Taj Mahal" in flashing red lights. Everywhere last-minute preparations were under way. Vans and pickup trucks still obstructed the driveway. Painters were touching up, electricians were focusing the lights, janitors were busily sweeping up behind them. And all of it amid a fantasy of excess and expense: everything was awash in thick candy colors—the liquid lines and undulating curves and scallops that stated its Oriental theme, the white battlements crowned with 70-foot minarets, each studded with fiberglass jewels. For sheer magnitude I had never seen its equal. The sidewalk at the porte cochere was lined with tourists and gawkers, pointing this way and that and moving in and out among the workmen.

In the midst of this carnival I spied Lynwood Smith and Jim Farr, Donald's burly Atlantic City bodyguards. They rushed over when they saw the car and met us at the curb. Lynwood shook his head. "Jack, they got a real mess in there," he said as he escorted us into the hotel lobby. "You won't believe what's going on."

At first, I didn't. The lobby was impressive and enormous. It was sheathed in white marble. The carpet was richly woven in lavender and gold and pink. The front desk must have been 75 yards long. Behind it were reservation clerks and cashiers in shiny maroon coats. The doormen were arrayed in high plumed turbans, embroidered waistcoats and gold sashes.

Then I saw the first sign of crisis. As we turned right and made for the casino floor we ran into hundreds of angry people who had been waiting three hours to get in. They were jeering and catcalling: "Donald! Donald!"

"C'mon . . . open up!" they demanded. It was almost a chant.

One woman cried, "Whatsa matter, Donald? Ain't ya got enough money?"

Lynwood and Jim each took one of my arms and one of Tony's and together we drove a wedge through the crowd. In the middle of it, Lynwood looked over his shoulder at me. "This is nothing," he said. "You should've seen it an hour ago."

We pushed through to the casino entrance. Two uniformed security guards saw us and quickly pulled back a velvet rope to let us pass. We walked down three short carpeted steps into the largest gambling palace I had ever seen. Here in this one huge room was nearly one-fourth of Atlantic City's entire gaming capacity. Row after row of green felt tables, too numerous to count. Phalanxes of slot machines, thousands of them, standing like an army at silent attention. Behind each table stood a dealer in a black brocaded vest. Cocktail servers in harem pants and pink fezzes and veils waited at their assigned stations. Everything was splashed with the light from giant clouds of crystal chandeliers high overhead. They were suspended below a great barrel-vault ceiling that blazed with gold leaf and hundreds of mirrors. Save for the dealers and waitresses, the room was empty. There was a dead silence. The broad aisles were deserted. It was like a vast, ornate mausoleum.

Lynwood led us along one wall, about 25 yards, to the security podium. Next to it, the Casino Control Commission maintained a booth. Up ahead I saw Donald near the booth in a huddle of maybe 150 men and women in business suits, Taj executives mostly, all whispering somberly among themselves. Donald was talking with commissioners Pat Dodd and Kenneth Burdge, and Tony Parillo, director of the Division of Gaming Enforcement, and Dino Marino, the division's operations chief. The conversation appeared pleasant enough from a distance. Robert stood off to one side with Harvey Freeman. Bucky Howard was there, so was Nick Ribis, Donald's senior Atlantic City attorney. Strangely, I didn't see the Taj's president, Walt Haybert.

Odder still was how everyone turned and looked at me. Some seemed hopeful, others bewildered.

Since we had no official status at the Taj, Tony and I had to present our gaming licenses at the security podium in order to receive temporary access badges authorizing us to operate on the casino floor.

While we waited, Nick saw me and came over. "Jack, thank God you're here," he said. "Donald is going crazy. This place is so fucked up. You've got to get this fixed."

Donald's infamous temper was clearly Nick's biggest worry. He couldn't tell me much more. But I began to get the sense that the operation was in the throes of a total breakdown. Nick told me that Don Wood, the vice-president of finance, was carried out that morning, literally carried out, on a stretcher and rushed to the hospital. A nervous collapse, brought on by fatigue. Which only threw Donald into a rage. The way he saw it, one of his top executives was a weakling. He was talking about wholesale firings. Nick was in a panic.

I greeted Robert, who was standing nearby. "What's going on? Is this as bad as it looks?" I asked him. Robert was calm, as always. He shrugged. "I don't know, Jack. It doesn't look good."

It was the sight of Harvey that was the most unsettling. Here was the seasoned veteran of Donald's greatest financial campaigns, the senior among his top lieutenants, and he was gazing at the carpet and muttering to me, and to himself, it seemed. "Not good," he was saying. "This is not good." He was mumbling about "make it or break it." He told me, "You don't know how big this is. We can't afford not to be making money this weekend. We've been spending like crazy. . . . We've got to reverse this."

Immediately I started over toward Donald. He had seen me and met me halfway. He looked haggard, which wasn't like him. His hair was hanging a bit, as though he had been running his hands through it. His suit jacket was wrinkled at the vents and creased at the knees and elbows. "Jack, you've got to get me opened," he said, and as he does when he is angry, he repeated it: "You've got to get me opened." And he repeated it again. Up close, I saw his eyes were lined and tired. My god, the man is really sweating this one, I thought. The heat is on and he looks terrible.

I said, "Donald, I don't know what your problems are at this point. I might get you opened in thirty minutes. I might get you open in three hours. But first—"

"No," he interrupted. "That can't be. . . . It can't be. Fifteen minutes, Jack. You've got to get this place open in fifteen minutes. Let's shoot for one thirty."

I knew it was useless to discuss it further with him. "Fine, Donald," I said. "Give me a few minutes, and I'll be back to give you a report."

I sought out Dino, whom I had worked with closely over the years and knew well. Dino was strict in enforcing the gaming laws, but he tempered that with a keen understanding of the business we were in. "The problem is that you folks cannot tell us how much money you have on the floor," he said. "Nothing's been reconciled from the last shift. You've had twelve hours to do it, and you still can't tell us, and we're not going to let you open until you can give us a number. All we want is a number."

The problem concerned the slot machines. As it gradually became clear to me that day, the Taj was a disaster area of muddled and insufficient planning.

In a casino, money has to be transferred on an "imprest" basis—that is, cash and coin must be replenished in exactly the amount that is withdrawn. State regulations and the casino's own accounting demand it as a safeguard against skimming by employees. If a change booth is to issue $500 to customers, exactly 2,000 quarters must be transferred from the casino's central cash office, the "cage," to the booth. Over the course of opening day on Monday, the Taj was deluged with thousands of players. Over $5 million changed hands. For a variety of reasons—poor planning, inadequate training and the flawed physical design noted earlier—the Taj failed to track and reconcile the massive transfers of money from the master coin bank to various locations on the floor.

It was a matter of simple accounting. By Tuesday, it was a nightmare.

The magnitude of the problem wasn't apparent to me at first. My initial response to Dino and the state regulators was, "Okay, let me go back to the master coin bank and see where they stand."

I expected to find the coin bank humming with lots of people busy counting coin and tallying numbers. What I walked into was a room, maybe 15 feet by 30 feet, suffocating with cigarette smoke and filled with people muddling along with no apparent direction, some of them studying their watches, biding their time until their shifts ended, others simply getting up and walking out when it came time for their breaks.

"Who's in charge here?" I said. The supervisors eyed us suspiciously. No one answered at first. It seemed no one knew.

Tony and I looked at each other in amazement. Here, at the nerve center of the operational problems, there was no sense of urgency, no awareness of the angry crowds waiting to get into the casino, and worse, no concern that just beyond these walls, Donald Trump was pacing like a caged lion.

It was at the entrance to the master coin bank that I first saw Walt. He was standing alone. He looked ill. His cheeks were a sickly gray. His eyes were bloodshot. "You holding up all right?" I asked him. He slowly shook his head. I guessed that he had taken so much abuse from Donald that he would be of no help from here on. "I don't want to get in the way," he said listlessly. "You handle it. I'm going to lose my job anyway, Jack, so what the hell's the difference."

It was an uncomfortable moment, the president of one property stepping in to help the president of another, and in his property. But he seemed to know his days as president were numbered. I tried to reassure him by telling him I'd be back to give him a report. "Fine," he muttered and he walked away.

Tony and I began to question employees up and down the line. We learned that no one knew how much money was on the casino floor, or how much should have been out there, or how much was out there before they opened yesterday—not within $50,000, not even within $100,000.

Donald was waiting anxiously when I came out. I went directly to Dino. Donald followed and leaned over my shoulder. Robert, Harvey, Nick and the rest of the executive staff closed in behind him.

"This is going to take some time," I said.

"How long?" Dino asked.

My guess would have been six hours at least, maybe longer. But I knew Donald would never accept that. "Give me an hour," I said.

Donald looked at me with anger and incomprehension. "What the fuck is going on?" he asked me on the side. "Why can't we get this straightened out now?"

"Donald, we have to count some money, we have to collect some paperwork. It's going to take a little time."

"This is fucking crazy," he said, throwing up his hands. "I don't believe this. . . . I can't be embarrassed like this. I got celebrities coming, I got all my friends coming." Which was a point he would hammer at constantly over the next three days.

"I'll do the best I can, Donald," I said.

He continued to wear a blank expression. His patience was even shorter than his attention span. He simply wanted his casino open *now*. To his thinking, if that couldn't happen, then someone had to be fired. That was his response. "Jack, you fucking fire people. You don't like somebody, fire them. Whoever's responsible. I want them out of my building."

It was clear to me that he was exasperated beyond anyone's

ability to calm him down or reason with him. If the state officials weren't there, I'm certain he would have exploded. That fact was driven home to me by those closest to him, especially Nick Ribis, who was on the receiving end of his private rages and was continually warning me, "He's going nuts, Jack. I'm afraid he's going to fire half the staff."

"Nick," I finally said, "I can't worry about that right now. You handle him. I've got to get this place open."

The rest of the afternoon was taken up with isolating locations on the floor, tabulating dollar amounts and filling in and gathering the required documentation. We assembled as many competent employees as we could and supplemented them with experienced supervisors from Trump Plaza and Trump Castle. At every location there were huge variances between our calculations and the state's. The total amount was off by nearly $2 million. Technically, the Taj Mahal was in tremendous violation of state-mandated procedures. I knew our only choice was to accept the variances, and the fines for those violations the state might levy as a result, and try to negotiate compromises on the biggest gaps. It was that or shut down until we could sort it all out, which would be indefinitely. I took the plan to Dino. Reluctantly, he agreed.

Now I had to take it to Donald, who had stayed close to the commission's booth to receive my reports.

As I walked over, Donald had cornered Walt to ask him about Don Wood, who was being treated at Atlantic City Medical Center. "Was that asshole fired?" he asked. Walt hesitated a moment, then tried to placate him by saying that Don would be reassigned as soon as possible. Donald flew into a rage. "No! I want him fired! I don't want to see his fucking face in this building again!"

By now, Donald had departed even further from the actual operational mess, of which he had no understanding. He was convinced that the difficulties at the Taj were the fault of an executive staff that was "soft."

"I'm gonna fire all you assholes," he said to Walt. "I want pricks in here. I want people in here who are gonna kick some ass."

He had finished with Walt. Then he noticed me. "Yeah, Jack."

I began to explain about the variances and tell him we had devised a plan. He listened absently. Then Nick came over on his other side. He suddenly turned on Nick, glowering.

"You! What am I paying you for? You're supposed to have some clout with these guys," he said, meaning the regulators. "You can't get me through this opening. I'm going to bring in somebody who can. I'm bringing in . . ." and he thought for a moment. "Mickey Brown," he said, referring to G. Michael Brown, the influential casino attorney and former director of the Division of Gaming Enforcement. "He's coming down here. I'm bringing him down here. I want him involved."

Which only infuriated Nick. But Donald loved to play this game with the lawyers, pitting one against the other to watch them battle for a piece of his pocketbook. He was badgering Nick in this way all day and continued to do it for the rest of the week, telling him he wasn't going to pay him beyond his retainer for the long hours he was working at the Taj. With the threat of another attorney, Donald was turning the screws tighter.

At 3 P.M., I reported to Donald that we had whittled the variances down to $30,000, simply negotiating on compromise figures. At 3:30, Dino met with his boss, Tony Parillo, and the two commissioners and their staff. They studied the paperwork and realized, as I did, that we'd never know how much money was in the building until the end of the shift, if then. So they called us together to meet—me, Donald, Robert, Harvey, Nick and Walt.

"Okay," Dino said. "We don't like it, but you can open whenever you're ready."

Donald said nothing. He let out a slow breath.

We were standing in the exact spot where I had entered nearly four hours earlier with Donald's bodyguards at my side.

At 4:20, the uniformed security took up the velvet ropes and the Taj Mahal was open for its second day of business, six and a half hours late. What would have been thousands of gamblers that morning had dwindled to a few hundred.

But the press hadn't budged. As soon as the casino opened, they descended on Donald with microphones and flashbulbs and television lights. How was he going to explain this one, I wondered. He squinted in the lights. But he didn't flinch. "This is the most incredible thing I've ever seen," he announced. "Tremendous numbers were done, and in doing the numbers we just wanted to make sure things were perfectly reconciled."

Then one reporter asked about a report of problems in slot accounting.

"The only problem we had was that we made so much money we couldn't count it fast enough."

I moved out of view and shook my head in amazement. At least he didn't crumble, I thought, almost with admiration. It was pure Donald: It was quick and it bore little resemblance to the reality of the situation.

(But even the state would back him on this. In an interview later that day, Tony Parillo said the "ebb and flow" of cash was so enormous on Monday that it slowed accounting procedures until the end of the day. "It becomes a very lengthy process to reconcile," he said. The Taj Mahal exerted a power of its own. The stakes were tremendous, for Atlantic City and the state as well. No one wanted the bad publicity of a botched opening.)

After Donald gave his statement to the press, he turned away, his customary signal that the interview was over. With his back to them, he walked straight up to me. I had never seen him look the way he did at that moment. His features seemed pulled so tight they would tear apart. Yet his face was blank, washed of all expression. It was the face of a man who had come to the edge of a cliff and barely escaped falling over.

"Jack, from now on, you're in charge here," he said. "You got carte blanche. You fire whoever you want. . . . Look at these jerkoffs. . . ." He motioned to all the lawyers and executives milling around us. "You can fire anybody you want."

It was the greatest power Donald could think to bestow.

"You bring in anybody you want from the other properties," he continued. "This is too embarrassing. I'm getting out of here. I'm going back to New York. Don't leave here, Jack. You've got to get me through my opening. I can't be embarrassed."

"Donald, I'll do whatever you want," I assured him. "But what about Walt?"

"*Fuck* Walt," he said, and he turned and walked away. But not before he repeated the words so easily reminiscent of that first time we ever met in my office at Trump Plaza. "Don't leave here, Jack," he said. "Don't leave me."

I didn't see him anymore that evening. He took a limousine across town to Trump Castle and left from there by helicopter for New York. He didn't return until the morning of the grand opening on Thursday.

For a few minutes after he left, I stood alone on the casino floor. There was noise and excitement all around me. The crowds, the shouts from the craps tables, the rattle of coins, the tick of the cards, the bells sputtering when a jackpot hit. Yet I was alone. I wondered if he meant it, that I was to be the third president of the Taj Mahal. Mark used to joke that the Taj would break a few presidents' careers before it was through. I thought of Walt. How was I going to handle that? More than anything, I wanted to talk to Lisa. I was beginning to feel the anticipation I felt before a marathon. I was familiar with it: the thought of running for three or four hours, knowing there will come a point in the race when the pain is excruciating. You try to imagine how bad it will hurt so you can prepare for it. At the same time, you hope it never comes. But you know it will.

Don Wood recovered and would be all right, I learned later that night.

Then another tragedy struck. On top of all the other problems, some of the change banks at the end of the aisles had not been bolted down properly. One of them, weighted with hundreds of pounds of coins, tipped over on a female attendant, who had to be rushed to the hospital.

At about six o'clock, I finally got a chance to call my wife. "Honey," I said, "you're not going to believe where I am."

She was surprised, especially when I told her I wouldn't be coming home that night. As it turned out, I didn't get to sleep. We worked straight through, even after the casino closed at 4 A.M.

Donald, in the meantime, had virtually barricaded himself in his office at Trump Tower in Manhattan. My promise to stay was his ticket to escape the media in Atlantic City and the colossal failure of the Taj opening. It was typical of Donald's management style, though later I learned that he had pressing business in New York, too. He was locked in negotiations with a separate army of attorneys over another epic business deal that threatened to go sour—his $25 million nuptial agreement with Ivana.

Shortly after daybreak, I called Lisa again to tell her I'd be sending a car to the house to pick up a clean suit and some necessities.

At 6:30, Donald called.

"What's going on?" he said. "You getting it squared away?"

"Well, Donald, we've got real problems here. We've been at it all night."

He was surprised. "All night, huh? You didn't sleep?"

"No."

"You're my man, Jack. You're the best. You're going to get me through this."

"Yeah, we'll get you through it."

"You're going to get all my machines open today?"

"That's what we're shooting for," I said.

It was an element of doubt he didn't want to hear. He said nothing for a moment. I could sense his anger rising again. Then he asked, "What's Ribis doing? Is Ribis fucking this up? Are you watching what's going on?"

They were senseless questions and I didn't respond. Instead I tried to make him realize the seriousness of the problems in the slot areas.

"Well, did you fire anybody?" he asked.

"No, Donald."

"Fuck. . . . Whoever it is, find out who's responsible and get rid of them. Goddamn it, Jack. I told you that. You need people? I don't care who you take out. . . . I don't care. I don't care what happens at the Castle. . . . I don't care what happens at the Plaza. You take anything. You take equipment, you take people . . . whatever it takes, do it. This is the main priority. I've got to have all my machines open. I can't be embarrassed tomorrow. Tell everybody who comes over they're going to get big bonuses."

"We'll get you open, Donald," I said.

"You're the best, Jack. Just hang in there. Get me through this and I'll have a big bonus for you."

Then he hung up.

I didn't mention bonuses to anyone. I had recently been through that humiliating game with him myself. And it had happened before that I'd tell my staff to expect them, and then he'd invent reasons for not delivering them.

More frustrating, though, was the knowledge that Donald, even now, had no grasp of the enormous operational problems at the Taj Mahal. We still hadn't determined how much money was on the floor from the previous day. Now we had upward of 60,000 customers passing through. There was still no orderly mechanism in the place to get coin to the floor. Then the coin "scalpers" appeared, people who had bought change at Resorts or the Showboat and were selling it at a premium on the floor of the Taj. It was more an embarrassment than a harm. But Dino and the regulators were losing their patience.

Then about midday, Ed Tracy, the president of Trump Castle, showed up. His presence was a mystery at first until I began hearing complaints from the staff around me that he was making himself available to the press and answering questions, though his knowledge of the problems could only have been cursory at that point. Naturally, by virtue of his position, he was being quoted. The rumors were flying that he was going to succeed Walt as president of the Taj. Ed had been spoken of for months after the crash as a candidate for Steve Hyde's position as chief executive officer of Donald's Atlantic City empire. So was I. Robert was no fan of Ed's and used to say, when asked about Steve's position, that Ed would only get it "over my dead body."

When I raised the question with Robert on Wednesday and again on Thursday his position hadn't changed. "No way, Jack," he said. "Don't worry about it. It's not going to happen."

But Robert knew better than anyone that his brother's decisions and impulses were unpredictable and were easily swayed by whoever was closest to him at the moment. So Ed's high profile in the press was a constant irritation to him. He knew, as we all did, that Donald was likely to be more impressed with that than with complicated operational successes.

I was too busy to get involved with the press, which probably was a mistake. Even Nick Ribis took me to the side at one point that day and said, "You're keeping too low a profile on this. You've got to start returning phone calls. Start talking to the press."

But I didn't react, maybe because I hadn't slept in 36 hours. I did manage to snatch two hours' sleep Wednesday afternoon. It was a good thing. For the rest of the night we were locked in negotiations with the state over the best way to keep the casino open. It was inevitable that all or some of the slot machines would have to shut down. The only questions were when and how many. The lawyers were adamantly opposed to it. And they informed Donald.

At 11:30 that night, he called me.

"How are we doing, Jack? We straightened out?"

"We're trying to work it out, Donald," I replied. "You know the situation here. We have to discuss this. We've got major problems down here."

But he wasn't interested. "What's this I hear about shutting down half the machines? We're not going to do that, right? You're going to have all my slots open tomorrow."

"Donald, this is the story . . ."

"Wait, Jack. Are all my slots going to open tomorrow? I want every machine open. I can't have half my casino closed. I can't be embarrassed like that."

"What we're thinking of doing is this. We're talking about roping off some areas . . ."

"No."

"Donald, the state . . ."

"No, Jack. We can't. No way. We can't. It's impossible."

"But they're going to let us open on schedule, at ten. We're going to go till four. They're going to let us have a full day. But we've got to limit access in some areas. This way, we can get some flow out of the master coin bank and isolate some banks on the floor and get these variances straightened out. I mean, you won't believe some of these numbers. It's ridiculous. You've got to get some kind of service loop going on or you're going to have big problems."

But I was losing his attention.

"What the fuck is going on, Jack? Is this Ribis? Is it Walt? What do I have to do? Do I have to fire these motherfuckers?"

"Donald, let's examine the options."

"No, Jack. We can't. I'm going to lose millions."

He did stand to lose a lot of money, hundreds of thousands of dollars, at the least. But at the time it seemed insignificant compared with the long-term stability of a billion-dollar property. Up to now I had only heard vague reports of a financial crisis within the Trump Organization. But then the laywers' whisperings, Harvey's mutterings—it all began to take on form. I sensed that Donald's situation was truly grave and that the success or failure of the Taj Mahal was crucial.

Donald repeated again on the phone that he "was going to lose millions." I didn't press him for details, and he gave none. But he was insistent about one thing: "I can't afford it." Then he asked me, "Jack, do you think these problems would have existed if Steve and Mark were here today?"

"No, Donald, I don't."

"The truth, Jack."

"Donald, that is the truth. I really think Steve and Mark would have been able to focus the financial people on what happened historically, what happened when Trump Plaza opened; and I think they would have been a little more thorough in training these people."

"I disagree," he said. There was bitterness in his voice. "I think these are Hyde's people in here, and I think that Hyde's people are responsible for this problem."

Ironically, the spectacle surrounding Thursday's grand opening only worsened Donald's problems. Desperately now Donald needed to believe in his own image. It had been his weapon in outmaneuvering partners and opponents over the years, in mesmerizing the bankers and bondholders and politicians. Unwittingly he had now turned it on himself. He was becoming the victim of the fiction, of his "truthful hyperbole." Just as he fat-uously named the top floor of the Taj's 42-story hotel the "51st" and claimed that it was the tallest building in New Jersey, and boasted that scores of celebrities were coming to the grand open-ing, he could not really believe that "Trump" was facing financial disaster.

But Donald was in high spirits when his helicopter touched down on the roof of Trump Castle at 8 A.M. Thursday. A silver limousine was waiting downstairs in the porte cochere to whisk him across town to the Taj Mahal. He walked into the hotel lobby at about 8:30, surrounded by his top aides, some Taj ex-ecutives and public relations people and Lynwood, Jim Farr and four New York bodyguards. The extra muscle was justified. He didn't get more than a few steps inside when he was swamped by microphones, flashbulbs and television cameras. He had huge commitments that day, among them Governor Jim Florio, who was on his way from Trenton for a tour personally escorted by Donald.

The slot areas were still in disarray, which only got worse when the casino opened and people poured in by the thousands to play the machines.

Upstairs, portions of the hotel roof leaked, room keys didn't fit the locks, room service was at a standstill, diners were waiting for hours for meals in the restaurants, the top floors weren't getting enough water pressure, the spa, the health club, the stores, the child-care center and the beauty salon were incomplete and wouldn't open for months.

"Jesus, Jack, isn't this great?" he proclaimed when our paths finally crossed that afternoon in the hotel lobby. I was on my way to a meeting with the slot staff when I bumped into him and his entourage. He was in a jubilant mood, though he appeared tired, his eyes a bit swollen and his cheeks pasty. Beyond the protective ring of his bodyguards, customers and fans were leaning in and shoving and shouting for his attention. I started to explain our plan for roping off some of the slot machines, while all around us flashbulbs exploded and camera shutters snapped nonstop. "You're doing great . . . you're doing great," he said as the lights washed over his face and his tousled hair. "Thank God you're doing this for us, Jack. . . . This is wonderful." Then he recognized someone in the lounge nearby and he pushed away from me to go in that direction.

All day Donald moved about within this haze, beckoned by reporters and fans, people wishing him good luck and telling him that the Taj Mahal was the most magnificent building they had ever seen. I think he genuinely believed that he had built the "Eighth Wonder of the World." And if there were problems, well, they were insignificant.

As it turned out, the grand opening that night was remarkable for how few celebrities did attend. Fashion model Carol Alt, a friend of Donald's, with whom the tabloids had linked him romantically, was there. Former heavyweight champ Michael Spinks showed out of respect for the memory of his friend Mark Etess. He brought along some associates from Butch Lewis Productions. Top heavyweight contender Evander Holyfield was there with his managers, Dan and Lou Duva of Main Events. It was barren by contrast with the rumors the Taj's PR factory was churning out all week: names like Jack Nicholson, Tom Cruise, Liza Minnelli, Brooke Shields, Don Johnson, Melanie Griffith.

The only celebrity with anything approaching universal recognition was Merv Griffin. He had a prominent place in the front row of the VIP section at the base of the Taj's lavish entrance outside at the head of Virginia Avenue. Merv sat on one side of Donald. Fred and Mary Trump, Robert and Blaine, Donald's sisters, Elizabeth and Maryanne, a federal court judge, and Maryanne's husband, the attorney John Barry, sat on the other side. Merv and Donald appeared to be getting along fabulously.

A fireworks show was launched on the beach side of the building. We couldn't see it from the VIP section. By then it had gotten so cold that blankets were distributed and we wrapped ourselves in them. The laser that was supposed to cut a giant red ribbon on the building misfired, leaving shreds of ribbon still clinging to the walls. Then came an especially uncomfortable moment when indicted Atlantic City Mayor James Usry was introduced. He was booed for an entire minute.

Inevitably the sad moment came for Lisa and me when Donald paid tribute to Steve and Mark and their families. He thoughtlessly neglected to mention Jon. We were shocked. Beth McFadden, Jon's fiancée, was sitting with us. By the end of the ceremonies she was in tears.

It was the last time I saw Donald that night. He went to a massive reception in the grand ballroom on the second floor. I had planned to have dinner with Lisa, Donna Hyde and a couple of friends. But a worried Nick Ribis stopped me in a hallway to tell me that the state had run out of patience and was waiting for us in a suite of offices they had set up in the hotel.

We gathered Robert and Harvey and the rest of the emergency staff and found Dino and a group of officials waiting for us in their suites. The slot areas were unmanageable, they said, operations were atrocious, service was a joke, and we still couldn't give them an accurate accounting of funds. We had done the best we could to buy Donald time for his grand opening. Now Dino wanted a long-term plan of action. The Taj Mahal was not going to get a certificate of operation from the state, he said.

We met among ourselves. Even Robert and Harvey had to concede that the best we could do was open with half the machines, about 1,500. We had already arranged to bring in contractors for major modifications on the floor—particularly the installation of more change booths and additions to the cage and master coin bank areas. We brought the plans to Dino. Over the protests of his own staff, he agreed to let us open on Friday.

It was 1 A.M. now. I got down to the restaurant in time to have coffee with Lisa, Don and the others. I had to get some sleep myself. I finally did at four o'clock when the casino closed. I left instructions to be wakened at six.

Donald slept in his apartment at the Castle that night. From the looks of him the next morning, he slept well. Michael Jackson was coming so he was sure to salvage some face. But he was surely informed that night that the lights were going out on half his slot machines. He would be furious. One of his bodyguards was overheard that evening saying he had never seen the boss so angry. Donald bitterly complained to them, "I'm getting no fucking answers from anyone."

First thing that morning, Friday, April 6, we were told that Donald wanted to see us—me, Robert, Harvey, Walt and Nick—in Walt's office.

We assembled there at about 8:30. We waited fifteen minutes or so, passing the time cheerfully enough with some small talk. Then Donald burst in, moving rapidly, as he always does. Harvey got up to make room for him and Donald immediately took his seat. There were no greetings. He crossed one leg over the other and tugged once sharply at the crease of his pants. He looked rested and fresh in a blue pinstripe suit and pink silk tie. He couldn't have been up that long. His hair appeared wet, or he had slicked it with more than his usual amount of hair gel.

He gave a stern look around the room. At Robert, seated on his left, at Harvey, who was standing now, at Nick, at me, and finally his eyes met Walt's.

"Am I going to have all my slots open today?" he asked.

Nick and I attempted to answer. But he quickly fired off a second guestion.

"Did Wood get fired?"

Walt answered, "He's taking a couple of days' rest. We're thinking about a reassignment somewhere."

Donald nodded rapidly and glared at Walt. "Oh, I know . . . I know all about it. I know he's been moved to an office somewhere in the back of the house, where I wouldn't find him. Hasn't he?"

"Well," said Walt, "we removed him—"

Robert lowered his eyes.

"Wait," Donald interrupted. "What do you mean 'removed him'?" His jaw tightened. "Is the fucking guy working for me still? Is the motherfucker on my payroll? Does he have an office in the back of the house where he's being hidden?"

"Donald," Walt started.

"Shut the fuck up! I tell you to do something, you don't do it. You move the guy in the back. . . . This is the most fucked-up operation I've ever seen!

"I heard about this plan. I can't open all my machines today. I'm not going to have all my machines this weekend. You guys are fucking crazy! I don't want it! I want every machine open this weekend!"

I said, "Donald, this is a deal we negotiated with the state."

But he shook his head and looked at us with disbelief.

"There's really nothing we can do about this," Walt added.

Donald exploded. "You!" he shouted at Walt. "I've listened to you long enough. You know what? You're a fucking idiot!"

At that I got up and walked out of the room. I looked at Walt's secretary, who was at her desk outside. She looked at me. I just shook my head. Lynwood and Jim Farr were lounging in a couple of chairs by her desk. They appeared matter-of-fact about it all, though I knew that they must have been chuckling to themselves. They would get Donald's order to "escort" Don Wood out of the building. It was a detail they especially enjoyed.

I went to Robert's office to wait. Donald was still shouting at Walt. His voice followed me, echoing down the hallway and frightening the secretaries, who were standing outside their doors, listening wide-eyed.

"You're the one who fucked this place up the way it is!" he

shouted at Walt. "I never wanted you in this job. I knew you didn't have what it takes. Everybody warned me that you were the wrong guy. Now this is it. Lightning strikes twice for me. This is the same fucking thing that happened at the Plaza . . . and it was your fault then . . . and you're responsible for it now!"

Then it quieted down. I went back in and returned to my chair next to Walt, who sat there silently, listlessly.

The conversation turned to some discussion of the actual problems. Harvey and Nick were doing most of the talking. Donald listened, his face still red with anger. "I can't believe this," he said. "Does anybody know how much money we're losing? We're going to lose a fortune!"

Robert said, "Donald you know there's just no way to predict these things."

"Robert, just never mind!" Donald snapped. He didn't look at his brother. "I'm sure as hell not going to listen to you in this situation. I listened to you and you got me into this. . . . You think you're clean on this one? You're the one that's been down here in charge. You're the one who wanted this guy"—he jabbed a finger at Walt—"in charge of the building. You're the one who said I should do this. I thought you could handle this. I must've been out of my mind. I let you make recommendations. I'm sick and fucking tired of listening to you. . . . I'm sick of listening to all you fucking guys!"

Robert blinked and said nothing. Harvey and Nick tried to come to his rescue by changing the subject. They reminded Donald of a meeting at 10:30 with the contractors.

Donald seemed content with that. I rose and excused myself and left them sitting there. I went down to the casino floor to run a last-minute check on operations. As far as I was concerned my job at the Taj was over. Then Nick caught up with me in a panic. "Robert split!" he said. "Right after you left. He told his secretary to get some boxes. He said, 'I'm getting out of here. I don't need this.' And he got on a helicopter and went home."

I was surprised. I knew that Harvey, who was close to Robert, would be next. As I guessed, Harvey was on a plane back to New York within the hour.

Nick was driven nearly to distraction. "You know what's going to happen now, don't you? I'm going to be the one stuck here. All these fucking guys are bailing out. . . . Jack, my clients are calling me, screaming at me. . . . I sacrificed everything for him. You know what's going to happen now. I'm going to get all the blame. Everybody's bailing out, and now I'm going to have to take all his shit."

That was enough for me. I promised to sit in on the meeting with the contractors; but after that I was going back to my casino. I hadn't been at the Plaza since Tuesday.

Nick walked off, muttering and swearing. I found a house phone near the Casino Control Commission station. I called Joellen at the Plaza. She was glad to hear my voice.

Then I noticed Walt standing behind me. I held the receiver and said, "That was tough, huh. You all right?" He just shrugged. I motioned for him to wait. But just as I hung up, I saw Donald coming toward us, weaving through the employees who were rushing in and out of the master coin bank and the cage area.

Donald walked straight up to Walt. He tapped him on the chest and said, "You're out. You're not the president anymore. I just put Bucky [Howard] in charge of the building. You're the chief financial officer, for now. I'll deal with your salary reduction later." And without another word he walked away.

Walt looked at me and said nothing. It was appalling. But on reflection I don't know why I was surprised. I had witnessed Donald humiliate people before.

Donald made a brief appearance at the meeting with the contractors. He was completely changed. Relaxed, joking and back-slapping with the construction bosses and with Bucky—the Taj's vice-president of casino operations when he woke up that morning; now, for the last hour or so, its president. To Donald's thinking, everything was fine now. He had taken action. He fired one executive and replaced him with another. He believed his problems were solved. And he was in a good mood in anticipation of Michael Jackson's arrival.

Steve Wynn had introduced Donald to Michael in December during the festivities surrounding the opening of the Mirage in Las Vegas. Donald returned convinced that Trump Plaza would be sponsoring a Jackson concert in Atlantic City at Convention Hall. He was going to "get Michael Jackson for me," he said.

At 2 P.M. Friday, I finally returned to Trump Plaza. Tired as I was, it felt terrific, like coming home. But I had slept all of four hours since Tuesday and my body was shutting down. I left at five, drove home, and slept in my bed for the first time in three days.

The slot machines at the Taj didn't open until 4 P.M. that day. They were shut down at 9:30 P.M. They stayed closed the entire weekend. On Monday, 1,000 machines were returned to service. Later in the week, another 600 opened. The rest, some 1,400 machines, were opened gradually over the next couple of weeks. Judging by the $1 million-plus win on Thursday, the day of the grand opening and the only day that week when the casino operated the full 18 hours prescribed by law, the problems must have cost Donald several millions. He did, as he feared, "lose a fortune."

On Monday, an official statement was released announcing the appointment of Willard "Bucky" Howard as president of the Taj Mahal. Walter J. Haybert would become chief financial officer. More notable was the appointment of Trump Castle president Edward M. Tracy as chief executive officer of all the Trump holdings in Atlantic City, the position last occupied by Steve Hyde.

None of the changes were related to problems in the slot areas, the statement said.

On *Saturday morning,* in the Emerald Ballroom on the second floor of the Taj Mahal, the "war room," as it was known, Donald assembled the casino's top managers— some thirty vice-presidents, directors and attorneys—for a staff meeting. He sat at the head of a long conference table. Walt Haybert, the second president of the Taj Mahal, demoted now— the announcement would be released on Monday—and his future uncertain, sat to Donald's right. Bucky Howard, the third president of the Taj Mahal, in an equally uncertain situation, sat to his left. Next to Bucky was Ed Tracy, the new chief executive officer of Donald's Atlantic City empire. Nearby was Al Glasgow. Absent was Robert Trump, who had resigned as chief executive officer of Trump Taj Mahal Associates that previous morning, when he angrily packed his belongings and returned to New York after Donald's tirade in Walt's office.

On the Taj's casino floor there was an ominous silence. Every one of the Taj's 3,000 slot machines was closed. The floor areas were sealed off with tape. Donald was still fuming over it, and still uncomprehending of what had gone wrong. He had called his executives together to demand to know again. He was no more satisfied by the explanation than he had been before. "I have to tell you all one thing: you're all weak shit. You're a bunch of assholes," he said.

At that moment, one of the attorneys appeared at the doors and attempted to walk in and take a seat. Donald looked up and ordered him to stop. "This meeting started at ten. Get out." The lawyer quickly turned and left.

He continued, "You're all jerkoffs. I've never had so much incompetent shit working for me. First of all, you hired scum. I got scum working for me here. . . . Walt was in charge, and he hired scum. Walt was stupid."

Walt sat impassively and listened, as he had the morning before in his office. But Bucky, his successor, took the opportunity to rise from his chair and say, "Yes, Donald, you're right. We do have assholes here, and I promise, we're going to deal with them."

Then Donald continued with more of the same for several more minutes. No one should expect a bonus, no one deserved one, and they would not be given out, he said. And it went on, as one witness told me, for what seemed like hours. It ended finally when he paused to introduce the new head of slot operations, a protégé of Bucky's who had just been hired from the Showboat with a big increase in pay on Bucky's recommendation. Donald looked at him and said, "We're happy you're here. . . ." And he turned to the staff seated around the long table. "But I don't know, maybe you're regretting it right now." Everyone laughed nervously.

"This is going to change after today," he concluded. "I want the assholes out of here. I want the incompetents out of here. I want people in here who are going to kick some ass. I want pricks. What I need are more nasty pricks in this company. Warriors."

The implication was not lost on anyone. In the weeks that

followed, there was a purge in the managerial ranks of those who were considered the "Hyde people."

I hadn't slept well the night before. Finally, at 6:30 Saturday morning, I got out of bed. Normally I would have run, then gone through a light workout in a small training room we had upstairs. But the events of the week had drained me. I didn't leave the house that morning. I simply wanted to recuperate. I couldn't relax.

On a table by the sofa in the den stood a small crystal prism in which I had mounted Steve's and Mark's and Jon's business cards, one on each side. When I slumped on the sofa I suddenly noticed it. I picked it up and turned it, studying it as though I was seeing it for the first time.

I had been aware all week of the maneuvering that would ultimately place Ed Tracy in Steve's former position. Actually, there had been rumors of Tracy's possible succession for weeks. Robert was on record that it would happen only "over my dead body." "But whatever position Tracy gets, Jack, it's not going to affect you," Robert told me. "We know you've got the only money-maker in the company. We're not going to risk that." But it was obvious, especially after the scene in Walt's office on Friday, that not only would Robert no longer figure in the future of the Trump casinos, he knew no better than the rest of us what Donald was capable of.

When the phone rang, I got up and went into the kitchen to answer it. It was Lauren Etess, Mark's widow.

"Hi, Jack, this is Lauren."

"Oh, hi, Lauren. What's up?"

"I want you to know that I'm calling in an official capacity with the Trump Organization." (As it turns out, Lauren was on her way to becoming executive vice-president of player development at Trump Castle.)

"Yes?"

"There has been a management change. Donald has decided it is in the best interest of the company to have Steve's position filled, and he's selected Ed Tracy. Now we want your cooperation in this. . . ."

I was incredulous. It caught me by surprise. But I should have known.

"Well . . . things moved pretty fast, didn't they," I said. I had assumed that there would be a regrouping in the wake of the disaster at the Taj. I had hoped that beginning Monday, we'd start conversations as to how we should go forward, whether there should be an active search for Steve's replacement, and if, indeed, Steve was going to be replaced. But I was unprepared for this. What really angered me in that moment, though, was the calculation behind it. Nick Ribis had warned Donald that he was certain I would quit if Tracy got the position, to which, Nick told me, Donald responded, "I pay Jack O'Donnell way too much money. He'll never leave me."

I had laughed at that. "You know, Nick, it is funny," I said. "We work for somebody for three years and it shows how little this man knows me. The money was important. But it was never what motivated me. I never even asked him for a contract."

Nick nodded and said nothing.

"I promise you one thing," I said. "If I stick around, my attitude is changing. This man is going to pay me based on a contract, and he is going to pay me based on the performance of my property, based on revenue and earnings. And he's going to pay me comparably to what the other COOs in town are making. That's it. I have a whole new attitude now if this is what he thinks of me."

But now it was silent on the other end of the phone. Lauren said, "Jack, we're counting on your support on this. We hope you're going to be a team player."

"Lauren, I can't believe I'm hearing this. I can't believe you're the one making this call."

"This isn't an easy thing for me, Jack."

"Donald Trump should be making this phone call to me."

She hesitated for a moment. "Well, I'm sure he will call you. . . . Look, they wanted me to do this."

I didn't ask her the identity of "they." I knew she had been put up to make this call to deflect the blow, to gauge my reaction and report back. "They" knew I wouldn't explode at the widow of a man who had been one of my best friends.

"Lauren, I have to be honest with you. I find this conversation offensive. How can you even talk to me about being a team player after this past week? Forget about this past week. What about the last three years? I have done nothing but what this company has asked me to do, and what I felt was in the best interest of this company."

She said nothing.

"Okay, fine . . . great, Lauren. This is why you called . . . I understand . . . thanks for the message."

Again she was silent.

Then she spoke. "It was nice to see you and Lisa at the opening. It made me think of Mark."

"Yeah, me too," I said.

"It's sad, isn't it?" she said.

"Yes, it is." Then I added, "Lauren, I apologize if I got angry at you over this. It's not you. You understand that."

"Well, I have to go now," she said.

"Yeah, me too. Remember, if you or the kids need anything, you know we're here. Just give us a call."

"Thanks," she said. "I'll talk to you later."

"Yeah, sure. Talk to you later."

After I hung up, I sat there for a moment and tried to figure out what to do next. I hadn't planned to go in to work until later that night. But I couldn't stay around the house now. I couldn't be idle. I went upstairs, showered, put on a suit and took my Jeep to Trump Plaza.

I arrived at Trump Plaza shortly after noon. At the other end of the Boardwalk, Donald had finished berating his executives. A second meeting had followed in the war room, with officials of the Division of Gaming Enforcement, to discuss the imprest procedures I had started to implement that week and the construction plans to install more change booths and enlarge the cage and coin holding areas. After that, he prepared to meet Michael Jackson, who had arrived on Friday and spent the night in the Taj's $10,000-a-night "Alexander the Great Suite." Donald planned to bring Michael down to our end of the Boardwalk for a tour of Convention Hall.

As the first week of April wore on and it became clear that the slot problem at the Taj might take weeks to rectify, Michael's visit became vitally important to Donald as a means of saving face. When he should have focused his attention on an operation that was in chaos, he went off instead for two days of entertaining his superstar guest, first on Friday and again on Saturday afternoon.

On Friday Michael Jackson's arrival at the Taj touched off a mob scene. The Taj security was unprepared for the enormous crowds pressing in on them from all sides, wildly shoving and jumping and screaming, chasing Michael and Donald as they toured the Taj. There were a few moments when things nearly got out of control. Michael looked petrified. Donald gloried in it at first; then even he seemed to lose his composure and joined in the shoving to get through the mob. Donald's guards roughed up a couple of wire service photographers rather severely.

The tour concluded inside the Etess Arena. Donald exuberantly pointed out various features of the state-of-the-art, 5,000-seat showroom. Michael listened passively to the hard sell, responded softly and asked only one or two polite questions in tones that were barely audible. He left the arena to retire to the $10,000-a-night suite. He did not come down until the following afternoon.

Not only had the tour turned out to be a harrowing experience for Michael Jackson, but he let it be known that he was very upset about Ryan White, the Indiana schoolboy whose bout with the deadly AIDS virus had captured national attention. When Donald heard the boy was dying, he saw an excellent opportunity to court Michael and garner a media boost for his own sagging image, and he offered to fly Michael out to Ohio on his private 727 to be at Ryan White's bedside. Michael, in turn, invited Donald along.

The next day, Saturday, Donald took Michael through Trump Plaza briefly on their way to tour the facilities at Convention Hall. After Lauren's phone call that morning, with major management changes in the offing, I had been waiting anxiously that day to hear from Donald. But I never did. I was in my office maybe an hour or so when I got a call from Tommy Sparks, our security director. "Jack, I want you to know that Michael Jackson and Donald just came in and passed through security."

"Where are they now?" I asked, thinking that I'd finally get my chance to discuss the Tracy promotion with him.

Tommy said, "They just went by the casino floor. They're heading for Convention Hall."

"Where are they going?"

"We don't have any idea."

"Well," I said, "keep me posted if they come back into the building."

I only hoped they came in separate cars. If they doubled back through the building, I planned to go down to greet them, after which I was sure I could get a few minutes alone with Donald.

"Tommy, if the crowds get too bad, bring them down to the executive level. There's three or four ways out from here."

"Right, Jack."

As crowded as the casino was that afternoon, there was no repeat of the mob scene at the Taj Mahal. We had a crack, efficient security force that knew how to control a crowd coolly and effectively.

I waited maybe twenty minutes. Then Tommy called back. "They're gone, Jack."

"Where the hell did they go?" I asked with disappointment.

"They went right to the street through a side exit. They're gone from the building, that's all I know."

"Yeah . . . thanks, Tom."

"Sure, Jack."

So I sat down behind my desk, the president of Donald Trump's most successful business, and I laughed to myself, realizing that at that moment I didn't exist in his thoughts, and he couldn't have cared less about my concerns. He was being Donald, spending time with a superstar.

At 2 P.M. or so, I was in the office of our counsel, Roger Claus, when I got another call from Tommy. The new chief executive of Trump Atlantic City had arrived and was on his way down to the executive level.

When I hung up the phone, Roger said, "What's up? Who is it?"

"Tracy's coming in. Do you believe it? He ordered a security escort."

Ed saw us from the open doorway when he passed. He stuck his head in. "Hey, what's going on?" he said in an effort to be cordial. He was nervous, I could tell. He wasn't looking forward to talking to me. But I wanted to talk to him. I got up to let him know I wanted to have this conversation in my office. He followed and we took a couple of chairs at my conference table.

"Well," he started, taking a slight breath. He rambled a bit for several minutes, while I waited; and then, almost as an aside, he mentioned, "Yeah, and now that I've got this job, I'm really going to need your help. I sure hope you're going to accept this. We're going to run this like a team. I hope you're going to be a team player here. . . ."

"I don't know what you're talking about," I said. "What's with this fucking 'team player' bit? I've never been anything but, as you call it, a 'team player.' I don't anticipate that changing right now. Do you? Frankly, Ed, I'm offended by this whole 'team player' business. And I'll tell you something else: I'm not happy that Donald hasn't called me on this. And I'll tell you another thing, I did not appreciate hearing about this from Lauren Etess first."

"Jack," he continued, "I just need to know if you are going to be on the team."

"Ed, I'm going to tell you something. I am here . . . and you are paying me for today, and I'm a man of principle; I always have been. You pay me, you are going to get one hundred percent from me. So, if that's what you mean, yes, I'm part of the team."

"I need to know that you are going to be part of the team for the future."

"Well, that's one of the things that I have to think about," I said.

He said, "I hope you'll let me know when you've made up your mind, whether you're going to be a long-term part of this team or not. I need you here. I expect big things from you."

"That's a joke, Ed. I'm already running the most profitable company in the organization."

"There isn't going to be a leader anymore. There is one casino group that is going to go forward," he said. Then he thought for a moment. "Uh, you know what I mean. I . . . anticipate big things for you. . . . You will let me know when you've made up your mind?"

"You'll be one of the first to know," I told him.

. . .

I left the office shortly after six and returned home. "You're home early," Lisa said, a little surprised to see me home so soon on a busy Saturday evening.

"Did Donald call?" I asked.

"No, he didn't," she said.

Later, we were in bed, watching TV. The evening news had just ended. The phone rang on the nightstand next to me. I reached over and picked it up.

"Jack, how're you doing? It's Donald."

"I'm doing all right, Donald. What are you doing?"

I looked over at Lisa. She sat up.

"I was just walking around. I'm in the building. I thought you might be here."

"No, I got out of there. I was beat."

"Oh, did you see Michael Jackson in there today?"

"No, I didn't."

"Unbelievable, Jack. It was beyond anything I've ever seen. You couldn't get any more people in there. Unbelievable. Standing room only. It was an event. Strange motherfucker, though, Jack, I have to tell you. When he got down from the room, we had a route worked out, you know, with security. 'Nah, fuck it,' I said, 'Let's go through the casino floor.' Let me tell you . . . the crowds . . . I thought they were going to rip us apart. And this sonuvabitch, he's getting off on it. Yeah, I'm serious. It turned him on. I know it. He really got off on the pushing and the shoving and the physical crush of people. I think he was getting a hard on."

Like Ed Tracy in my office that afternoon, he did not want to get to the point.

"He loved Convention Hall," he continued. "I told him about the acoustics; it's just a great room. I told him about the Rolling Stones. They loved performing for Trump.

306

"You want Michael Jackson at Trump Plaza, you got him. He's in my hip pocket. I'm going to have him perform at your place. He's going to sign a contract. I'll have it done in a week. Well, what do you think?"

"Good, Donald. That's good. Do it," I said.

The fact is, since it was my property that would foot the bill, I knew no serious negotiations had taken place for Michael Jackson. He was never signed to perform for Trump.

"I'm going to do this just for you, Jack," he said. "You guys deserve it. You've done so well."

For a second I started to believe him. "Donald, it would be great for the property, great for Atlantic City, great for everybody."

"That's it," he said. "You're right. It's good for everybody. That's why I had to make this move. You know, the thing about this change I had to make. I really felt like I had to do something for the image and had to have a guy who could coordinate some projects for me."

"I think you moved too fast on this, Donald," I said.

"No, Jack, that's where you're wrong. I had to do this. This is a positive. Long-term, this is going to be a positive. But it is not going to affect your reporting structure. Because you're still with me. You're still going to report directly to me. This is the way it's always been and it's always going to be that way. C'mon, Jack, you're the best. You know how I feel about you. You're my man. It's still me and you."

"But, Donald, you're saying two different things. You've got a CEO that will coordinate things, but it's still you and me. I don't understand."

"What do you mean? You're still my man. This other guy isn't your boss. We're still going to be running the Plaza the way we always have."

"Donald, I have to tell you, this whole situation has got me a little confused. I don't think it was a particularly good time to do this. And I have to be honest with you, I have some problems with your selection."

"No, c'mon. The guy is good. I need somebody in there who's going to kick some ass. He's a warrior. I need warriors. He really is the only guy. Don't you think?"

"No, Donald, I don't. And I have to tell you—"

But he cut me short. He knew how I felt. He didn't want this conversation, not any more than Ed Tracy had.

"Listen, I have to go," he said. "We'll talk about this next week." And he hung up. The next morning, he left for Indiana with Michael Jackson to be at young Ryan White's deathbed.

Lisa looked at me questioningly. "Well?"

"It's official. It's Tracy. This is what he wants."

"So what are you going to do?" she said.

"I don't know what I'm going to do. I need to think. I'll see what happens on Monday. I'll deal with it when it happens. Right now, I don't know. I've got some serious thinking to do."

Actually, his phone call that night stirred thoughts that had been turning in my mind for some time, probably since the day that helicopter went down and my friends went with it. For six months, I had been watching Donald drag down the memory, too, as his world collapsed faster than anyone could have predicted.

20

*"Sometimes by losing a battle you find a new
way to win the war."*
　　　　　　　　　—DONALD J. TRUMP

During one of our conversations Donald had told me that
he "was tired of hearing people saying no to him." The
implication was clear: whatever he decided, however damaging or irrational, it was to be followed. This was a man fearful
of a future he knew he could no longer control, one in which he
knew he was going to suffer some degree of public humiliation.
As his financial crisis closed in on him, what he struggled hardest
to maintain was his image. As it had all along, appearance mattered more than reality.

But reality was closing in on Donald Trump. At Trump Castle
some $42 million in interest and principal payments on its mort-
gage bonds was coming due in May. The future there looked grim,
according to documents filed by the Trump Organization that
spring with the Securities and Exchange Commission: "The Partnership does not expect its cash flows from operations to exceed
its financing and capital requirements for 1990 and possibly several years beyond. . . . Balancing cash requirements beyond 1990
will be dependent on . . . the Partners' ability and willingness to

continue to make additional capital contributions, and the ability of the Partnership to obtain additional financing on acceptable terms."

At the same time another $47 million in interest was due on the Taj Mahal. *Forbes* magazine observed, a bit belatedly, I thought: "[Donald Trump] can no longer count on steady capital appreciation to help offset the relentless drain of interest costs which almost always exceed the cash flow from his properties." Then the publication ruminated, "Does Trump command an impressive pile of assets? Yes. Do his assets exceed his debt by a comfortable margin? That's a different question."

It was around this time that something happened which at another time might have been comic but now, with the walls crashing in on Donald, took on greater significance. Donald went over to the Taj one day to inspect one of the new limousines that the three casinos had jointly ordered. He climbed into the back seat, and saw that the interior was too small, and that the side panels were cheaply made and configured wrong so that they cut off the leg room. He flew into a rage, swearing loudly, punching the ceiling and tearing out a light fixture. He clawed furiously at the upholstery, ripping out handfuls of it. Then he called me at my office at Trump Plaza. I could tell he was boiling over with an anger he could not suppress. "These fucking limos! Did you see these cars? What the hell is going on here, Jack? Goddamn it! These are the worst things I've ever seen in my life."

"Yeah, Donald, I know," I replied calmly.

"Idiots! Nobody down here knows what the fuck they're doing! My idiots at the Castle, my idiots at the Taj, they all accepted these cars. What kind of idiocy did you guys do? How many did you take?"

"None," I said. And we hadn't. We had already inspected them before Donald and saw the same shortcomings he did. We didn't wreck the cars, though; we just refused to take delivery. I called the marketing departments at the other two properties to suggest they do the same. They decided to accept them, however. I told Donald this on the phone. "We sent them back. We tried to tell them to send them back, too."

Suddenly there was silence on the other end. In a calmer voice he said, "How come you guys always do it right and these other assholes do it wrong?"

I could hear in his voice that he wasn't happy. He sounded as though he wished that we had accepted the limousines, too. Illogical as it seems, he wanted to berate me as well. After all, it was Tracy whom he had promoted, not me, and Tracy had screwed up.

With Ed Tracy now my superior, I decided that my relationship with Donald would be determined by an employment contract, something I had never asked for in three years at Trump Plaza. I meant to speak to Donald about it at the first chance. But the week after the Taj opening, Donald fell ill for the first time since I had known him. He was bedridden in an apartment in Trump Tower for days, I was told, with the flu. But he called that week to congratulate me on our performance. We had held well at the tables and had made a little money. "God, you guys are doing tremendous," he said. March had been a disappointing month for the industry as a whole, but Trump Plaza had led the town again, winning more than $27 million. We had recovered from Akio Kashiwagi's $6 million hit, and our games had righted themselves, holding a healthy 16.9 percent.

I took advantage of having Donald on the phone to raise the contract issue. "Donald, about the change."

"Yeah, Jack."

"I have to tell you, whoever you wanted to put in Steve's position, that's fine with me. That's your call. But I have to tell you, I don't know how to view this job anymore. This used to be a personal challenge and an emotional challenge. I really enjoyed it. But I think I have to start treating it for what it is, and for what I am. I'm a commodity. I'm the cleanup hitter on a baseball team. And even if I'm hitting a lot of home runs and driving in a lot of runs, if the owner thinks it's time for a change, he does it. So screw it. My record stands. I'm proud of that. I think it's time I took advantage of it. I want that formalized in a contract."

To my surprise, he immediately agreed. "Absolutely. You want a contract? You got it. Jack, you want a lifetime contract with me, you got it. You just write it up. You write up the terms of the contract."

He never mentioned any need to discuss it with Ed Tracy. But that same day, shortly after I talked to Donald, Ed Tracy called. At first, I expected a continuation of our discussion from Saturday. I almost looked forward to it. But that didn't happen either.

"How are things going?" he said cheerfully.

"Just great. Things are going fine," I said.

"Good. Glad to hear it. Let's talk next week, okay?"

"Fine," I said.

Marla made her first public appearance that week since the divorce announcement, coming out of hiding to give a television interview to Diane Sawyer for ABC's *Prime Time Live.*

But there was virtually no public sympathy for Marla—or for Donald. Ivana won the support of the public hands down. Immediately preceding the Taj opening and four weeks afterward, Donald complained bitterly that the press was treating "Trump" unfairly.

The local daily, the *Atlantic City Press,* became a prime target of Donald's frustration. Its coverage of the Taj was a particular sore point with him. He never mentioned any article specifically, but he called me one day and ordered the paper banned from all his properties. This was not entirely unusual for Donald. If he read an unflattering story in any publication he'd yank all its editions. He had complained to me about his coverage in the

Press several times while he was in Tokyo. First, he told me to call the publisher to register a complaint about "their unfair treatment of Trump." He called again later and, over my objections, ordered an end to all our advertising in the paper. I complied. Trump Castle, oddly enough, simply ignored the order. But this was the first time that he banned the *Press* unconditionally from all the rooms, gift shops and newsstands.

"Fine, Donald, if that's what you want," I said. "But I'll tell you, I don't think it's a smart move. You're not taking into consideration our guests. We have customers who are coming from out of town, and it's our policy to deliver the local paper to all the rooms."

"I don't give a shit about that. Just get them out," he said.

Midway through the month of April, with financial crisis steadily closing in on him, he seized on the idea of slashing costs. Given his cash shortage, this might have made some sense if applied as a component in a reasoned long-term strategy. But it was not. Al Glasgow believed 20 percent cuts in the casinos were feasible without hurting operations or impairing our ability to generate revenue. Twenty percent had a nice simple ring to it for Donald. And in Ed Tracy he found a man willing to wield the ax.

Donald himself delivered the bomb by phone. "I want you to cut expenses by 20 percent," he said.

"Donald, where did this come from?" I said. "What do you mean, cut expenses 20 percent. That's a lot of money."

"Get rid of some staff," he said.

"I don't understand. Where do we get rid of staff? Are you talking about the hotels?"

"Yeah, the hotel . . . the restaurants. You can start in the restaurants."

"Do you think that really makes sense right now? Donald, this is April. We're moving into a peak season. If we cut staff now we're going to sacrifice service."

"No, no, no. The way it works, Jack, is this. If you have a waiter in a restaurant, and he is working six tables, you fire a third of the staff, and you give him all ten or twelve tables. He'll make more money, and that will make him hustle more. Everyone's happy, and we'll save money."

I was dumbfounded. Here again he displayed a total lack of understanding of how things happened operationally.

"Donald, what about turnover?"

"What?"

"Donald, in a restaurant, you've got to turn over the tables. . . . It's all in how many covers you serve in one evening, which takes a certain number of people and a lot of timing between staff and kitchen. We lose that, then dinners get prolonged. Instead of serving 350 covers, say, maybe we'll only serve 275. Which only means we're not generating the revenue. . . . Most important of all, we won't be getting gaming customers in and out of the restaurant fast enough."

He was silent for a moment, then he said, "Well, we have to cut staff, Jack. We have to cut staff. We've got to become more efficient."

"Donald, we're always looking at ways to become more efficient. But think about it. Specifically, what do you want? Do you want to cut flights? Programs? We've got $200 million in expenses. You're talking about $40 million. This isn't a question of efficiency. It's not just a matter of saying, 'Okay, we'll cut staff by 20 percent of expenses.' That isn't the way we do business."

"Just do it, Jack. Just do it. It's going to be a positive. Believe me."

Then Ed Tracy called me as he said he would the week before. But he wanted to emphasize Donald's instructions. "Jack, you need a plan to reduce expenses," he said. "I think you should start with staff."

"Well, I think you're wrong," I said. "I think there is a better way to start. Maybe there are some other things we can do. Let's step back for a minute and try to take a look at this in perspective."

As Ed and I traded information, I began to outline for him some things we had been working on anyway, what I considered a sensible approach to restructuring certain departments, and which in the long run would have led to reduction in staff, mostly at the middle-management level, and would have enhanced efficiencies in certain areas. I believed this was a strategy to allow us to apply the right response at the right moment instead of trying to save money in the short run through wholesale layoffs.

I had some of the details committed to paper and sent across town to Ed. But he was not happy with what he saw. He called me a short while later and said, "There are not enough staff cuts here."

"I really don't know what you're saying," I replied. "But I have to tell you, I'm not going to implement mass layoffs. Right now, it doesn't make sense."

"Jack, this is all Glasgow. He's got Donald all wound up on this expense thing. I want you to know that I had nothing to do with this. But you have to understand, Donald is really pushing this now."

"Yeah, I know," I said. "I've already talked to him about it."

"Let's get together for lunch, huh? Why don't I come over there. How's Monday sound?"

I agreed.

The course Donald was pursuing could only be disastrous. We had already had a ludicrous budget imposed on us. With unrealistic expectations on the income side, now the order to slash millions from the same budget turned unrealistic goals into impossible ones.

That weekend, I did not sleep well. My wife, Lisa, noticed the effect this was having on me. She was concerned and we talked about it. I told her that the fun was going out of the business. But I felt an obligation to the people who worked for me and who had made Trump Plaza a success. We solved problems as a team. We were pioneering a style of management that promised to be the most productive in the industry, one that combined hard work with an understanding of personal needs and communication.

All of this was contrary to the way Donald operated. He was a terrible communicator and didn't know how to sort out his thoughts on a daily basis, let alone provide long-term corporate direction. But Steve Hyde always told me, "Your greatest job is to isolate the people from Donald. It's up to us to carry the corporate lug." Mark used to joke about it, using a reference to Disney's success: "You've got to protect the mouse." So I did, at every "Employee of the Month" awards ceremony, at every employee function. We knew that to motivate people to give us their best they had to believe that Donald Trump was the best person in the world to work for.

The following Monday, Ed and I had lunch at Roberto's at Trump Plaza. After we sat down and ordered, the discussion started. He said, "Jack, I don't think you understand how serious our problems are. Donald is facing severe cash shortages. This is a very critical situation we are in."

"Well, believe it or not, it is obvious to me that he's in a very critical situation," I said. "If not, I don't think anyone would even be talking about cuts as radical as you guys are. I know you're starting to lay off at the Castle. . . . The problem I have with this approach is that this isn't just shooting from the hip—an obscene shooting from the hip—this is like shooting from the hip with a machine gun."

At that moment, his beeper went off. "Excuse me," he said, and he glanced down at his belt. His face suddenly reddened.

"Hmm, this number isn't familiar. I wonder who the hell this could be?" He read me the digits. "Does that sound familiar to you?"

"No, not at all," I said. But now I was curious, since it seemed to me that he knew quite well who it was but was embarrassed to think I might know. He called for a telephone. I quietly took a pad from my inside pocket and jotted the number down.

Ed dialed and I waited. He got an answer. "Hey, how'ya doing, buddy. . . . Yeah, yeah . . . yeah, okay, good. . . . Yeah, be about an hour. . . . Right, Bye." He hung up. "I'm sorry, Jack. You were saying."

"I was saying, this attitude is going to get us into trouble. Because what's going to happen is, you're going to see a big drop in revenues overnight."

He said, "You've got to understand what I need to do in this situation."

"Ed, sometimes when you cut costs, you can do it so that at least for three or four months it doesn't have a significant impact on the top line. You do it the way you're talking and you're going to have significant decreases in revenue almost immediately. The service levels are going to go down—like that. Twenty percent. You know what that means? You can't just throw out a number like 20 percent. I told Donald the same thing. We've got $200 million in expenses. You can't just cut $40 million out of the budget. It's insane. You're saying, 'Okay, we don't run any more programs.' . . . We're running twenty airliners a week. Do you want to cut the air program? But it's impossible to just say, 'Cut out $40 million.' You're talking about cutting the kinds of programs that will have people stop coming in the door immediately."

"Jack, I need a plan. What can I tell you? I need a plan. I've got to have something to take back to Donald to show where we are cutting staff. He wants to see staff."

"All I can tell you at this point, Ed, is this: Let me begin to work on some things that I think will incorporate some cuts but in a way that won't affect us immediately. . . . But I have to say, and I can't emphasize this enough, it's going to have a long-term impact on results. So if that's what you want to know, then yes, I'll go back and try to find you some more money."

"That'll be great. Thanks, Jack. Listen, you know, I really need you here. I have to tell you, I don't understand marketing in this town. I'm looking for you to be the guy that is going to give us corporate direction for marketing in Atlantic City."

I had to laugh to myself. So far he hadn't attended one of our executive committee meetings. Instead the staff at Trump Castle became his liaison to obtain information from us and to issue directives. We were the ones who understood the business, who had established the record of success; now we were expected to take direction two and three levels down from a business that had lost money two years in a row.

After lunch, when I returned to my office, I phoned the number I jotted down from Ed's beeper. It was the offices of *Atlantic City Action,* Al Glasgow's newsletter. I put the receiver down.

It was around that time, in a luxury suite at the Taj Mahal, that Donald stepped into the white television lights and made himself comfortable in a chair. Sitting opposite him was his friend Larry King, host of the syndicated television talk show *Larry King Live.*

When King turned the subject to the Taj Mahal and its disastrous opening, Donald explained, "I had a choice who I wanted to run this hotel. I listened to other people. I decided to listen to other people for the first time in my life. The choice turned out to be what I thought." Referring to Walt Haybert, the former president, he said, "We had a Type C personality running the hotel. I've never made money in my life with a Type C personality."

King: "What's a Type C?"

Donald: "Type C is low key, you know, people that fall asleep."

King: "I thought B is low key."

Donald: "Well, B is low key, but C is very low key."

King asked: "Had you not had that tragic helicopter accident killing three key personnel, this would have been maybe different too, right?"

"Well, they were really friends of mine," Donald responded, "and it wouldn't have affected it from a business standpoint, because I have the best people working for me, and other than the one particular manager . . . It showed me once again how fragile life is."

And he again told the fiction of his narrow escape from death that fateful October day. I thought the tale couldn't have gotten any more distasteful than it had a month earlier when he told it again, recollecting the day of the crash in an interview with *New York* magazine.

"It's an amazing story," he said. "They were sitting right there"—he pointed to the chairs in front of his desk. "I almost went down with them, but I was too busy. In a way, I can thank my work. They said, 'Are you coming down?' I was this close to saying yes. But I said, 'You know, I'm just too busy.' That's how close it was."

Two days later, I sent a letter to Donald on Trump Plaza stationery, with copies to Harvey Freeman and Ed Tracy.

Mr. Donald J. Trump, President
The Trump Organization
725 Fifth Avenue
New York, NY 10022

Dear Donald:

As per our conversation last week, please find enclosed an employment contract for your review and execution. In pre-

paring this contract, I have taken into consideration my successful past performance as well as the expectation of the future
and the management changes which have recently taken place.

Donald, I am not happy with the fact that for the first time
in my career I feel the need for a contract in order to feel
comfortable with the company in which I am now employed;
but, as you know, much has changed over the past six months.

If you have any questions regarding this matter, please feel
free to contact me directly, or if you feel more comfortable,
your attorney can contact my attorney directly. I have enclosed
his name and telephone number.

Sincerely,

Jack O'Donnell
President
Chief Operating Officer

I signed it, "Jack."

The only thing that upset him was that a copy had been sent
to Ed. "This is between you and me," he said. "I don't want
everybody to know what I'm going to pay you. It's just between
you and me."

I agreed to that. But he asked me to swear that anything we
negotiated from then on would be confidential. I did.

Then he said, "Good. Now we can reduce this to paper. And
yes, Jack, I'll sign it. But I don't want another soul involved in
this other than myself."

"Fine, Donald," I said. "I don't have a problem with that."

The contract was to run for three years at a salary, exclusive
of health insurance and fringe benefits, of $450,00 the first year—
a raise of approximately $190,000 over my current salary—
$550,000 the second, and $600,000 the third, with a $100,000
signing bonus, like a professional athlete. I designed it to be
excessively high on purpose, knowing that Donald would nego-

tiate relentlessly to reduce it. Recalling the treatment I got over my 1989 bonus, a clause was written in guaranteeing me at least $150,000 annually, again knowing that I'd probably wind up with less.

Early the next week, Donald called me from New York. "I've got no problems with this," he said, "except for one thing, and that's salary. I feel it's a little high, Jack. I feel you should think of a lower number."

"Well, we can talk about that," I said.

He quickly added, "But not significantly lower. I think there's room for negotiation on that."

"If you say so, Donald. I don't have a problem negotiating."

"I don't think we're far away," he said. "I just think it is a little high."

"Okay. Fine. Let's sit down," I said. He said he was flying down on Friday, April 27, and he suggested we get together early that afternoon at the Taj Mahal. I agreed. "Two o'clock fine?" I asked.

"Yeah, that's good," he said. "Two o'clock."

But for Donald, this was only the commencement of the negotiations. He called me the next day and screamed over the expense issue. "I've talked to Tracy. Why can't we get moving on this? I want to see cuts, Jack. I don't give a shit. I want cuts . . . cuts in staff."

"Donald, what is this? What's going on?"

"I'll tell you what's going on," he said. "You know what I've been doing for the last fucking hour? I've been on the phone with a reporter from the *Times*, Jack. What are you guys doing down there. That's what I want to know."

"What are you talking about?"

The reporter was Diana B. Henriques, a business writer for the *New York Times*, who had reported back in February on the precarious worth of Donald's casino bonds and now was delving deeper into his Atlantic City operation. Apparently, what Henriques had quizzed him about was Trump Plaza's "provision for losses on receivables," also known as the "provision for doubtful accounts"—in layman's term, uncollected gambling markers. As bad debt, the loss is recorded as a line item in the casino's annual financial report to the Securities and Exchange Commission, a document known as a "10K," required by law as a condition of a public bond sale. In 1989, Trump Plaza provided $3.8 million for uncollected markers, 52 percent more than Trump Castle, which had set aside $2.5 million. Because we attracted more high-stakes play, including many high-rolling foreign nationals, we always ended up writing off more bad markers. Henriques wanted to know why our provision for bad debt was comparatively higher as a ratio of revenue than the Castle's. Donald had no answers for her. So he demanded to know from me, "What's this about our bad debt ratio?"

"What about it?" I asked.

"It's the highest in town!"

"What are you talking about?" I said. I don't know where Donald got that idea. As a ratio of casino revenue, or the gambling win, Trump Plaza's bad debt was not the highest in town. It was slightly above 1 percent. Three gaming halls were higher. Also, it was only slightly higher than the Castle's—three-tenths of 1 percent higher, to be exact.

But Donald went on angrily, "What I'm talking about is, you guys are giving away the fucking store!"

"We're not giving away the store, Donald," I said. "When you're giving out more credit than anybody else you're going to have more bad debt. Right? Did you tell her that?"

"Jack, she's a sharp girl. This is the smartest bitch I've ever seen."

"Well, great, she's a good reporter, Donald. Did you tell her about the cost of business last year? What about our level of international play? All explainable stuff."

"No."

"Well, for godsakes, tell her to call me."

"Yeah, yeah, I will," he said. But he never did. Instead, he called me back a couple of days later. Henriques was armed with the 10Ks, and he could not make her go away. They had spoken again. From what I could make of Donald's latest tirade on the phone, among other things she had wanted to know why Trump Plaza's operating income after expenses had decreased in 1989 from the year before as a proportion of revenue. While total revenue was up $8 million over 1988, our operating income was down from $71 million to $60 million. Donald hadn't the faintest idea why. But there were several reasons. One major factor was $7 million more that we spent on promotional allowances—the retail value of the complimentary food, beverages and hotel service we dispensed to our customers—which reflected not only the increased cost of doing business in 1989 but Donald's obsession with beating Caesars in the revenue war. Another important item was "hold percentage," the portion of all the cash and markers placed in circulation that we won from the customers. We had simply played luckier in 1988, which was beyond anyone's control.

"This fucking broad," Donald grumbled.

Friday, April 27, broke warm and clear, a luxurious spring day. It was the perfect morning for a long run, so I logged eight miles under the bright sunshine and a big blue sky. I showered and dressed and drove to Trump Plaza refreshed and full of vigor, ready to hammer out the future terms of my employment with Donald. I arrived at 9 A.M.

Within a half hour, he called from Trump Tower. "Jack, we're on for two o'clock, right?" He sounded anxious, a little edgy, but beyond that it was impossible to determine his mood. He said, "Good. Because you and me, we're going to get this resolved today. We'll put the final touches to this contract and we'll be on our way. We're going to put this behind us."

"Yeah, I don't think we're far apart," I said.

"Yeah, I don't think we are far apart either," he agreed. "This should be very easy."

He mentioned Diana Henriques again, but only to say they'd talked one more time, and he was not feeling very good about the conversation. I reminded him again to have her call me. He seemed satisfied with that and said he would.

Not long after I hung up, Ed Tracy called. He was troubled. Donald had just spoken to him, "in a horrible mood," Tracy said, and Donald had berated him unmercifully over the expenses.

I was a little surprised. "That's funny. I talked to him not too long ago. He sounded a little wound up, but it wasn't horrible. As a matter of fact, I'm supposed to meet with him this afternoon. He still wants to do that."

"Phew, well, that's good," Ed said. "Maybe he's all right." I figured Donald must have ridden him hard because he was trying his best to be solicitous toward me.

Shortly after, Donald called again. I could hear the engines of the Aérospatiale Super Puma roaring in the background. He was in the air aboard his sleek military-style helicopter, painted across its black fuselage with the broad gold letters of his name, like everything he owns. He was heading for the landing pad at Trump Pier outside the Taj Mahal, where the old Steel Pier used to stand. The commercial helicopters of the Trump Air shuttle—Manhattan to Atlantic City in 48 minutes—land there, laden with gamblers for the Taj.

Donald's mood was completely altered from an hour earlier. He was furious, just as Tracy had described him. He hollered over the engines, "I'm coming down there . . . and I'm telling you we have got problems. You're talking about all this fucking money when we've got real problems down there . . . and I want to see costs cut, and you're giving me a hard time. I tell you to do something, and you don't do it. Jack, when I want you to do this, just do it. . . . And on top of everything else I got this fucking woman from the *Times* who is breaking my balls."

"Donald," I said, trying to stay calm, "just let her talk to me, and I will explain what is going on if you can't."

"You? You got me into this, for chrissakes! You got me into this fucking Rolling Stones deal. I must have been out of my mind."

"Do we have to go through this? We've been through this time and time again."

"Yeah, well, it was my ass. My money you lost."

"Hey, all I did is renegotiate the deal, Donald."

"Well, I had nothing to do with it," he said.

"Donald, that is just not true. You had a lot to do with it."

"I didn't have a damn thing to do with it!"

"Well, I sure didn't."

"If you didn't, who did?"

Then I realized where all this was leading.

"Donald, look, I don't want to be pulled into that," I said.

"Oh, yeah?" he said. "Well I want you to tell me."

"You know who negotiated that deal, and who laid the foundation for that, and I'm not going to be pulled into it."

"Tell me!" he screamed.

"Donald, you and Mark did the preliminary work on that. . . . Are you happy now?"

"That's right," he said. "Mark cut a lousy deal."

Now I was angry. "Are you happy that I said Mark did the negotiations on this deal, which turned out bad? Are you happy that I said something bad about my friend?"

"What did you say? That Mark didn't know what he was doing?

That's right, he didn't. He was a poor negotiator who spent way too much money."

"Wait a minute, Donald!" Now I was shouting. "You were involved with the deal, too. . . . And I'm really tired of you putting down my friends. I'm fucking sick of you treating these people this way. . . ."

"You're fucking sick of it!" he cried. "Well, I'm fucking sick of the results down there, and I'm fucking sick of looking at bad numbers . . . and you telling me you can't do this, you can't do that . . . and I'm sick and fucking tired of you telling me no!"

"Donald, you can go fuck yourself!" I cried. I slammed the phone down. The roar of the engines ceased. Instantly, there was silence.

I started out from behind my desk, then I stopped, then I stepped out again. The next thing I knew I was pacing the office, so angry at first that I couldn't think. But then I knew what I had to do. "Joellen! Come in here, please!"

Joellen walked in with a worried look. She had heard me shouting on the phone.

"I'm out of here," I told her. "I'm done. Get a pad, take this letter."

Joellen looked at me for a moment. I looked at her and said, "Well, you're going to take this letter, so you're going to know what I did. It's a letter of resignation."

She nodded grimly. "I thought so," she said.

There would be no notice. I was not going to be frisked and escorted out of the building by Donald's bodyguards. I searched in the next few minutes for just the right words, but I couldn't find them. So I dictated this:

Dear Donald:

Effective immediately, I resign my position as president and chief operating officer of Trump Plaza Hotel & Casino.

Jack

Then I turned to Joellen. "What do I do now?"

"Just go," she said. "You've done it. Just go now."

I rooted through the top drawer of my desk but decided to take nothing out. I came upon the book containing the list of Trump Plaza's best customers, the list we'd given to the Taj Mahal. I turned it over to Joellen with instructions to give it to our attorney, Roger Claus. Then I signed the letter and a copy, sealed them in blank envelopes and handed them to Joellen. "Take this to Donald. Be there when the helicopter lands. Give this one to Tracy."

After Joellen left I sat at my desk alone. The Super Puma would be touching down at any minute. I dropped my appointment book in my briefcase and walked out a back stairwell that led up to the casino level. I left Trump Plaza the way I came in, through the gaming hall.

Joellen called VIP services for a limo to take her to the Taj Mahal. By the time she got there the Super Puma had already landed. On the Boardwalk she was stopped at the security booth that guarded the pier. Donald was out on the pier waiting in a Trump Air bus, a school bus painted in maroon, black and gold. Harvey Freeman was with him. They were waiting for Donald's security escort. Joellen waited, too. When she saw his bodyguards, she noticed that Nick Ribis was with them. She handed one sealed envelope to Nick to give to Donald. Then she went into the Taj to deliver the copy to Ed Tracy. But when she got up to the office she found that he was out on the pier with Donald. He had flown down with him from New York. She left the letter with Tracy's secretary.

Joellen wasn't back at her desk at Trump Plaza fifteen minutes that afternoon when Donald called. "What made Jack do this?" he asked. "Was it me?"

Strangely enough, Lisa wasn't surprised at all when I called from the car phone near midday and told her I was on my way home. She was relieved. When I got home we sat together quietly for a time. She had already called Steve's widow, Donna Hyde, who was on her way over. I received several calls from Trump Plaza's executives that afternoon. But the call that made the greatest impression was from Norma Foederer, Donald's administrative aide. "Oh, please, Jack, tell me it's not so," she said.

I had to tell her it was.

"This is so awful," she said, "You were the last good man he had. But I know you'll find a future with someone who appreciates you. Because he sure didn't. God bless you."

When Donna came by the house early that afternoon, the three of us went out on the back porch. But it was such a nice afternoon we moved outside and sat together on the porch steps. We talked about Steve and about old times. After a while, the sun shone high in the sky. There was the softest breeze blowing off the ocean ten miles away. It brushed the tips of the new grass as it followed the slope of the yard up a slight incline toward our swimming pool. From there the yard falls gently down to a copse of trees, a tall pine guarded by the spindly trunks of a few young maples, planted that spring and no more than saplings. It occurred to me as I sat there how quiet and pleasant this place was and how little time I had had to spend in my own backyard in the last few years, surrounded by the things Donald Trump had bought me.

I wondered, would I lose them all now before I ever had the time to enjoy them? But at that moment I realized it did not matter. I wasn't much for yard work anyway, not like Steve Hyde, for whom gardening had been a favorite hobby. So much that I remember that on the day of his funeral someone brought it up, saying, "There are enough seeds in that garage to last several years."

I thought about that. And I knew there were.

Epilogue

The *Taj*, which was supposed to have been Donald's financial triumph, turned out to be a pit of quicksand that sucked dollars until they disappeared.

The Taj had broken every Atlantic City record for win in April 1990, its first month of operation, recording $34.4 million in casino revenue. But the Taj was not expanding the market, as Donald and Al Glasgow claimed it would. Instead it was simply cannibalizing the competition. Casino win industrywide in April rose $12 million over the year before, a 5 percent increase. Considering that the Taj had added 20 percent more capacity to the market, that meant the Taj was drawing money away from the other casinos. The win at eight other casinos was down a total of $19 million in April, an average decrease of 10 percent. And what Donald swore would never happen did: the properties that took the biggest beating were his own. Trump Plaza dropped from first place in win to eighth—a 23 percent decline, the worst in town—and Trump Castle fell from sixth place to ninth place, down 11.4 percent.

Trump Plaza bounced back in May, but there's a story behind

that. My efforts and Ernie Cheung's paid off as Akio Kashiwagi returned and lost $10 million at baccarat. Although I was gone from the property by then, I felt vindicated. On this second trip Kashiwagi gave the casino four solid days of play, and, as I was sure would happen, Trump Plaza won back the $6 million it lost to him in February and $4 million more besides. But Donald sweated the action all the way, pacing the baccarat pit with Ed Tracy and Al Glasgow while Kashiwagi played. Finally, when he was ahead the $10 million, Donald shut down the game even though the Japanese tycoon still had $2 million in credit left to play. Kashiwagi left the casino in a rage. Caesars—which Donald claimed would not allow Kashiwagi to play—sent a white limousine to pick him up at Trump Plaza's door and take him to their casino.

Vindication of a different sort came when the holders of some $600 million in Trump Plaza and Trump Castle bonds sued Donald that spring, claiming the transfer of customer lists to the Taj improperly sapped revenues from the other two gaming halls. They further alleged that the transfer of lists was a breach of contracts, and, by failing to disclose it, Trump may have violated the securities laws.

The Taj Mahal would win $305 million in 1990, an impressive performance for only nine months of operation. But that was still $5 million per month short of the $39 million a month the casino needed to win to turn a profit.

The industry as a whole won $2.95 billion for the year, a 5.7 percent increase over 1989. But nine gaming halls posted lower wins in 1990 than the year before. Removing the Taj from the picture, the town actually suffered a decrease in win of 5.2 percent. Worst hit was Trump Castle, where casino revenue fell 11.7 percent. Trump Plaza, the once mighty cash machine that powered the Trump empire, saw its win plummet 8.8 percent from $306 million in 1989, when it led the city, to $279 million.

The banks came to Donald's rescue after he failed to make $43 million in interest and principal payments due June 15 on his Castle bonds. Technically, the bondholders were empowered to wrest the casino away from him, which would have brought Donald's mountain of debt crashing down.

For several weeks that summer, his advisers huddled with representatives from scores of banks, all desperate to salvage the $1.9 billion they had lent him in the days when his star was on the rise. What came out of those meetings was 1,000 pages of documents providing for an emergency loan of $65 million and a deferral of interest payments on most of his bank debt, which enabled him to pay the Castle bondholders and forestall a potential firesale of hotels, casinos, condominiums, mansions and airlines. In return Donald pledged his three casinos as security to the banks. He promised to submit to regular audits, and he agreed to appoint chief executive and financial officers to manage the teetering Trump empire.

The hope was that the loan would give him time to get his financial house in order through an orderly sale of some of his biggest money-losers, like the Trump Shuttle, the Plaza Hotel, the *Trump Princess* and his private jet. A bank-ordered audit at the time tallied his debt at $3.2 billion, against which he held assets that, had he sold them all at that moment, would have left him in the hole for more than $290 million. But he still owned everything, at least for a while.

No sooner was the ink dry on this complicated arrangement than Trump officials announced that the Taj Mahal would not be able to make a $47 million interest payment due in November on its $675 million in first-mortgage bonds.

As the year drew to a close, the Taj Mahal reported huge losses. The interest payment on the bonds was out of the question, and the bondholders forced Trump to give up half the equity in the property as part of a "pre-packaged" bankruptcy. The deal, which was concluded in November, granted Donald a reduction in interest rates, part of which he could pay with new notes, while the maturity date on the bonds was extended from 1998 to 2000. Under certain favorable conditions, Donald could buy back up to 30 percent of the equity. But if the Taj fails to perform to the bondholders' expectations, he could lose control of the property entirely.

On December 17, according to various reports, a lawyer acting on behalf of Donald's father, 85-year-old Fred Trump, entered Trump Castle, deposited a certified check in the casino's cage, bought $3.35 million in gray $5,000 gambling chips, put the chips in a bag and left the casino. The next day, Fred Trump wired another $150,000 to the casino and bought more chips that were never gambled. That same day, Donald announced to everyone's surprise that he would make an $18.4 million interest payment due that day on his Trump Castle bonds. The new director of the state Division of Gaming Enforcement, John Sweeney, promised an investigation, since the twin transactions amounted to an interest-free loan, which may have violated both state regulations that require approval of all casino financial sources and the terms of Donald's massive bank bailout back in the summer.

Meanwhile, on December 11, Ivana Trump was granted an uncontested divorce in New York state court in Manhattan on grounds of "cruel and inhumane treatment." An April 11, 1991, court date was set on a property settlement including a decision on the couple's $25 million nuptial agreement, which Ivana is contesting. She wants half of everything her ex-husband owns— which may be nothing.

In the meantime, she reportedly signed a $3 million publishing deal for two "novels" not yet written: one of them promising to be a veiled autobiography, including, presumably, details of her life with the somewhat tarnished master of the deal.

Then on December 19 Liz Smith broke the news of my book

in the *New York Daily News*. I was told by some of his closest Atlantic City associates that Donald went on a rampage for days afterward. On December 23, he responded in the *New York Post*, calling me "a disgruntled former employee." That didn't surprise me. But at the same time Norma Foederer, Donald's spokesperson, gave a statement which did. Speaking of my three years at the highest levels of management of the only profitable company her boss ever owned, she made the ridiculous statement that I was "never in the mainstream" of the organization. This from the woman who called me the day I resigned to tell me I was "the last good man" Donald had. But working too long for Donald has that effect on people.

Donald was at work behind the scenes, as well. On the morning of December 19, I was paid a visit by Joseph Fusco, a Trump Casino attorney with the Atlantic City firm of Ribis Graham Verdon & Curtin. He came to my office at Merv Griffin's Resorts Casino Hotel, where I had taken the post of executive vice-president and chief operating officer.

"Jack, I'm here for three reasons," he started. "First, to say 'How ya doing' to an old friend."

"I'm doing fine, Joe," I said.

"The second is to tell you that the feds are proceeding with their investigation into ———," referring to a gambler I knew from Trump Plaza.

"You know," Joe continued, "they're pretty hot to get him."

"Yeah? So why are you telling me?"

Joe didn't answer that. But he went on, "And the third reason is your book. . . . I just want you to know that Donald is going off the wall about this. He doesn't know what's in this book. He doesn't know what you might say. He's expecting the worst. He is going to react, he's going to fight this as hard as he feels he must. Accordingly, I'm here on his behalf. He does not want this book published, and if you proceed, he's going to look for anything he can to discredit you. . . . You know, he's going to say you had an affair with one of your executives—he's already got that information on you—and he's going to go public with it. He's also going to tie you into illegal business dealings with ———," referring to the same former Trump Plaza gambler.

"This is not good stuff, Jack," he continued. "I'm just here to warn you, this is what's going to happen."

I was furious, and not only because both allegations were completely false. I was outraged that Donald would send one of his lawyers with whom I had worked in the past, when I was with the Trump Organization, to stride into my office threatening me in this way.

I told Joe I intended to report this visit to state authorities and document it in my book. His face went blood red, and he begged me not to.

"Count on it, Joe," I said.

Later that day, Nick Ribis called me. "Jack, I just want to say good for you. You write your book, print the truth and fuck Donald."

But then he asked me to keep Joe Fusco's name out of it.

"Jack, he was just doing what Donald wanted," Nick said. "I begged Donald to stay away from the personal stuff . . . not to get involved in that type of activity; but, Jack, you know Donald; he's uncontrollable; I can't stop him."

On December 21 I went to the state capital in Trenton to meet with Division of Gaming Enforcement Director John Sweeney specifically to report the threats that Fusco had conveyed.

The state DGE said, however, that they could not make a "credibility determination" between my account of the meeting with Joe Fusco and an apparently different version given by him and Ribis. A DGE official also responded that he could not conclude that the DGE had jurisdiction over this matter.

Then a couple of weeks later, came the most astounding call of all. It was from Ed Tracy of all people.

"Jack," he said, "I want you to know that I owe you nothing and you owe me nothing. Man to man, Ed to Jack, I need to tell you something. . . . If I knew someone was doing to me what they are doing to you, I would kill."

"What are you talking about, Ed?" I said.

"They're tailing you, they're digging into your past, and more. I'm uncomfortable with this, and I want you to know that I have nothing to do with it. Every man has his limits, and they've gone way beyond mine."

He added, "Things have really gone crazy in Trump Land. I can't predict anything on a day-to-day basis anymore."

Immediately afterward, I called my attorney, who called Nick Ribis to complain. Nick denied the allegations that were described to him. Instead he proposed a meeting between Donald and me. I said I would consider it but I was not going to walk into such a meeting blind; I wanted a specific agenda. That was the last I heard about a meeting with Donald.

But interesting things were happening to Ed Tracy, Nick Ribis and all the people I knew from my days in the Trump Organization. Back in June Bucky Howard, who had succeeded Walt Haybert as president of the Taj Mahal, was himself replaced by Donald's friend, I. G. "Jack" Davis, one-time president of the old Resorts International, who was fired when Merv Griffin took over the company.

Then the new year, 1991, brought the "Atlantic City Massacre." Donald purged his casino leadership again.

Roger Wagner, president of the Claridge Hotel & Casino, was named president of Trump Castle. Anthony Calandra, who had been named Castle president when Ed Tracy was promoted, was demoted to a "marketing position."

At Trump Plaza, Gary Selesner, who had replaced me as president, was likewise demoted. An executive with Steve Wynn's Mirage in Las Vegas, Kevin De Sanctis, was named the new president.

The most dramatic change came when Ed Tracy was "reassigned," as one news report put it, to the presidency of the Taj Mahal. Jack Davis was demoted to vice-president. Mark Etess's joke that the Taj had the potential to devour a few presidents' careers proved truer than either of us could have known. Tracy was the Taj Mahal's fifth president in sixteen months, the fourth since it had opened only ten months earlier.

The top job as chief executive officer of all Trump's Atlantic City holdings went to Nick Ribis, Donald's lawyer.

It was around that time that I received an unsettling, anonymous letter one day in my office at Resorts. It was hand-printed on Trump Castle stationery:

"Watch your back!" it warned.

"Donald Trump is desparate [sic] to find out exactly what your book is going to have in it. . . . Donald is outraged that Ivana Trump may have more information on his affair with MM than he originally thought. He's afraid there is enough to void his agreement because MM was in the picture before Dec. [sic] 1987, as you also know. . . . He is going to try some 'typical Trump tactics' to make sure that none of the pre-publication excerpts are not [sic] printed before April 11, his court date with Ivana Trump. . . .

"Jack, be careful. . . . Don't put it past Donald to have your office or home broken into. I'm positive its [sic] on his mind quite a lot.

"Good luck. I'm looking forward to a good read."

Late in the summer of 1990, I was called to give a deposition in Pratt Hotel Corporation's antitrust lawsuit against Donald over the Penthouse site. I related the facts as I knew them. But apparently Donald's lawyers reported back that my testimony had been favorable to his case. Shortly after, he called me at Resorts and thanked me.

"All I did was tell the truth, Donald," I replied.

"Yeah, but you didn't have to," he said. "A lot of guys in your shoes would have gone in there with a different attitude."

"Well, that's not me," I said.

Then he said, "I want you to know that I consider you my friend."

I didn't know how to respond to that dubious honor. I just wanted to end the conversation, so I thanked him. Of course, he didn't know about my book, and I didn't tell him. I thought it better to leave it this way. I figure Donald needs all the friends he can get.

Index

339